Both Sides of the Circle

The Autobiography of Christmas Humphreys

Both Sides of
the Circle

The Autobiography of
Christmas Humphreys

ⁱ¹ⁱ

London
GEORGE ALLEN & UNWIN
Boston   Sydney

First published in 1978

ISBN 0 04 921023 8

Printed in Great Britain
in 11 on 13 point Baskerville
by Cox & Wyman Ltd,
London, Fakenham and Reading

Dedication for **Puck**

This story is a journey of the heart
Renewed awhile though long ago begun;
Inseverably each to each one part
Until the sleep of fresh oblivion.

A twofold climb to wider still becoming,
With eyes awake to heights as yet unwon;
With strong intent all obstacles consuming;
Our ordered duty strenuously done;
For fifty years we loved and laughed and laboured
And every moment of the way was fun.

Preface

The only sources of information for these memoirs are three volumes of press cuttings, mostly about criminal trials; a series of photograph albums, mostly of holidays; a miscellany of menus, programmes and the like; diaries of some of my travels in the East; a bound set of *The Middle Way*, the journal of the Buddhist Society; and memory, no longer reliable. There must therefore be errors of names, places and dates, and even of the order of events, and to all affected I apologise.

I am most grateful to all who read chapters in the state of their first creation and corrected and titivated from every point of view. In particular, Mr Ronald Cohen fiercely commented in red ink on my English, meaning and even sense; Mrs Ella Smith's comments on my punctuation were followed by much retyping, while Dr Irmgard Schloegl not only made helpful comment but in the intervals of her own writing retyped for me whole chapters. The illustrations were not easy to obtain in a form suitable for reproduction, and I am grateful to Mr Fred Dustin for expert assistance. Finally, I should like to thank Mr Peter Leek and Mr John Hardy of George Allen & Unwin for dealing with these memoirs fairly and with a firm and able hand, and Mrs Lucy Pollard for preparing the index.

But in the end I accept all blame, and hope – I cannot put it higher – that there still remains in scattered places material deserving the faint bloom of praise.

Contents

List of Illustrations

Alan Watts, Dr D. T. Suzuki and Dr Irmgard Schloegl at the
   Rembrandt Hotel in London
His Holiness the Dalai Lama at the Buddhist Society, London
Christmas Humphreys and his wife at the Shrine of the Buddhist
   Society

Introduction

There are many reasons for writing memoirs: boredom, if retirement means a life of less mental activity; conceit, to make sure that such an important person shall not be lightly forgotten; the need of money; or a blend of all three. I have other reasons: to recall events and people which few remember and the younger generation never knew – London in 1906–14, the First World War, Peking, Sikkim, the Japanese War Trials, the last case tried in the House of Lords, and the World Congress of Faiths; or to describe areas of activity in present life unknown to many, such as the life of a City Guild, or a criminal trial. There are matters about which I think that I have something useful to say, such as unorthodox medicine, or the real identity of Shakespeare, or the place of religion in the modern world; and there are fields of pure nostalgia, which include French cathedrals, Chinese art and the Russian Ballet. An old man loves at times to enjoy the sweet agony of recollection, and to share it with others for their mutual delight. But I fully agree with a remark made to Queen Alexandra by the Earl of Rosebery: 'Nothing can recall the past, but it should be a shrine to which we return at times, not the cell in which we live.'

I have written some twenty-five books and scores of articles, but for my memoirs I must devise a different style. Most of the books were written to make known to the Western mind principles of Oriental philosophy, and hence with such clarity and precision of wording as I can command. These memoirs, however, make no attempt to teach, and any account of Eastern thought and practice is incidental to a description of my own development. I have therefore imagined myself reminiscing to a circle of interested friends, and it follows that the style and quality of English is appropriate to such an occasion.

Having never, I am glad to say, grown up, the schoolboy still at large within me allows me to be frivolous at times. The arrangement of the material is a blend of the introverted and extroverted aspects of my mind, of adventures within and without. As I planned an outline for the volume I saw the material as an anatomical diagram, two parallel spines and on either side a dozen or more ribs of collateral interests. The spines were those of Theosophy/Buddhism, covering some sixty years in time, and of English criminal law, which ended with my retirement from the Bench at the Old Bailey. The ribs, as interests absorbing time and energy on various planes of being, have been briefly catalogued already and are remarkably diverse. On each I could write a chapter, whereas here they had to be compressed to a few pages. To interests those already mentioned I would add books and all to do with them; collecting, whether of Chinese art, Persian carpets or antique furniture; poetry and writing it; psychology and arguing about it; travel in the Far East and Roman archaeology in England; gardening with my wife and the making of compost amid 'the murmur of innumerable bees'. For detective work, in addition to reading scores of specimens in fiction, I would like to know who wrote Shakespeare, being quite satisfied that the man of Stratford-upon-Avon never wrote a line. In nearly all these my wife, Puck, the intimate companion of my heart and mind for fifty years, joined me fully, adding on her own behalf skill with gold and silverwork wrought in the basement of our house, her drawing, painting and gardening, and looking after me.

Some readers may complain that I have not given more space to Buddhism, with which my name is often linked, or to the practice of the criminal law, to which the same applies. But this is a book about me, and I was never wholly wedded to either. They have, of course, relationship. Buddhism, and the Ancient Wisdom of which it is the noblest child, have in this life formed or, as I would prefer to put it, further developed my character, and the administration of justice according to the law has been the profession in which that character has been expressed. It might equally have been applied, and nearly was, in teaching or in medicine. I have written much poetry and, with a craftsman's cool dispassion, consider some of it good. I have included a small variety of poems for those who may agree with me. The illustrations called for anxious choosing, and I am grateful to my publishers for their generosity.

I have always written in a condensed style, and it may be that I have compressed too much material into the space here available.

The alternative was a work of two volumes, and my typewriter and I are growing old.

And so to my reminiscences, before creating at least the material for more.

St John's Wood

I
Beginnings

Most writers begin an autobiography with their date of birth. I can begin a little earlier. In the last days of 1900 my mother and her sister were walking along the Bayswater Road when my mother stopped, sighed and said heavily to her sister, 'Oh dear, I do wish baby would get out and walk.'

I obliged, so to speak, on 15 February 1901, and our address of the time inflates my ego. It was 7 Royal Crescent, but its glory was later tarnished for me by the discovery that the Crescent is built on the site of one of the plague pits of 1665. My arrival does not seem to have troubled my mother unduly, physically or in any other way. She kept an engagement book – 'Ladies' Year Book', I see it is called – and I have preserved that for 1901. On Friday 15 February, I read: 'Hairdresser 10.30. Baby arrived 2.20. Weighed 9 lb 5 oz. £1 11s 8d Emma's wages.' Emma was probably the cook. My weight is recorded weekly thereafter for a while but soon there is merely a note of who was coming to tea.

I was christened a month later, the event being considerably enlivened by my four-year-old brother, who released a clockwork mouse which made rapid circles round and round the font. Thereafter my name was added to the Family Bible and my life officially began.

The family bible is enormous and, together with its oak bible-box, is an armful to carry about. It was begun as a family record in 1758 with the name of James Christmas Arthur Humphreys, presumably the purchaser, who was Master of Saddlers in 1777. This explains the

Christian name I bear today, which many of my family, including my father, have borne. But for reasons unexplained I appear at once in my mother's diary as Toby, and so to my friends I have remained. The record at the end pages of the bible is interesting to compare with those of the Saddlers' Company, for it is the practice there for any new member 'admitted to the Livery' – whether by patrimony (because his father was a freeman of the Company at the young man's birth) or by redemption (through the trade of saddlery) or, rare indeed, by invitation – to sign a register. In this one may see not only one's ancestor's name and date of entry but his own handwriting. I am, it seems, the last survivor of the oldest family in the Saddlers' Company, of which there is evidence that it is not only Saxon in origin but also the oldest of the City Guilds.

My father and his family were apparently all lawyers, or solicitors as they are now called, he being the first to be called to the Bar. He was born in 1867 in Doughty Street, near Charles Dickens's house, and the families were great friends. Dicken's son Henry was the Common Sergeant at the Old Bailey when I was called to the Bar in 1924.

My father told me that he met my mother when she was but five weeks old. When she died in 1953, therefore, they had known and loved each other for over eighty years.

My mother's father was Belgian, an artist from Antwerp. He was, he claimed, a descendant of Van Eyck, but of no such account as an artist in his own right. He was, however, a *bon viveur*, a man of enormous charm, always bubbling with humour and refusing to take life seriously. My mother's mother was a daughter of Keighly Briggs, the well-known Yorkshire artist. How and where she met her husband is not known, but she was herself a pupil of a pupil of Chopin, and certainly a most lovely pianist.

My mother, a tall, handsome, stately woman, was a strange mixture. Witty, gay and charming, she was devoid of original thought on matters of the day and, so far as I know, she never read more than an occasional novel. Yet in the First World War she rapidly organised a Belgian Red Cross, to do for the Belgian refugees what the British Red Cross was doing for the British Army. She collected a band of women volunteers, who all wore nurses' uniform, and in borrowed premises they began turning out vast quantities of hospital clothing, bandages, splints and comforts, some of which were distributed for wounded Belgians in England, and the rest sent to the tiny corner of Belgium still held by the Belgian Army round its king. In the Second World War she opened a canteen in the front garden of the house at Ealing for all night workers, fire fighters and the like, and was on duty herself until the early hours of the morning. Such a woman had no difficulty in forming a Holloway Discharged Prisoners' Aid Association to match that existing for men's prisons, and she later became the first woman to be chairman of the Ealing Bench of Magistrates.

My parents were married in 1896, and their first-born was my elder brother Richard, known as Dick. Being four years older than I, he was always one school ahead of me, and save in the holidays we saw very little of each other. When the family had moved to Chepstow Place, Notting Hill Gate, my nanny used to take me to Kensington Gardens where I was soon behaving myself disgracefully. I well remember waiting until she was occupied in gossip with other nannies and then walking up to a pram and shouting 'Boo' into some sleeping baby's ear. The baby woke and screamed, the appropriate nanny came running to her darling charge and no one gave a second glance to the fair-haired, blue-eyed little boy in a sailor suit who was strolling off into the distance.

I remember another example of early misbehaviour. I must have been brought into a dinner party before being taken to bed, and then for a moment forgotten. I crawled under the table and began having fun with the ladies' shoes. In those days they were worn very tight, to show off the smallness of the foot, and they would often be discarded under the table. At the end of the meal there would be much hurried fumbling as, at their hostess's glance, they rose to retire to the drawing room. If I did really muddle them up . . .

In those days the streets of London were covered with dusty gravel, for not even woodblocks had yet arrived. Ladies wore enormous veils to protect themselves from the dust when they were out walking, or on the open tops of buses, or in carriages. When it rained the street was covered in mud and the crossing sweeper was a real necessity. As every vehicle was fitted with iron tyres, the noise must have been horrible, and I remember traffic jams as large as anything seen today. The main shopping streets would be filled with men and women earning their living with much noise. Muffin men, with a tray on the head and a loud bell to advertise their wares, would vie with paper boys shouting the latest news of an ''orrible murder' and the like; barrel-organs made more noise still; German bands marched slowly down the side of the road with every variety of brass instrument. Add to all this street singers, trying to make themselves heard, knifegrinders with their noisy machines, and the quieter chair menders and pedlars of trinkets on their trays, and one wonders how there was room for such traffic as there was. In the side streets would be telegraph boys with their pillbox hats, and postmen delivering six times a day – Sundays included, according to my older cousin. I know that my mother would send the parlourmaid to post a letter after breakfast to invite a friend to tea that same day.

Finally, with coal as the main source of heating every building, from basement to the top floor, fogs in the winter were frequent, dense, choking and frightening because people could be totally lost by day as well as by night within fifty yards of home.

I adored shopping with my mother in Westbourne Grove. If we went by the penny horse-bus, as like as not I would be hoisted up to sit beside the driver. The shop at the corner with a stuffed polar bear in the entrance was the famous Bradley's. My mother would stand for hours being fitted for a new ball gown in a room entirely surrounded by mirrors. I could make unlimited faces at myself in them, and when that palled I could pick up the mass of pins on the floor, for which task no doubt some menial was specially employed.

At the other end of Westbourne Grove was Whiteley's, then half its present size. Regular customers had access to Sir William himself for their shopping problems, and my mother was troubled to find that on the day when he was shot dead in his office in connection with a family quarrel she was probably the last person, save the murderer, to see him alive.

In 1907 we moved to Ealing, to a pleasant detached house in Montpelier Road opposite Princess Helena's College for Girls. Because I was too young for the considerable walk to the nearest boys' school I was admitted to the college kindergarten, one boy among 150 girls. I do remember smacking girls' bare legs through the banisters but it was not, I think, for that reason that I went a year or so later to Harrow View, where I learnt enough Latin to form a reasonably early grasp of the richest language in the world, English.

By now we had acquired a small house at Filey, and our own Yorkshire coble, manned by Jim Wyvill and his son 'Crump', from whom I soon learnt a splendid Yorkshire accent for production on chosen occasions. My father and I would go sailing before breakfast and spin for mackerel. Filey Bay on a summer's morning in a soft breeze and a rising sun was a glorious holiday for a small boy.

In 1910 my father, as a junior Treasury counsel at the Old Bailey, was sent for from London to help the police at Hilldrop Crescent where the hunt had begun for one Dr Crippen. It was then the practice of the Director of Public Prosecutions to brief at an early stage the counsel who would be the junior at the trial. He would advise on the sufficiency of the evidence available for an arrest, as distinct from the later details added for committal and trial. My father was actually present at the finding of Mrs Crippen's furs in a cupboard, a fact difficult to square with the suggestion that in winter she had willingly gone away from home for a long period.

In the same year he accepted a brief in Jamaica to defend in a murder trial. He crossed the Atlantic in the ill-fated Lusitania, had a delightful winter holiday in Kingston and came home crowned with success. While he was away, and my brother at boarding school, I was 'head of the family', and as such just old enough to attend a grown-ups' dinner party at my uncle Bobby's house. He was R. H. Humphreys, head of his father's firm of C. O. Humphreys and Son, who were incidentally, solicitors for Oscar Wilde when my father, as one of his earliest briefs, was junior counsel for that brilliant poet and wit. The guests numbered at least twelve, and my aunt's damask table cloth was all of twenty feet long. I alone, in my innocence, squealed with joy at an incident which befell it. Dudley Hardy, a famous artist friend of the family, who had already dined well, was clumsy enough to upset some salt. Without a moment's hesitation he seized the decanter of port and poured it over the salt. That salt on port is helpful to save the cloth cannot be denied, but the reverse . . . My aunt, I remember, just covered her face with her hands. Talking of dinner parties, my father's cousin, Peter Grain, then a Judge in Shanghai, was asked how he produced such lovely coffee. He clapped his hands for the houseboy responsible, and asked for information. 'I just boil', the Chinese servant explained, 'and strain through one of Master's socks I get from laundry basket before go wash. . . .' Another dinner party story, of my uncle's house but earlier. The ladies had retired, and the men were alone with the port when the door opened and a very young lady member of the household walked in, quite naked and holding her very wet nighty over her arm. 'Which of you men left that lid up?' she demanded through her furious tears. ''Cause I's fell in!'

All these years my mother would take me about with her when I was not at school. We went to the Flower Show, which was held then in the gardens of the Inner Temple; but more often to variety at the Coliseum, or Gilbert and Sullivan, or the Carl Rosa Opera where I must have seen *Cav.* and *Pag.* a dozen times, or to the immortal Follies, with Pelissier and his wife, Fay Compton. Marie Lloyd, as 'one of the ruins that Cromwell knocked abaht a bit', will live for ever, though my visual memory of Nellie Wallace and her moth-eaten fur tie is more acute. Albert Chevalier sang in the strong nasal whine of a genuine cockney. I know not when Harry Champion began to sing 'Any Old Iron', but he must have been ninety when he sang it last. Memories come fast: Albert Whelan, whistling a waltz as he entered and took off his white gloves; Alfred Lester in 'The Village Fire Brigade' and immortal for 'I've gotter motter, always merry and bright'. These men had no need for dirt. They were funny and clean. So was Harry Lauder, a phoney Scot but a great enter-tainer, and singers like Vesta Tilley, whose patriotic 'The Army of Today's all Right' was a powerful recruiting force in the First World War. Some were silent, as was Rebla the juggler, who threw up plates and caught them and then, with six in the air, walked to let them fall with a series of crashes, to the huge delight of the entire audience. Was Goldin the first conjurer to saw a woman in half? Were Humpsty and Bumsty the first trick cyclists or were they the ones who silently tied themselves in knots in a series of bentwood chairs? At Maskelyne and Devant, at the York Hall near the old Queen's Hall, one saw marvels and mysteries unending. Perhaps the greatest was Psycho, a head, alone on a glass cylinder, which would, as ordered, smoke and even answer questions with puffs of smoke. Wires? No, as it would be moved about the stage as wished by the audience. Wireless? Surely too early. I dare say many would like to learn the know-how. Not I. It is far more fun to discuss it still.

But two men stand out above all, and lasted until well on between the wars. George Robey, a cultured man who in his spare time made his own violins, was at the worst vulgar and at the best a brilliant clown, so frequently explaining: 'I was more than surprised. I was amazed.' The other was Grock, something of a scholar in real life, who did precisely the same turn for thirty or more years, ending always with some lovely music on the accordion.

I had already been steeped in music in an unusual way. One of the governesses who looked after me, and my brother when he was there, was a pianist. She loved Chopin, and would play on the up-right Bechstein by the hour. I, in a white jersey and shorts, playing pirates, with the sofa as a ship in mid-ocean and a crew of teddy bears and golliwogs, would stop when she began to play, and lie curled up and listen. To this day I could correct a false note in a wide range of Chopin, and can whistle it to myself in the car by the hour.

But childhood was passing, and in 1911 I went to Ascham St Vincents, Eastbourne, a private school which became the preparatory school for Eastbourne College. 'Bug', as the Rev. W. N. Willis was nicknamed, was a first-class headmaster, and in work and play I was supremely happy. I sang in the choir with a lovely treble voice and was soon the choir leader. I never learnt to read music and was taught my part in the Sunday service by a mistress in the drawing room. After that I would sing like a lark with, or harmonically against, all comers. I think those hours of singing were probably the most utterly happy of my life. There is something virginal, angelic in a boy treble, and I have the same reaction to others today, such as the choir of King's College Chapel, Cambridge.

In 1912 scarlet fever swept through the country and the school. I contracted it, and picked up measles at the same time. I was taken home, put to bed in a cleared top bedroom with a sheet soaked in carbolic over the door, and there nursed devotedly through high temperatures which at one time, I was told, very nearly left me blind and deaf. But the heart held on, and in due course I was convalescent. One night my father came into the room with the evening paper and in hushed whispers told my mother of the loss, with 1600 lives, of the 'unsinkable' *Titanic*. The news of Captain Scott at the South Pole and of Bleriot flying the Channel produced no such stir.

It was then found that I had septic tonsils and the family doctor set to work to remove them. A kitchen table was scrubbed and placed in the bedroom window; a table of instruments was placed beside it. The doctor gave me the usual anaesthetic of ether and chloroform, and the tonsils were removed with an instrument which I examined while waiting (but before sterilisation with a kettle of boiling water). And, with a little scraping of incipient adenoids, that was that.

Also in 1912, I think, came three memorable occasions. The first was the White City Exhibition at Shepherd's Bush. It included a splendid water-chute down which, holding tight to all and sundry in a small boat, half a dozen of the public hurtled to the water below and arrived with a quite glorious splash. (I was reminded of this in 1946, when landing on the Nile in a flying boat in which I had flown from India: there was the same exhilarating dive and an even larger splash.) The Great Wheel did not interest me, but the first occasion of 'Smashing up the Happy Home' taught me something of the repressions, though I did not know the term, suffered by many husbands. They took off their coats, collected the six balls and, with gritted teeth, hurled them at the kitchen dresser and smashed up cups and plates, mingled with tin plates to make more noise, and then, resuming their coats, felt better.

In that same year, I went to France by mistake. My father was seeing off a friend on the Boulogne boat from Folkestone. The whistle blew, so we turned to go ashore. We must have missed some previous signal for we found that we were a hundred yards from the shore. No trouble! No passports were needed in those days. My father bought two return tickets from the purser, we had a wonderful lunch in the station at Boulogne, I raced round the ship on the way back and was, not surprisingly in a rising swell, very sick.

The third excitement was a car, or motor as they were still called. It was a French Charron, with a let-down hood, and as my father did not drive we had a chauffeur, Vincent. When war broke out he at once volunteered and the car was sold, but while we had it I was very impressed by the way AA officials saluted on seeing our badge. They saluted to draw attention to the fact that they were not *not* saluting: if they failed to salute it meant a speed trap ahead! I believe they were actually prosecuted for this habit later, and their reply to the charge of interfering with the course of justice was rightly held absurd. They were helping it, they claimed, by seeing that their members did not break the law by driving too fast!

After the war everything became mechanised, from a dustcart to a milk-float, and one non-mechanical sight we shall never see again. I was in the Bayswater Road when I heard a fire-bell in the distance, and the traffic began to pull into the side of the road to let the engine through. It came and passed, large, scarlet and drawn at full gallop by two magnificent horses. The driver, an old and heavily-built man with his grey hair streaming from under his golden helmet, stood to his task as the thundering hoofs sped over the gravel road. It was pagan, mythological, classical in its majesty, and glorious to behold.

Tennis parties on Sundays in those days were an institution and had a certain efficient discipline of their own. Two visitors would come in the morning and cut and roll the lawn; my father would mark it out. After lunch the fours went on non-stop, save for a brief tea-interval, till six or seven o'clock. There were queues for a wash and brush-up while the net was brought in and help given for the supper table. Then we sat down a dozen or so, with a whole ham at one end of the table and a couple of chickens at the other. Drink was a cup prepared by my father, and after supper one or more of the ladies, usually Sophie Rosa, daughter of Carl Rosa, or Muriel Pope, the actress, would move to the piano. The songs were all old favourites, and we sang until it was time for the visitors to rush down to Ealing Broadway for the last train home. Yes, there was always a lot of music about.

So ended my childhood. I remember it as utterly happy, and I often thought of it when I heard in court, year after year, of the tragic broken lives of parents and the pathetic, unloved wreck of a youth, now steeped in crime, who stood before me. Lucky? No, I do not believe in luck; I believe in cause and effect. I had earned my own conditioning as he had earned his, but that is another story.

Then came the war, the First World War. When the news broke I was on the Thames at Lechlade with a master from Ascham and another boy in a camping punt. The master at once joined his Territorial unit, and that holiday was over. Back at Ascham I began knitting scarves for my mother's Belgian Red Cross depot in Ealing. Twenty or more did I knit, with lovely tassels at the end, and I persuaded other boys to do the same. I did not forget this simple craft and at Cambridge, when in lodgings in Portugal Place, I amused my landlady by knitting a scarf for her seven-year-old daughter. But my Ascham days soon came to an end, and I was due for Malvern College. My brother had gone ahead of me, but when I arrived at Malvern in 1915 he had just left for the army and the war.

2
Malvern and After

In 1915 I left Ascham and went to Malvern. At that time all English public schools lay under the shadow of war. No one still believed that it would 'all be over in six months'. The whole college was being slowly geared to provide a fresh contingent of 'the public school boy' who had officered the British Army in Flanders in 1914 and would, by sheer force of the authority born of breeding and its consequent tradition, save the country yet again.

I went to No. 1, where Mr Berridge was the admirable house-master. Before I left in 1918 I came to realise some of the problems with which he had to contend. Food had never had to be rationed before, with the result that it was inadequately supplied and distributed. In No. 1 we were lucky therefore that Mr Berridge seemed to have access to an unlimited supply of eggs and golden syrup. I remember one day eating five eggs at a single meal.

I was pleased to find myself on the Classical Side, but I was soon switched to the Army Side, where we concentrated on those subjects which would be used in the short course for Sandhurst or some similar establishment. There were games, of course, and I enjoyed keeping wicket, and playing full back, as at Ascham, in soccer and outside wing three-quarter in rugger. I also boxed at bantamweight for the House, but I never learnt to 'box' in the special meaning of the word. At an early stage of my training I asked how to approach my opponent. 'Just go and hit him,' I was told. So I did and to my surprise, and his, he went down. But I had no defensive technique, nor have I today in situations where I find it right to be the aggressor.

If the job was done the consequences to me were immaterial. This was excellent in the ring where my opponent was my size, but when in the finals I came up against a boy from No. 9 House who was a good two inches taller than I the result was one injured thumb and a nose with a bump. I was cross when my seconds threw the towel in, but a round of applause for me assuaged my somewhat bloodied esteem.

There was of course much time given to the O.T.C. We all had uniform and were, I believe, technically a battalion of the Worcesters. We learnt rifle drill and the use of the bayonet. We went on route marches round the Worcester countryside, singing the songs the army sang, such as 'One man went to mow'. When we reached a particular heath the officers manoeuvred the march into two rival sections which faced each other. We were given the order to charge with fixed bayonets but the whistles went in good time as the ranks approached each other.

But for me the joyous memory in a darkening world is of voluntary runs on the Malvern Hills which rise to 900 feet above the college. With my bosom companion, Redvers Coate, we were out in the minimum of clothing and up on the hillside. We went straight up, over and if need be through the bushes and over the rocks until, panting, we reached the Beacon. Lying on our backs, spread-eagled, there was no land in sight, or so we said to each other. Then for a run along the ridge and home, the better in wind and limb and, so I came to believe, in something more. I already had the urge to get up higher, look up higher, be higher, not in an egotistical sense but to be able to observe things from above and not from the middle of the confusion and struggle of the daily round.

For the rest, I worked, and actually ended head of the Army Side in geography. I do not know why, for although I have been round and up and down the world I need an atlas on my return to see where I have been.

We learnt to shoot, and I proved to be so good that I thought there was no need for me to obey orders and turn up as required for practice. One day a new prefect was in charge and I was given the traditional choice of doing so many lines or wiping them off, so to speak, over the prefect's table. I chose the latter, quite possibly because it would have needed greater courage to choose lines. I never offended again. And, today, would not the thousands of youths who have never learnt to obey or to behave themselves learn obedience and thereafter self-control from a few of the best over some convenient table?

The war deepened through the desperately cold winter of 1916. Every week or so some boy in No. 1, and presumably in all other houses, would be called to the housemaster's study to be told of the death on active service of a brother, father, uncle, or close family friend. I heard from my parents of my cousin Dudley's death. He was one of the last three of my name. The training went on, unashamedly to prepare us for our turn in the trenches. Even the use of my hands in some form of craftsmanship had to be abandoned. In the carpentry hour I just made splints and more splints for my mother's Belgian Red Cross. The war became visible, albeit beautifully, when in a clear, moonlit sky a Zeppelin flew across the college on its way west into Wales.

I was by now, and had perhaps been always, a confirmed and deeply practising Christian, attending Communion on Sunday mornings at the cost of an early rise before breakfast and a long walk, very often in the snow. My companion was I. W. E. Dodds, a College prefect and an officer in the O.T.C. We walked together, knelt at the rail together and came back to the House together, as two Christians, all other comparison laid aside.

On the first of October 1917 the blow fell. I was sent to Mr Berridge's study where he gently broke the news. My brother had been killed in Belgium two days earlier while standing talking with his orderly. During a lull a stray shell had landed and killed him instantly, leaving the orderly completely unhurt. His men, I learnt, adored him, partly on account of the fact that he had refused a staff job in another battalion, preferring to stay with them. And so 'Mad Jack', as they called him for his bravery, was gone, and I could not believe it. Silently I went 'up coll.' to my class, for such was the tradition, and many boys, with a well-meaning pat on the shoulder, sympathised. I thanked them but explained that it was all a mistake and would be cleared up soon. I believed that, for my mind would not take in the alternative.

The wound went much deeper than a schoolboy's learning of a beloved brother's death. I was already silently shouting 'Why, why, why?' What was my beloved Jesus Christ, to me a sort of super

Boy Scout Chief, doing about it? And God? Was he not the fount of
love and mercy and were we not all, in every way, as I was reading in
Tennyson, 'bound by gold chains about the feet of God'? From that
hour I began a journey and it has not ended yet, a search for the
purpose of the universe, assuming it has one, and the nature of the
process by which it came into being. Maybe this inner shock and
turmoil helped to make me ill. My parents brought me home from
Malvern in the summer of 1918.

When I was better I went to a crammer for the Sandhurst exam.
During this time I was still searching, in and out of the bookshops in
Great Russell Street, and in one of them I found *Buddha and the
Gospel of Buddhism* by Ananda Coomaraswamy, published in London
in 1916. I read in the preface that the author's aim was 'to set forth
as simply as possible the gospel of Buddhism according to the
Buddhist scriptures, and to consider the Buddhist systems in relation,
on the one hand, to the Brahmanical systems in which they origin-
ated, and, on the other hand, to those systems of Christian mysticism
which afford the nearest analogies'. Here was the sort of book I was
looking for, a setting out of one great religion, on a broad basis, and
a comparison with others. I read it and said to myself, 'If that is
Buddhism then whatever else I am I am a Buddhist.' Then, even as
I was making the copious pencil notes on the flyleaves which I have
made in many of my religious books, came the Armistice.

It was in itself a shattering experience. At 11 a.m. on 11 November
1918 I came out of a building near Piccadilly Circus, where I had
been sitting the last exam in the short course for Sandhurst. There
was a blend of mass hysteria and manifest shock. For example, a
large, well-dressed woman stood on the kerb wrapped in a Union
Jack and silently crying. A taxi passed with a man standing on the
roof, his legs held by two others crouching beside him, while he fired
off his army revolver in the air. As I stood bewildered and thinking
of my brother, I met a school friend, older and much larger than I.
Together we struggled through the crowd into Del Monico's Restaurant. I found myself standing on a table with my arm round a wait-
ress, drinking a glass of champagne. After a while I crept away into
the Underground and went home to Ealing where I solemnly told
my parents the news, as if they did not know. For days hysterical
rejoicing alternated with stunned silence and thoughts of those who
would never come home.

My entry to Sandhurst was cancelled and my father arranged for me to go up to Cambridge to his own college, Trinity Hall.

It was at a matinée at the King's Theatre, Hammersmith, in April 1918 that my mother and a great friend, Mrs Donne, introduced me to the latter's daughter, Irene, the last of the Donnes in direct descent. We fell in love and remained close friends for fifty years.

Rene was the only child of well-to-do parents who lived in a large house in Ealing. As her father was at business all day and her mother was largely occupied with social engagements, she was much alone. She was tall and beautiful. Three or four years later we each met our own life partner: for her, Geoffrey Burton, a noted engineer, and for me, Puck Faulkner. As two married couples we remained close friends for the next forty years. Rene was a strange girl. In her own room, the one-time schoolroom, an Egyptian mummy, obtained I know not where, stood in its open coffin. It may be that, as I did, she had made friends with Wallace Budge, then at the British Museum. I had begun collecting curios at Ascham and these included a substantial collection of small Roman–Egyptian hand-lamps of pottery. I solemnly presented them to the great man, who gratefully accepted them and gave me an official receipt.

These links with Egypt, with no logical connection, nevertheless made it easier for me to accept the immemorial teaching of rebirth, and to be impressed with a dream, vision – call it what you will – of an incident in Egypt when Rene and I were together in the reign of Rameses II. I was immensely proud of my gold breastplate as an officer in the royal bodyguard, and she was a Virgin of Isis. We loved, somehow, and unlawfully to the point of death for both of us. As I lay dying on a stretcher, we passed the steps on which the chief priest was waiting. Rene, having seen me dying, made a wild attempt to strangle him with her plaits of hair. Then a black-out, as she was presumably killed at once. In this life Rene's father was a highly placed Mason, and when we appeared in his life as two teenagers very much in love I wondered if there was personal memory in his amused and bright blue eyes. There it is, a good story, to be explained away no doubt by psychologists in Greek words of many syllables, or true!

Meanwhile, the war being over, we danced, Rene with her tall slim figure and long legs a perfect dancing partner for me. And the music was often classical, as we danced for hours round her father's drawing room to a gramophone which of course had to be rewound every few minutes. It was an experience of its own to dance with a perfect and beloved partner to the music of Bach or Beethoven, letting the music and its changing rhythm itself dictate our moving. In the winter we would go with a group of youngsters to dances, local or in London, choosing each other as partner for every waltz. The rhythm is unique and has a strange and unmistakable power of its own. Those who loved it loved it indeed. It needed space, for one moved very fast in the full, old-fashioned waltz, and young men changed their stiff collars more than once during the evening. We danced on our toes, and I would nearly wear out the soles of a pair of pumps while the heels remained unaffected. And so home, if from London taking a hansom cab or a 'four-wheeler' from Ealing Broadway station to Rene's home and then my own.

Our young minds looked, for such is the power of life, to the future, but my father could not forget his elder son. He and I and my mother, Rene often with us, went more than once to Belgium, where from our usual hotel at Ostende my father and I would drive to Ypres and with the full help of the authorities search for Dick's grave. We stayed in the ruins of Ypres in the one habitable hotel and explored with hand-drawn maps in the waste ground of the fighting where one kicked up the bones of the unburied dead. From Ostende the four of us visited Zeebrugge to review the immortal attack on St George's Day in 1918, and Bruges, unharmed by the war, where I bought the Brussels lace I coveted for its unique beauty. In a shop in Brussels I astonished the shopkeeper, when chattering in my highly unorthodox French, by telling him that I had a collection of lace at my home in England displayed in 'mon cabinet'! Well, why should not a china cabinet be a *cabinet*?

And so I faced Cambridge, with a deeply shared love and the first of the three books which profoundly influenced my life. What did this volume give me?

The answer is principles, thought-forces as I call them today, which, allowed to sink deeply into the mind, grow roots and push their way up again, affecting in the process the whole structure of the mind/emotions/action of the individual. It is not easy to look back and say just what of the vast field of Buddhist thought first operated on my wounded consciousness, but here, I think, are some of those thought-forces.

I found an alternative concept, or belief, or 'view', to that of an Almighty yet Personal God who created the universe and still controlled at His will the least act of all his children. In the Buddhist scriptures we read of an 'unborn, unoriginated unformed'. The Hindus call it by many names but surely the best is THAT, the Namelessness. It imports an inconceivable – yes, an inconceivable – Wholeness with neither anything created nor a Creator, beyond time and space, beyond all difference. This appealed to me as a great improvement on God, even on Eckhart's 'Godness' of which I was aware in my omnivorous reading.

All that lives is alive with the one life of which the universe is the manifestation in form. I am still discovering the vast implications of this fact. If indeed 'life is one' then men are truly brothers. I needed to go no farther. Clearly there could be nothing dead, save as that particular form of the one life.

Here at last was a dim vision of a Plan. The universe was cosmos and not chaos. There was a vast cyclic, rhythmic 'coming to be, ceasing to be'.

And the Plan was operated in a field of total harmony, and therefore justice. This was a word of great importance to me. I had found a book-plate in one of my grandfather's books which bore the family coat of arms, and underneath the motto 'Be always just'. This seemed to me a fine ideal for a family of lawyers, and the concept of the justice of things as utterly beyond any man-made law was deeply built into my character.

I was only at the beginning as I took in this small part of the actual recorded teaching of the Buddha set out in the Pali Canon of the oldest school, the *Theravada* or Teaching of the Elders. But I was extroverted at that time, looking about me for an answer to my shouting question, 'What is it all *about*?' I was therefore little interested in the Three Signs of Being: Change, which is obvious; *Anatta*, which is translated as 'There is no self', and was to me nonsense; and Suffering, which I understood only too well, as rooted in myself and all around me. True, I later found that the Buddha nowhere said that there is no self, only that what we fondly imagine to be a separate self is not, for nothing is truly separate from anything else. The same applied to some extent to the Buddha's famous

Eightfold Noble Path. Ethics I understood; deliberate mind development I had not yet reached. I was still looking for any reason why I
should begin! But the 'Middle Way' appealed to my sense of justice.
No fixation at any extreme, a middle way between all opposites, and
the supreme Buddhist virtue of total tolerance for a different point of
view. There is no evidence in all Buddhist history of a Buddhist war,
nor of a Buddhist persecution. This alone in the light of history should
endear it to all reasonable-minded men.

Yes, if that is Buddhism, I said to myself, already I am a Buddhist!

3
Cambridge

When I arrived at Trinity Hall, where I was given rooms in college, I found that nearly all the men were either my own age, eighteen, or at least twenty-two, having gone to and survived the war. A very large proportion of those between had been killed, and the survivors took time to recover a sense of reason, of normal life in a civilised, clean, gentle environment. I remember sitting with a group of them making daisy chains on the lawn outside the old Elizabethan library of the Hall. They were still slightly stunned and the dons treated them kindly.

Life for me had the quality of heady wine. I sat in my room and gazed about me. I had in fact two rooms, and although the block of buildings had no bathroom I had only to walk across the court to find one. In this respect I was better off than the members of a larger college not so far away. When it was proposed at a meeting of its governing body that bathrooms should be built, the Master replied, 'Baths! What do they want baths for? They are only up eight weeks at a time!' But, bath or no bath, I was filled with the spirit of possession. This is *my* coal in *my* coal-scuttle, I said to myself, and *my* pictures on the wall. True, they were in appalling taste, but later I was taken firmly in hand by Philip Fores, who patiently improved my taste in the matter of pictures. Mr Blackwell, the owner of Hills and Saunders, the picture shop in King's Parade, followed this up. He was an artist of ability himself and he helped me to appreciate quality in etchings, as he sat beside me and watched my face while I went through a pile. He was delighted when I chose what he regarded as one of first quality and thus I built up my own collection and was proud of it.

I joined all three political parties, for the sake of hearing the great speakers of the day, but remember only Winston Churchill as a man of obviously very high quality. In due course I resigned from all three parties, and have taken no interest in politics since. The Eternal, as it functions and expresses itself in vast cycles of becoming, and on the other hand the infinite complexity of relationships between human beings and other forms of the one life, seem to me sufficient for this life. How one group of human beings gains power in order to tell others how to behave has never held my interest.

I read Law. With my family record and my brother's death I could hardly do otherwise, but I never worked for more than five hours a day and never after dinner. In the evenings there was so much to do. There were debates at the Union or in the College Debating Society. At the Guildhall I heard Pachmann playing Chopin with his keeper beside him on the platform to prevent the old gentleman rambling on about what he was going to play next, and why. I heard Clara Butt and her husband, Kennerly Rumford. I went to revivalist meetings in which we stood up, or some of us did, to show that we were saved. Friends came to hear my records on the large horned gramophone that stood in the window. I spent 2s 6d on obtaining my horoscope by post from R. H. Naylor, then of Harrogate. It was excellent, and as I looked at it I saw two forecasts which gave me joy. 'In the matter of earned income you have nothing to fear,' and 'Your troubles with the other sex will end with marriage, a reversal of the usual rule.' How true!

I read omnivorously and bought at Heffer's, at 7s 6d a time as I could afford it, the collected works of Walter Pater. And second-hand works, selected on the top floor of the old premises, dusty, dingy and dark, but containing most admirable mental pabulum. It was then, I think, that I met *The New Psychology* of Tansley, which led me on to read Jung.

In my never-ending search for spiritual comfort and further knowledge of Life's Plan, I tried available religions. I went to Mass at the Catholic Church, to the Quaker's Meeting House in Jesus Lane, and listened to sermons on Sundays in Great St Mary's. But I think it was the music in King's College Chapel, either in the flickering candlelight of winter or in the liquid colour of the setting sun as it shone through the vast west window, which gave me abiding spiritual comfort.

For exercise I played golf and tennis, annoying my opponents, then as later, by my strange indifference to the score. I punted on the Backs, and well; it was perhaps the only sport at which I was really good. And I ran, disgracefully. It was said in disgust that not only did I and a Burmese friend come in last of our heat in a quarter-mile race, but that we trotted in discussing a point of law. I rowed, as my father had before me, but I never got further than stroking the Hall fourth boat. Then I hurt my back, slightly dislocating the fifth lumbar vertebra, the weak spot of any back in a heavy twisting movement. I crawled back to my lodgings and called on the doctor next day. He recommended ointment. A month later I was in worse pain, and in the vacation my father got me a first-class masseur. He massaged me, in vain. The dislocation stiffened up and I had to live with a permanently bad back. I managed to scull a little on the lower river, but soon took to a bicycle. As I was deep in Rupert Brooke and as Grantchester was but a few miles away, I cycled there and lay on the church wall. Yes, the church clock still stood at ten to three.

Being somewhat crippled, I mentally turned within myself and did little work. My tutor was firm. 'Humphreys, you must work harder and take a first in June. Remember you are the son of a famous lawyer and must be worthy of him,' and more to the same effect. I listened politely and as politely replied, 'Yes, Sir, but as a matter of fact I have always understood from my father, Sir, that when he was up he rowed – just rowed – for eight of his nine terms and in the ninth took a special.' Silence from the tutor. What could the poor man say, for that was true'? But as I had by that time become Secretary of the University Law Society and was soon to become President, I did work a little harder.

As I was going to the Bar I had to eat 'dinners' at my Inn, the Inner Temple, for three consecutive nights as a token attendance at the Inn for each Law term. I would spend the two nights at home, and on one occasion found my mother ill as a result of nothing less dramatic than a mysterious attempt to murder her. She had attended some charity fair at Kensington Town Hall, and placed a bundle of purchases on the steps at the entrance. On the way home by car, having had no tea, she opened one item, a box of chocolates and ate two or three of them. That night my father, who slept next door, found her violently sick and all but unconscious on her dressing room floor. The doctor at once diagnosed arsenical poisoning, and gave the opinion that only the violent vomiting had saved her life. General Sir William Horwood, then Commissioner of Police at New Scotland Yard, received a similar box of chocolates as from his daughter, with much the same result. No explanation for the poisoning was ever forthcoming, and although one can always conceive of an enemy for the Commissioner of Police, who would wish to kill my mother?

At some time prior to 1920, when the Attorney-General, F. E. Smith, became Lord Chancellor, I paid my first visit to the Old Bailey, and there in the famous No. 1 Court, which I was to learn to know so well later, was F.E. arguing a point of law with the judge. I was scandalised at the casual way in which the Attorney-General leaned back against the corner of the seat, a stance that I in all my forty years in that court never dared to assume.

In 1921, during vacation, I met my father's uncle by marriage, Lord Halsbury, who had been three times Lord Chancellor at the beginning of the century. He was then 98, and clearly remembered an incident in 1830, when he was seven. He was standing on the cliffs of Dover with his tutor, and watched the English fleet coming up the Channel under sail in the sunlight. 'A glorious sight, my boy,' said the tutor. 'They are going through the Straits to take part in the celebrations on the formation of a new country. They are going to call it Belgium'. Also I heard from my father that Frederick Meade, a well-known Metropolitan magistrate, who stayed on the Bench to an advanced age, was actually present at the funeral of the Duke of Wellington in 1852. I myself lunched with the first Duke of Connaught, who was a godson of Wellington. Sir Harry Brittain was a hundred years old when he came to lunch with the Sheriff and judges at the Old Bailey. When he had chosen a drink I asked him whether he would like to sit down while waiting for lunch. 'Why?' he inquired.

Meanwhile at Cambridge there were a series of rags, excellently organised because there were plenty of older, army-trained men to prepare them. The first was a cleverly planned theft of a captured

German field gun which ornamented a court in Jesus College. A group of Caius men engaged the attention of all police who might be in the streets, while others slipped it out on muffled wheels, and ran it successfully through the streets, a mile I would say, through the porter's lodge of Caius, and proudly set it up in their own First Court. This being before midnight, how the Caius or the Jesus porters come into the story was never revealed.

The second rag was a brilliant reconstruction of the extraction of Tutankhamun from his tomb, the public lavatory in the market place. The procession, emerging at noon one Saturday, was led by a dozen squirming and half naked 'women', crying piteously under the lash of violent guards. Then came palace officials and others until 'Tut', a superbly robed tailor's dummy, borne on a gorgeous bier, emerged to the sound of trumpets and was paraded round the square.

A third rag, enormous fun at the time, came to mind again when we knew more of a Hindu lawyer who became Mahatma Gandhi. It was called the Pavement Club and all 'right-minded gentlemen of studious habits but in need of occasional rest and refreshment' were invited to join. The rendezvous was no less than the whole of King's Parade. Bold pioneers laid rugs on the kerb and then spread farther and farther out into the road. Soon the traffic was brought to a halt and had to be diverted to another route. The street was rapidly filled with members of the club. I sat cross-legged in a group who allowed me to join them and helped to fry sausages on a primus stove. Men played cards, read books, or contentedly smoked in the summer sunshine. There was little noise save from some soft instrument. Then, at one o'clock precisely, all rose and departed, leaving not a vestige of any rubbish behind. In this case no one was hurt and only a few inconvenienced, but the germ of mass civil disobedience was born. Its power is frightening for it can be, or be made to appear to be the will of the people, a force that none can successfully oppose.

I was still dissatisfied, still wanting to *know*. I remember walking along King's Parade when something burst out of me, and I think I actually shouted, 'What's it all *about?*' I was beginning to get an answer, probably because I was beginning to look within and not without for what I wanted. At this time I made two more friends who became important to me in my search. The first was Ronald Nixon, who had been a fighter pilot during the war and was now reading

English at King's. Quiet and scholarly, he was a heavily-built man who was forever smoking a pipe. He later went to India on his own search, teaching for a while as Professor of English in Lucknow University. There, *karma*-led, he came in touch with his guru and spent the rest of his life in his *ashram* in the Himalayas. He became famous in the West as the writer Sri Krishna Prem, the author of *The Yoga of the Bhagavad Gita*, which opened up for me one of the world's greatest scriptures. In 1966 he produced *Man, the Measure of All Things*, a commentary of his own on 'The Stanzas of Dzyan', on which, under the instruction of her masters in Tibet, Mme Blavatsky had published her own *The Secret Doctrine*. Much later I was told when in India that he was regarded there as one of the leading minds in the spiritual teaching of that most spiritual of countries.

My second new friend was Phiroz Mehta, an Indian from Bombay who was reading Science at Trinity. He was a beautiful pianist, and was the first professional to make a tour of India, entirely on Beethoven. In 1956 he published his work, *Early Indian Religious Thought*, but his breadth of vision appears even more clearly in his boldly entitled *The Heart of Religion*, published, after long years of intensive study, in 1976. Here was the gentle scholar, meditating and practising his realised precepts. To this day, though in no way wedded to Buddhism, he is one of the most cherished teachers to honour the Buddhist Society at its annual summer school, and at times at the Society's meetings.

I discovered Theosophy at the Cambridge Lodge of the Theosophical Society, founded by H. P. Blavatsky and Colonel Olcott in 1875. At the time, the Society was undergoing an unfortunate phase, suffering from a group of what I rudely thought of as limpet organisations, such as the Liberal Catholic church, Co-Masonry and the Star of the East, which supported the then young Krishamurti, all of them no doubt admirable organisations for those interested. But they obscured the teaching given to Mme Blavatsky by her Teachers in Tibet with a view to offering the West an outline of this 'accumulated Wisdom of the ages', as taught in the esoteric schools of the East under many names but one invariable essence. Some of Mme Blavatsky's wisdom is contained in her two substantial volumes of *The Secret Doctrine*, published in London and New York in 1888. So far as I know this volume is unique. I knew of no other which sets forth the vast process of cosmogenesis and anthropogenesis, not as a pastiche of doctrine found in one form or another in the religions of the world, but as their common source. Not all their scriptures combined describe with the clarity and totality of *The Secret Doctrine* the Wisdom of which each is a partial and generally mangled expression. Here is no place to summarise its contents, but for me in 1920 it made sense of the universe with its 'coming to be, ceasing to be', in enormous cycles of the illusion of time, cycles of life-forms too small to be seen and too large to be cognised. It gave me a new sense of life as one and inseverable and of every thing alive and conscious. It was heady stuff for a keen young brain in search of a purpose in the life newly begun. Here was a Plan or conscious Process, governed and worked out by an infinite series of 'lives', from vast almost formless ganglia of matter down to the smallest and unseen, even by science, inhabitants of the teeming atom. Astronomy, as it extended its boundaries every year, all fitted in; and so did astrology, if even the stars were seen to be living entities. There was no need now to laugh at the Hindus' computation of a *maha-manvantara*, a definite era of time for them. What if it comes to fifteen digits; what is that to a million 'light-years' of distance? And all is Harmony. Remove one grain of sand from manifestation and THAT would burst asunder, for every thing is part of every thing and every thing is Right! And in all this man as a form, an animal still but housing a flame of the Light or what the Buddha called 'the Unborn, Unoriginated, Unformed'. Yes, Coomaraswamy and H. P. Blavatsky between them gave me what I wanted, a Plan, a purpose, and a way!

Can we today laugh at occult powers? I never knew Mme Blavatsky, but I knew well at least six men and women who did, one of them the leading Buddhist missionary of modern times, to be mentioned later, the Anagarika Dharmapala. All of them spoke of her occult knowledge and powers with profound respect, and of her with veneration.

However, the Theosophical Lodge, of which in course of time I became President, was not concerned with the deeps of *The Secret Doctrine*, but with more digestible aspects of the range of Theosophical teaching. A Mrs Yates, of the Folkestone Lodge, would regularly come up to Cambridge and teach us meditation, and help with a healing group, using thought-power on patients whose names were put in a chalice on a stand in the middle of our circle. I found, almost incidentally, that I was psychic, in the sense that I had developed

powers which I believe to be innate in all of us. I was sufficiently
interested in these powers to see how far they were developed in
myself. Having obtained the proof I wanted I have used them less
and less. But we made of telepathy a frequent entertainment.

Three in particular of our Theosophical Lodge, Philip Fores,
Robert Firebrace and myself, would sit round the fire, and two would
make their minds a blank screen, as though watching that of the
cinema. The third would visualise as strongly and clearly as he could
some simple form. After some minutes he would ask for results. They
were consistently remarkable. In one case, for example, I saw an
enormous flight of steps leading up to a vast cathedral entrance. I
said 'St Paul's'. 'Not bad,' said Philip Fores, 'though I had in mind
the entrance to St Peter's, Rome, which I know better.' But I needed
no such silent preparation for the transmission of thought. Later on,
in the early twenties, my wife and I would meet for lunch near the
British Museum, she coming from the Central School where she was
learning to be a silversmith, and I from the Temple. If I could not
come I would think strongly of her sitting at table, saying inwardly,
'Can't come, can't come.' After a while she would say to the waiter,
'My friend can't come,' and order her meal. And this was thirty
years before the term E.S.P. was invented!

I never spoke at a Cambridge Union Debate, as the subject was
generally politics, which held no interest for me, but in my last term
I thought I would make a gesture. Being then President of the
University Law Society, and knowing so many of the great lawyers
of the day, I offered to introduce them to a Union audience. I
borrowed the Debating Hall from the committee and held a debate
on the subject of 'Practice in the Courts', with speeches by Sir
Edward Marshall-Hall, Sir Henry Curtis-Bennett and Percival
Clarke, then one of the senior Treasury counsel at the Old Bailey. Of
the speeches I remember little, but the preceding dinner was according to my menu good, and the evening, as the audience of three
hundred showed noisily at the end, went well.

In the Law Tripos I ended with a respectable second and was
given, the last to be given one gratuitously, an LL.B. as well as a
B.A. When to this was added, three years later on demand, for the
sum of four guineas, an M.A., I was rich indeed in letters which,
however, meant nothing at the Bar. They were, nevertheless, a

memento of four years of great importance in my life, in which my character was, as some would say, moulded and, I would say, helped to re-emerge.

A final note on Cambridge which puzzles me. While up I was already writing poetry, and in a poem entitled 'Moriturus', a strange theme at the age of nineteen, I included the following verse.

> Few enemies I had, and fewer friends
> And no regrets for what has gone before.
> Who leans upon the name of friendship lends
> To hostile fortune so much power the more.
> And how should I regret who round me saw
> Nought but the workings of a perfect Law?

The true seeker is not confined to the language of any one religion for expression. The following poem is in Christian terms, but is none the less sound Buddhism of the Mahayana school.

Full Cycle

God, to know himself as God
Breathed and produced a Son.
And all that is, or great or small,
Is member of that One.

And each is Self, unsevered Light,
And every Self a flame,
And you and I, the eyes of God,
Are Self without a name.

But in the Darkness yet unseen
And now as yet divine
The voice of folly cries aloud
'I am, and this is mine.'

And so we suffer, self-deceived
And bitterly complain,
Until we rise and take the road
From God to God again.

4

The Early Twenties

I came down from Cambridge in June 1923, leaving the fascinating sphere of self-contained life which is a great university to face London and a career. I had already begun the round of joyous activity which filled my life for the next ten years. I had met Puck – Miss Aileen Faulkner as she then was – sometime in 1922 in the flat of a mutual friend. She was some years older than I, all Irish, her father being a doctor from Co. Tyrone and her mother a Tickell from Clontarf, Dublin. She was loved by all, except those who crossed her sense of integrity. She was of sturdy build and a skilled user of her hands, had green fingers in a garden, and possessed a wide range of talents in jewellery, woodcuts, pastel and oil painting. She was noticeably fearless. One of only sixteen women in the First World War to win the Military Medal (while working as an ambulance driver for the FANYs), she did not need the stimulus of war to prove her indifference to fear. She was well into her sixties on one occasion when, as she was about to get into bed with me in our house in St John's Wood, we heard noises, or thought we did, downstairs. 'I'll go,' she remarked, and strolled downstairs to cope with any burglars there might be.

We met again, and again, and soon were saying to each other, 'Hullo, you again?' As we had already independently arrived at both Theosophy and Buddhism, the thought of a renewed association from the long past was not new to us. When could we marry? Alas, not until I had earned enough money at the Bar, and that, as it turned out, meant a wait of over three years. But from then on we were never separated in thought, and what to us was already a vaguely sensed joint enterprise was taking shape. Thereafter we were as two halves of a whole. None came between us, none seriously tried. We worked and played and never separated the two; and we found it all enormous fun. We shared what Gerald Gould in an immortal line called 'a careless trust in the divine occasion of our dust', and we agreed with D. H. Lawrence:

> There is no point in work
> unless it absorbs you
> like an absorbing game.
> If it doesn't absorb you
> If it's never any fun, don't do it.

Rene Donne had likewise found her true life's mate in Geoffrey Burton, and we two couples remained firm friends until her death and Puck's, which occurred within the space of a month.

In December 1923 I went to Davos with Puck for winter sports. In those days one climbed on skis all the morning, for there were no mechanical overhead ski-lifts, had lunch from a rucksack, sitting in the snow, and ski'd down in the afternoon to the hotel for tea. The skating rink, a dozen tennis courts flooded afresh each night to make clean ice for the morning, was nearly as much fun. While Puck was being reprimanded by her skating teacher – 'Would Madame mind enjoying her glüwein *after* the lesson rather than *before*?' – I was being taught to waltz by a tiny little lady who somehow held me upright until I got the knack of it. My fear was not of falling but of falling on her and flattening her! But I learnt on skis the merit of the answer to 'Why does one climb a mountain?' – 'Because it's there!' There was a short slope in the trees up the hillside set at a terrifying angle and straightening out sharply at the bottom. I paused at the top of it, and was much too frightened to go down. But it was there so I went. I went down perfectly until I arrived at the bottom, failed to adjust my balance at the sudden change of angle, sat back, bounced in two complete somersaults forward and landed at Puck's feet with blood trickling down my forehead. I got no sympathy. 'Damn fool,' she said, but I was still – to my surprise – alive.

1924 was to prove a year of double destiny. In January we paid a fleeting visit to the Wembley Exhibition, where all Puck's exhibits were sold in the Palace of Art. On display was her first and perhaps her finest work, a rose bowl of hammered silver, ornamented with gold and enamel and much besides. Then I went off to my father's boat, a small motor cruiser which he had built for him up Thames and kept at West Mersea. His engineer was Ronald Powell, later a Metropolitan magistrate, and we had great fun. 'All you need for a marine engine', said Ronald, 'is a two-pound hammer. If she won't go, hit her hard.' Excellent, maybe, if you remember to fasten the propeller shaft into its socket after taking down the engine. If not, when you start the engine the propeller flies off like a torpedo, as it did. Once, through insufficient knowledge of the mud banks we ran aground on the falling tide, and as the water went down we rolled over to some 45 degrees. My father calmly went ashore in the dinghy, saying he would return when she refloated. He did, but slipped off the hard into the mud when getting into the dinghy. When he climbed on board we stripped him and the next day sent the mud-soaked clothing back home to be cleaned. Terrible error! My mother burst into tears and assumed that the parcel was all that was left of her husband. Much telephoning cleared the air.

Of great importance at this time was Puck's insistence that I go to her osteopath, Ralph West, to see what could be done for my back, now steadily growing worse. At last I went. He examined me and gave me a choice. 'You could hang a hat on the nob of your fifth lumbar, as it sticks out of your skin,' he said. 'Shall I put it back now, at the risk of spoiling your fun with a girl friend for a week or two, or do it gently in a month?' Now,' I said and in twenty minutes it was back. It did not, of course, stay back. After the vertebra had been four years out of place the space made by the lesion had been filled by nature and it took years before my back was wholly well. But I had now firmly entered the field of what has been called 'fringe medicine', and I worked hard for osteopathy, as I did later for the Society of Herbalists and homoeopathy and radionics, and continue to do so to this day.

My back was soon well enough for me to take up judo. But as 'ground work' in judo was apt to hurt I turned to kendo, Japanese fencing. I was amused when my teacher explained that the relation between the two was that of the Navy to the Army in England. Certainly the elaborate ritual of donning the helmet, the bowing and the play of drawing the sword was superior to that of throwing each other about and rolling on the floor, as he put it. I found kendo a very fine means of self-control, of speed and skill in action, and, in my life at the Bar, an excellent substitute for any other form of sport.

In April 1923 I had founded in London, with some of my Cambridge and other friends, a Youth Lodge of the Theosophical Society, gaining permission to hold our meetings in the English headquarters, then at 23 Bedford Square. Its objects were admirable: 'To provide a means of expression for the ideas, needs and methods of the younger generation of the Theosophical Society in London, and to initiate new methods of spreading Theosophy'. And lots more, clearly meaning to teach the older generation what is Theosophy, to clean up the T. S. by training for better leaders, and to put these new ones in control! Other objects reveal my early love of capital letters and what to me was already integral in all activity: 'To reveal Beauty in Action by combining Service with Efficiency.' Little did I know that I was almost inadvertently founding a world-wide movement in the Society.

To our delight the then General Secretary, Major Graham Pole, secretly backed us in our impertinent activities, and at least we did some good in our loud expression of ideas. During the next few years I was instrumental in founding three other Lodges, including the Buddhist Lodge, of which more later.

My search in the fields of Theosophy and Buddhism continued. I would dearly have liked to have met Ananda Metteyya, born as Allan Bennett, who had taken the Buddhist Robe in Burma. He had come to London in 1908 to make known to England that Buddhism was a way which all might follow with advantage. To this end he used the Buddhist Society of Great Britain and Ireland, which had been formed under Dr Rhys Davids for the purpose. In 1923 he published his *Wisdom of the Aryas*, and died that same year. Francis Payne, a Buddhist evangelist, carried on the dying first Society, and, in a memorable series of thirty-six lectures at the old Essex Hall, kept the flame of the *Dhamma* alive until a new group, of which I was the leader, moved in to form a new Buddhist society, the Buddhist Society of today.

In August 1923 I went with Basil Howell, the Chief of Staff at Headquarters, to a European Theosophical Congress in Vienna. There we met Krishnamurti, to whom I expounded the virtues of

Youth Lodge, and he agreed to be the President of a European Federation of Lodges, which I promptly founded. This spread to become the International Federation of Young Theosophists. I returned via Berlin. It was an unforgettable period of really acute financial depression, although a few wise men in London are trying to revive a memory of it as a warning of what this word can mean. We are troubled today about the pound, but I have kept the bill of the Adlon Hotel where we stayed and it is frightening, amounting for two nights to 2,248,000 marks, and I changed a million mark note to buy a book at the hotel bookstall. There were armed police at every street corner, and we heard of university professors dying of hunger in their houses. The psychic atmosphere – of fear, rebellious emotion suppressed, agony of the present and despair for the future – was truly horrible, and we were relieved to pass the frontier into the clean, sane air of Holland.

Back in London I took part in my first trial at the Old Bailey, sitting behind Sir Edward Marshall-Hall in the defence of Mme Fahmy, a Frenchwoman who had shot dead her Egyptian husband in the Savoy Hotel the previous June. Here was a trial in the grand manner, and the great man was at his greatest. It was said of Marshall-Hall that he lost as many cases as he won by his melodramatic technique, but he knew the value of that last speech. He told me once, when I went to 'view' with him as deputy for his junior, Roland Oliver, 'Show me the witness for the defence worth my right of reply!' For in those days if you called a witness for the defence you lost the right of reply.

Mme Fahmy said that she had shot her husband in self-defence, with an automatic weapon. In the witness box, she held it at arm's length with her eyes tightly shut and said, 'It just go pop, pop, pop . . .' Marshall, according to Edward Marjoribanks in his *Famous Trials of Marshall-Hall*, in his final speech for the defence 'performed the most wonderful physical demonstration of his forensic career'. Repeating Mme Fahmy's description of her husband 'crouching like an animal and bounding forward' (at which she had pointed the pistol and pulled the trigger), he pointed the pistol at the jury and let it fall with a crash to the floor, as she had said that her husband fell. Then came the peroration. Referring to the scene in Robert Hichens's *Bella Donna*, he drew his parallel. 'Members of the jury, I want you to open the gates where this Western woman can go out, not into the dark night of the desert but back to her friends, who love her in spite of her weaknesses; back to her friends who will be glad to receive her; back to her child' – with a slight drop in that wonderful voice – 'who will be waiting for her with open arms. You will open the gate and let this woman go back into the light of God's great Western sun. And he dared on the closing words, to point, to the sunlight pouring through the skylight of the court on to the spellbound, utterly silent crowd that hung, from judge to jailer, on those final words. This oratory in any day has tremendous effect in a theatre; here a woman's life was at stake. I have heard many attempt to imitate this speech but it needed a Marshall-Hall to get it over, and none, I think, would succeed with it today. Mme Fahmy was acquitted.

In January 1924 I was called to the Bar at the Inner Temple, and I entered my father's chambers in 1 Temple Gardens as a pupil of his one-time pupil, Roland Oliver. As such I studied his briefs and went with him everywhere, asking innumerable questions and digesting the replies. Then I had a brief of my own, for two whole guineas, and for the first time stood up in court and heard my own voice. I believe friendly counsel next to me really were holding my knees. I was very upset when my client, appallingly guilty, was convicted, but one soon gets used to that. And so to the exciting, ever-new life of a criminal lawyer, where in fact we were little concerned with law! The law was generally clear enough. What mattered was to prove, or see that the prosecution failed to prove, the guilt of the accused.

But not all my practice lay in criminal courts and I would add a few lines on licensing. In the thirties the sale of liquor, either on or off licensed premises was strictly controlled by the Licensing Acts, which were applied by Licensing Justices, being an elected committee of the justices for the area in which the application was made. Off-licences, furiously fought for and as furiously opposed by those brewers and wine companies already at work in the area, were valuable assets, but the hours of opening and sale were maddening to the consumer. One could order drink at any time, but only take possession of it during the prescribed hours for public houses, which could, however, sell 'off' when open. Public houses were very different establishments from those of today; many had sawdust on the floor, at least in the public bar, to allow for the general habit of spitting. The first mention at a Licensing Meeting of a public house where the bars were furnished with oilcloth aroused mention in the press; with carpeting sheer astonishment!

All applications were made at Brewster Sessions, in February, or at the adjourned sessions in March; those few counsel who specialised in this practice worked almost night and day during these two fortnights. They might apply before the Hendon Justices in the morning and in Croydon in the afternoon. For a while I actually had a chauffeur, so that I could read briefs on the journeys and not be quite so tired at night when I would have to read, very often, the next day's brief. Brewers contended for every new site, such as a crossroads on the then extending 'Woodford Spur' into Essex. Four would produce their plans and witnesses, others would cry them down and produce their own. 'Is there *any* space for a bar in the middle of the women's lavatories?' someone asked me in court, a trifle too loudly, about an applicant anxious to please the justices' latest whim. Some brewers won and others lost, but we all, brewers, architects, solicitors, counsel and experts on this and that would meet at lunch as friends, and renew the battle in the afternoon. Then came Confirmation, some months later, when the battles might be fought all over again before Quarter Sessions. Financially, this was for many of us the jam on the bread and butter of our criminal practice, and defendants had to wait!

The most incongruous venue for a licensing session was Buckingham Palace, where the licensees of premises 'within the verge of the Palaces' met at the Board of Green Cloth, a room in the palace itself. The Chairman of Justices for the occasion was a court official, and I remember Sir Henry Curtis-Bennett rising to his feet to request a slight change in the licence of a public house at the top of Whitehall. But alas, the baize cloth on the table was blue. . . .

There were, however, moments of embarrassment. Once after the Court rose at Ascot, a woman magistrate came to speak to me and said, 'You won't remember me, Mr Humphreys, because the last time I saw you I helped to bath you!' Such are the possible entanglements at law.

At the Bar one must speak, yet strangely enough a barrister is never trained for public speaking. He is not taught how to choose his words, nor does he receive any lessons in elocution. I learnt something of both when I acted as a steward at public lectures given at the Queen's Hall by Annie Besant, then President of the Theosophical Society. She was described, I believe, in the *Encyclopaedia Britannica* of the day as one of the finest orators living. I would watch her looking at the clock in the room off-stage, and as the hand moved to seven she would walk on to the platform, place her hands on the curved brass rail, and then speak without notes for an hour. A shorthand note of the speech was made, transcribed and sent straight to the printer. She said that having thought out the matter of the speech to her satisfaction the phrases 'rose up in her mind', and she had but to repeat them. She was a very remarkable woman.

About this time I had the first of several brief interviews with great men which had a profound effect on me. This was with Nicholas Roerich, Russian explorer, geologist, artist, herbalist and much else. For some reason I was asked to help him with his passport and I called at his hotel. I helped as I could and then, as we stood in the room, looking out of the windows on to the Haymarket, the conversation turned to my current mental condition, which must have been one of mild despair. 'No,' he said, 'look!' And somehow his following words almost literally lifted me up into his own magnificent vision of the far ideal. I saw, as through his eyes, that it was ALL RIGHT, *everything* was ALL RIGHT! I saw it so, and have never ceased to see it so, even as what the Buddhists call the 'three fires' of hatred, lust and illusion still obscure my spiritual view. It was not what was said but the immense power of the man to enfold my mind in his and lift it for a moment to the level of his own at its highest. This power is surely the mark of a highly developed man, one of six I have been privileged to meet and who have helped me in this particular life.

Meanwhile much was happening in Buddhist-Theosophical affairs. Earlier in the year *The Mahatma Letters to A. P. Sinnett* had been published, and Puck and I, and members of our loosely formed study group were studying them deeply. These were letters written by the two Masters who had trained H. P. Blavatsky in Tibet to A. P. Sinnett, then editor of the *Pioneer* of Allahabad, in answer to those which H. P. B. helped him to send to Tibet. In the long replies the Masters tried to explain to an educated but totally Western mind something of the wisdom-religion which was in the keeping of their Brotherhood. The letters make fascinating but difficult reading as I found when studying the originals in the British Library for a third edition of the book.

The pressure grew, and through me the group applied to become a Centre of the Theosophical Society, in preparation for becoming a Lodge. Our Charter was signed at 7 p.m. on 19 November 1924. I was the first President, and still am. My wife to be was Hon. Secretary. Mr C. Jinarajadasa, a Sinhalese Buddhist, then Vice-President of the T. S., who happened to be in London, smiled as he gave me the Charter. 'It is a good omen that a Buddhist Theosophist should present the charter to a group of Theosophically-minded Buddhists'.

And so Puck and I were launched on our life's main adventure, feeling it then, as we felt each step thereafter, as part of a pre-ordained and in a vague sense guided task which had to be done and was for us, in a phrase I have used too often since, the 'N.T.B.D.', the next-thing-to-be-done. And we never found anything more important to do than that, to do completely and utterly, and with the whole soul's will, the next thing to be done, large or small, pleasant or unpleasant, rewarded or unnoticed, or even the subject of abuse. Such was our great adventure and I repeat that as we saw it for the next fifty years it was always enormous fun.

The Lodge first met at a friend's house near Paddington, and received immediately two presents, the one of practical and the other of symbolic value. The first was a very fine gold-lacquered wooden image of the Buddha from Burma, which became and is the much-photographed heart of the Society. It is housed in a lacquered teak shrine made for us by G. Koizumi of the Budokwai, and the hinges are of silver wrought by Puck in our home. The other present was a framed photograph of the North Col of Everest, one of the first ever taken. There was the mountain, and we from the bottom could unceasingly work to reach its summit. It has been done on earth, but as a climb to the Ultimate?

5

The Later Twenties

The Buddhist Lodge began its career with meetings on alternate Mondays, and very slowly began to gather members. So far Buddhism in London was that of the *Theravada*, sometimes called the Southern School, of Ceylon, Thailand and Burma, and at this time the Lodge had only a single shelf of books to cover the entire range of Buddhism. Scarcely were we established when we were called on to receive the most famous Buddhist missionary of modern times, the Anagarika Dharmapala of Ceylon, who wrote in September 1925 to say that he proposed to devote two of his declining years to making known the *Dhamma*, meaning the Buddhism of Ceylon, in England. We joyfully received him and his nephew Daya Hewavitarne. We found the old gentleman a house in Ealing and helped him to open a London branch of the Maha Bodhi Society, which he had founded under the inspiration of H. P. Blavatsky and Colonel Olcott in Colombo in 1891. Here was a famous Buddhist Theosophist in London aiming to make known the teachings of Buddhism as he held them to be, and we naturally joined forces. But his strength was all but spent, and in 1927 he went back to Ceylon where he died in 1933.

I protested mildly that the establishment in London of the British Maha Bodhi Society effectively halved the energy available to each society, but despite this early split in English Buddhism the two groups worked in harmony until the Second World War when the B.M.B.S. closed down. In 1928 three monks were sent from Ceylon by the Anagarika to found the first Western *vihara* or monastery; and the work was revived in 1954 when the present incumbent, the Venerable Dr H. Saddhatissa, opened a Vihara which still flourishes in Chiswick today.

News of the Buddhist Lodge spread to Buddhist countries. One of the first people to write to us from the East was U Kyaw Hla of Mandalay. He had acted as an agent for the disbanded Buddhist Society of Great Britain and Ireland and he now began to work for us as a collector of much-needed funds and as an agent for *Buddhism in England.* Time and again when we were in financial trouble a cheque made up of small sums from our readers and friends would arrive from Burma. But it was not until I met U Kyaw Hla in Rangoon on my way back from Japan in 1946 that I was able to thank him personally.

In 1927 Japan gave the Western world its first authoritative work on Zen Buddhism, a *First Series of Essays in Zen Buddhism,* by Dr D. T. Suzuki. Born in 1870, Dr Suzuki underwent an intensive period of Zen meditation under the famous master Soyen Shaku, author of *Sermons of a Buddhist Abbot.* From 1900 until his death in 1966 he worked unceasingly, with a stream of books in Japanese and English and his magazine *The Eastern Buddhist,* to teach as much as can be taught in words of the purpose and remarkable technique of Rinzai Zen Buddhism. This Japanese professor, for he was never a monk, was given by his teacher the additional name of Daisetz, which means 'great humility', and so we found him. Indeed, Dr Suzuki was the greatest, in the sense of the most spiritually developed, man that I have known and dared to call my friend. I was proud to become the agent in Europe for his writings published here, and I have reverently kept them in print since I returned from Japan.

The *First Series of Essays* did more than teach us about the branch of Zen Buddhism founded by Rinzai in the ninth century. They opened to the public mind the glory of *Mahayana* (Great Vehicle) Buddhism, with its doctrines largely expanded from those already in the *Theravada* of the Southern School, and the great heights of what I call the mystical metaphysics of the *Madhyamika* (Middle Way) School, founded by Nagarjuna and expanded through several centuries into the ultimate concept of *sunyata*, 'no-thing-ness'. Here was a door flung open to the splendours of a vast field of thought and spiritual achievement, comparable with that of the Vedas and

Upanishads of India. Here was the fourth volume to influence my life profoundly.

In 1928 the Venerable Tai Hsü arrived in London in the course of a world-wide attempt to collate and unify in friendly co-operation the many schools of Chinese Buddhism. His organ, *The Voice of the Tide*, already penetrated into all corners of the Chinese Buddhist world. As President of the Buddhist Education Association of Nanking, he toured Europe having in mind an International Buddhist Union. He succeeded in founding Les Amis du Bouddhisme in Paris, under the leadership of Miss Constant Lounsbery, and my wife and I were present at the founding meeting. He did his best to amalgamate the various Buddhist units in London, and we were at least stimulated by his energy. He was one of the great men with whom, though speaking through an interpreter, one seemed to unite on a high plane of awareness.

The time had come for the Lodge to produce a journal, and the first issue of *The Buddhist Lodge Monthly Bulletin* appeared in October 1925. It was composed of twelve sheets of foolscap paper roneo'd to produce the few copies needed and 'bound' by the process of laying the twelve sheets in piles round the floor of Puck's flat and then, as they were collected into a set, just clipping them together. After six issues it was decided to venture into print, and thus *Buddhism in England* was born. Later it became *The Middle Way* with Arthur March as editor.

I myself was beginning to write, my first attempts being a series of articles for the *Theosophical Review*. It was at this point that I learnt a lesson which ever since has affected all my writing, comprising twenty five books and hundreds of articles and reviews. Mr S. L. Bensusan, the editor, agreed to the series I had in mind and I submitted the first article. He glanced at it and said, 'I said two thousand words. This is at least three. Please shorten it.' I crept away and worked on the draft, excising many a splendid paragraph, and took it back. 'I said 2000 words', he said, 'and this is still at least 2500.' I crept out, all but in tears, and nearly murdered the poor thing, returning with the remains. 'Excellent,' he said. 'Now for the others at the same length.' He meant it as a lesson for a young writer, and I learnt it. Today my motto to myself in all writing is, study the draft and cut, cut, cut – an unnecessary adverb, or clause, or even paragraph. It is all part of self-control and for the writer a necessary part.

The two books which followed the articles were a success. *What is Buddhism?*, compiled largely from my drafts at meetings of the Lodge, was a pioneer volume, being written for the Western layman interested in trying to live the Buddhist life. We published it ourselves, and in my top hat I would call on my way to the Old Bailey to deliver orders to the trade entrance of Simpkin Marshall, the wholesalers. The book sold steadily until 1951, mostly at the bookshops stocking such material. These at the time were J. M. Watkins of Cecil Court, owned by Mr John Watkins, who had worked for Mme Blavatsky and would reminisce about her; Luzac and Co. in Great Russell Street, where Mr Knight-Smith was a keen supporter of our work; Probsthain's, where we had the help of Mr Probsthain himself; Kegan Paul's; and Salby's, now closed. In 1950, when preparing at the request of a director of Penguin Books an entirely new work on Buddhism, I used a good deal of *What is Buddhism?*, turning the question and answer form into straight prose. The heart of the later work, *Buddhism*, has therefore been selling steadily for some fifty years which, compiled as it was by a small group of amateurs from very scant material, is a temptation to self-congratulation. I therefore at once remind myself of a passage in *The Voice of the Silence*: 'Self-gratulation, O Lanoo, is like into a lofty tower up which a haughty fool has climbed. Thereon he sits in prideful solitude and unperceived by any but himself!'

My other work, in a very different vein, was *The Great Pearl Robbery of 1913*, written at the suggestion of my father, who used it in a public debate organised for charity on the theme 'Truth is stranger than Fiction'. His answer to fiction was to tell this story, and the reviews wallowed in the real-life details of a pearl necklace worth £150,000 being sent by post from Paris, and ending up in the thick soup of a London receiver of stolen goods while the police were vainly searching his house on suspicion that he held it. I then wrote a pot-boiler on circumstantial evidence, *Seven Murderers*. I smile to myself on looking at a third, *The Menace in our Midst*, written in conjunction with R. E. Drummond, a Metropolitan magistrate, with whom I planned it at lunch at the Garrick Club. The book drew attention to the scandalous behaviour of a section of the younger community who, insufficiently educated and controlled, were causing serious injury and damage, and becoming 'a menace in our midst'. With the figures today as they are, what a pity no one listened to our warning!

I was also trying my hand as a playwright, and in blank verse. For the occasion of the fiftieth anniversary of the Theosophical Society, which was 17 November 1925, I wrote a short play on the life of the Emperor Asoka of India, called 'The Conversion of the King', and we gave two performances at the Mortimer Hall. Muriel Pope, a famous actress and an old friend of my family, kindly produced it for us, and Ella Collings, who was a professional pianist, played appropriate Brahms before the curtain went up. It went well, considering we were all amateurs, and I as the king a poor actor. But, as someone pointed out, I was only being myself and clearly improvising in blank verse when I fluffed my lines. Reading it now with an impersonal eye, I find the play contains some lovely verse, and the principles expounded are unimpeachable!

At a lower level, Puck and I frequented family seats at, I think, two shillings in the Victoria Palace, where soon afterwards we began to revel in Gracie Fields. More sophisticated evenings were the parties given by the osteopath Ralph West and his wife in Hertford Street, Mayfair. Here was great music and lovely people, including Paul Robeson, still shyly waiting for a hand to be held out to him before offering his own. Equally well known at the time was Val Rosing, the principal tenor of Les Chauves Souris, a White Russian Company which put on a highly popular programme of music, singing and ballet. The soprano, Olga Alexeeva, possessed one of the three most beautiful voices I have ever heard. Later she sang frequently at our house. At her request I fitted words to Chopin's Étude in E major as a poem, 'O Leaves of Love', and we were proud indeed as we listened on the radio.

In 1925 my parents moved to 47 Castelbar Road, Ealing. The house had a fine garden and tennis parties continued, I now taking a larger part in running them. I was never a good performer, partly, I think, because I seemed to have been born without a sense of competition, and often when serving had to ask my partner for the score! But many of the players were very good, including Harold Abrahams, my Cambridge friend who became a famous Olympic runner, Clifford Mollison, the actor, a delightful 'silly ass' off the stage as on it, and Betty Nuttall, who became a bright young star at Wimbledon.

In 1926 there was a sudden call to action, the General Strike, and, as my duties at the Old Bailey would all but cease for a while, I volunteered as a special constable. Bearing in mind a splendid oath administered at the Ealing police station, I armed myself with a truncheon bearing the arms of the City of London which had been used in the Chartist riots, and paraded for duty.

In due course it became clear that this strike was a landmark in the history of English politics, but at the time it was light-hearted fun, as a crowd of public-school boys and others rapidly took over the running of public services. Notices, such as one on a bus, 'To stop bus ring conductor's neck once', were prevalent. I can only add a potentially alarming memory of my own. On each spell of duty I and others were taken by car to the Park Royal power station, where presumably we would oppose any dastardly attempt to blow it up. Our chief was Lord Lawrence, who was prepared to stand no nonsense. The very first day a shot rang out, and we, mostly gawping at a worker who had remained on duty and was shovelling coke while we tried to learn how to do it properly, leapt into action. We found that the shot came from the noble lord himself, who was firing at a figure on the skyline then approaching the central office of the establishment. 'Hi,' yelled the worker, as his Lordship took aim for a second shot. 'That's the postman!' His subordinates firmly removed the ancient weapon and peace was restored.

And so to December 1927, when at last I could afford to marry Puck, my income at the Bar being then some £600 a year. A Buddhist marriage? Of course, even though no such thing existed; I wrote it myself and it proved extremely successful! Puck, as a jeweller, made her own engagement ring of a single sapphire and her wedding ring of a sovereign with a hole bored in the middle and then worked out to become a smooth, well-fitting ring. The service was designed so that anyone could act as the 'officiant', and A. C. March, almost a co-founder of the Society with Puck and me, functioned with due weight and dignity. We had already been married that morning at a registry office, and enjoyed a reception at my parents' home at Ealing, where Sir Henry Dickens, then Common Serjeant at the Old

Bailey, obliged with an appropriate speech. After this triple ceremony my wife and I went off to Folkestone for the night before
crossing to the continent for winter sports in Davos, a honeymoon
which included my first visit to that natural capital of Europe,
Paris.

We received many presents, including a beautiful *sang-de-bœuf*
porcelain Chinese bowl from the Lodge, and one at which we
shamelessly giggled, a present of a splendid crystal bowl from the
family dentist. With one accord on opening the parcel we shouted
'Please spit!'

We found time on the honeymoon to make plans for the extension
of the Lodge activities, and returned to the maisonette where we had
been married, in St George's Way, Pimlico, where we should remain
for some six years, and the Lodge with us.

In February 1928 my father, who had been knighted in 1925, was
made a Judge of the High Court of Justice, and soon established the
reputation, expressed in the public comments on his retirement, of
strength allied with justice, courtesy and humour, and a sound
knowledge of the basic principles of English Law. These in my
humble way I endeavoured to apply when my own time came on the
Bench, as a Recorder and later on as one of the permanent judges at
the Old Bailey.

Judges in those days went round England, as they had done since
the reign of Henry II, on prescribed Circuits three or four times a
year. They could take with them a Marshal or aide-de-camp companion, who in the old days would have been armed to the teeth and
act as the judge's bodyguard. I went one Circuit with my father, but
more often Harold Abrahams would accompany him and amused
him when sitting beside him in Court by producing an enormous
race-track stop-watch to time the undefended divorce cases. 'Hurry,
Judge,' he would whisper, 'this is a record – twenty, thirty, forty, it
is, 2.40 precisely!' 'Shut up, Harold,' the judge would mutter back
before publicly pronouncing the needful judgment.

6
The Early Thirties

I was nearly thirty, and found it a solemn thought. Indeed, I wrote a
sonnet called 'Farewell, my Youth' and recited it at one of Ralph and
Marie West's great evenings. None seemed impressed, but they were
mostly middle-aged so I left it at that, and obeyed the Zen Master's
injunction when asked 'What is Tao?' 'Walk on!' I came to love this
phrase and its spiritual injunction so much that I wrote a book on it,
Walk On!, which has sold steadily for forty years. But Puck and I no
longer literally walked. We bought a car for £15 from Geoffrey
Burton, my friend Rene Donne's husband, and I learned most
incompetently to drive. I had not been made sufficiently aware of the
necessity of declutching when stopping in traffic, so the engine stalled
and my barrister pupil, Stephen Langdon, had to get out again and
again to wind her up. After which, for a while, in our beautiful top
hats, we pursued our way.

The Buddhist Society was now well founded. We had left the Theosophical Society, finding that the leech-like minor movements about
it stifled the teaching it was founded to proclaim, and that henceforth
those who liked their Theosophy neat, as it were, could find it in the
works of H. P. Blavatsky and a few others, while the Buddhist
Society, as the Lodge soon became, would proclaim what Puck and
I held to be the finest extant application of that ancient wisdom. In
1930 we founded a Meditation Circle, at first by correspondence,
with members all over the country. This coincided with, or may have
been one of the causes of, a sudden Western interest in meditation,

which had long formed a large part of the training of the Buddhist Order in all its schools. Partly to correct the sudden appearance of undesirable literature on the subject, we wrote and ourselves published in the same year *Concentration and Meditation*, which again is still in print after forty years. In it we concentrated on right motives. Meditation produces power, as many would-be teachers fail to realise, and unless this power is developed and used with the purest possible motive it turns back upon the user. Its misuse, as a spiritual force developed for selfish ends, is a form of black as opposed to white magic. The misuse makes the ignorant user of it a focus for evil forces and entities, and can drive the ego-ridden mind into insanity. Hence the need for perpetual warning, needed then and needed far more in the second wave of interest at present manifesting itself throughout the Western world.

We published more. To the Marriage Service written by me for our own marriage we added a Funeral Service which many, attending occasions when it has been used, have found deeply impressive. Then A. C. March gave up his accountant's job to work whole time for the Society, and in the course of five years' work produced in 1935 *A Buddhist Bibliography* with over 2000 items. We also published *A Buddhist Students' Manual*, which included a brief history of the Society, now expanded into *Sixty Years of Buddhism in England*, a *Brief Glossary of Buddhist Terms*, now expanded by me into *A Popular Dictionary of Buddhist Terms*, and *An Analysis of the Pali Canon* by A. C. March.

We were receiving valuable presents, including, from the eldest son of Sir Edwin Arnold, the armchair in which his father had written much of *The Light of Asia*, which, until the publication of my *Buddhism* in 1951, had interested the Western mind in Buddhism more than any other volume. Dr Arnold also gave us a fine portrait of this pioneer Buddhist, which hangs over the mantelpiece in the Society's library. We were given images of the Buddha of all provenances, and in all materials. Many we lent to members for their personal shrines, but the collection at our present headquarters is a fine cross-section of the range of Buddhist art.

More beautiful, though more ephemeral, were a series of calendars published by the Society with coloured illustrations by Puck, using her Japanese name, Hasuko. She had learnt the craft of wood-block carving from Take Sato, a Japanese artist then resident in London, and devised a set of illustrations of famous Zen *Koans*, such as 'the sound of one hand clapping' or 'Walk on', or 'The bridge it is which moves upstream'. Mounted on hardboard with a Buddhist quotation beside the calendar for each month, they proved extremely popular, and it is difficult to believe that they were sold at a profit for 3s 6d.

Puck and I were now in double harness in a condition such as only the most fortunate couples achieve, that of almost perfect happiness. We had no children, as her work in the war as an ambulance driver had meant in practice, whatever the theory, that young girls lifted men in stretchers high into the back of the ambulance, and her physical mechanism had been strained to a serious degree. The absence of children never seemed to worry her, and it never for one moment worried me. If we felt the need of a child we had the Society, which called for our full attention for all the years to come.

   By day I worked in Magistrates' Courts or at the Old Bailey, and she in her workshop or in housewifely duties. By five o'clock, unless I had a conference in chambers, we were ready for a Buddhist meeting in our drawing room, or for a concert or the ballet or the theatre, or a meal with friends at L'Escargot Bienvenu in Greek street, or for one of our own parties. By night we curled up happily together until that occasion, nearly fifty years later, when I had to agree to her being taken to a nursing home where, some four years later, she died.

Soon I met the third of the great men with whom I had a memorable and profitable hour. This was Meher Baba. Born in India in 1894, he had had an immense spiritual experience or breakthrough at an early age, and later formed a school in which, as he put it, he trained his pupils individually 'to rouse people, to awaken them', striving to arouse their feelings as distinct from their intellect. His view was that emotions in the West are like a veritable jungle of untamed animals, and they must be released in order that the mind may come to terms with them. However the emotions are defined, they are one expression of the vast force of the human entity, and must be controlled even as the intellect must be trained and controlled before it becomes a first-class instrument. Meher Baba's emotion was love. I sat beside him cross-legged on a sofa and we talked on love, he through an alphabetical board, as he had taken a vow of silence. He literally radiated love. It was a physical sensation of warmth and I have never experienced anything like it. The effect on visitors varied from garrulous chatter to silence, from halting questions to healing tears. And what fascinated me, who am not an emotional person, is that the love was far above the emotional plane, nearer to the divine compassion which is the supreme quality of *Mahayana* Buddhism at its best. Would there were more who attempt to develop this one virtue, even though it be still an earthly, personal love, that has at least purged itself of the corrosive force of hate.

In the Society a new arrival was Alan Watts. We first heard of him when he wrote to us from King's School, Canterbury, and we assumed by the tone and content of his letters that he was at least a senior master. In due course he turned up at a meeting, aged seventeen, and talked to us on Zen with the voice of authority. When still only nineteen he wrote one of the best books on Zen by a Westerner, *The Spirit of Zen*, which John Murray published in their Wisdom of the East series. When he went to the U.S.A. with his bride in 1938 we missed him sadly, as a deep student and as a delightful young man whom Puck and I would take on holidays. He was for a short while editor of *The Middle Way*, handing over when he left the country to Clare Cameron, who for the next ten years played a large part in the expansion of the Society.

The *R 101* disaster of 1931 was as dramatic as that of the *Titanic*, twenty years earlier, although with less loss of life. This enormous prototype dirigible set out on its maiden voyage to France with much publicity and with a distinguished list of passengers, including the Air Minister. It crashed at Beauvais, killing all aboard. At the mass funeral procession in London, which started from Palace Yard, Westminster, I was on duty as a special constable in Parliament Square. I remembered what I had heard of the powerful and clearcut prediction sent in to the editor of the *Sunday Express* by my astrologer friend, R. H. Naylor, as specimen material for a weekly article. It contained the words, 'the coming weekend is a grave period for all aircraft and the *R 101* is doomed'. The editor, John Gordon, was shocked. 'We can't print this sort of stuff,' he said to his staff. But before the article could be published, with or without amendment, the news came through. Dick Naylor's column became a leading feature of the Sunday Express for many years to come.

.   .   .   .   .

At the Bar I was becoming established as a criminal lawyer. My practice was slowly built up by a wonderful clerk, Billy Hollis, who served both my father and myself and later also Sir Henry Curtis-Bennett when he took over the chambers on my father's elevation to the Bench. Obeying his orders, and they were orders, I went from court to court ready to cope with such briefs as had been sent from the police solicitors, or which he had secured from private solicitors for the defence. Most of my work was prosecuting because I preferred it. Witnesses called for the prosecution are generally telling the truth as best they may, and the prisoner is generally guilty. Most defence briefs aim at cross-examining witnesses for the prosecution to persuade them to say the opposite of what they have just said, and then to call the defendant to tell a story palpably untrue, and to persuade the jury, if possible, that at least the case for the prosecution is not proved. It is a job which must be done, for all are entitled to help from trained lawyers to put forward their defence, but I preferred the dispassionate calm of prosecuting, as others revel in defence. I think that the average police officer is telling the truth. I refuse to believe that the 'planting' of evidence or the physical bullying of defendants is more than a very rare occurrence. I admit one does not need to believe the very words reported by the police as coming from a defendant on arrest. Tony Hawke, son of Mr Justice Hawke, used to tell a story which must be allowed space here.

A police officer was giving evidence of the arrest of the prisoner who was in bed at the time. 'At 8.42 p.m. on 9 November last I entered the prisoner's bedroom at 19 Paradise Crescent, Wapping. He was in bed. I said to him, "Is your name Albert Gordon Smith?" He replied that it was. I said to him, "Will you please dress and accompany me to the police station where you will be asked questions about a robbery at the Shackleton Produce Works in Skye Lane on 15 August last." He dressed and accompanied me to the station. That is my evidence.' The prisoner was gazing at him, fascinated and tongue-tied. 'Well,' said the magistrate, 'you've heard his evidence. Do you want to challenge it?' With heavy deliberation the prisoner asked the witness, 'Is that what you say I said to you?' 'Yes,' said the officer. 'Coo,' said the prisoner, 'I'll tell you what you did say. You bust in my room and said, "Come on, Ginger, hop into your pants. You're for the nick!"'

I have said that I preferred prosecuting to defending, but I was fortunate to be briefed to appear for the defence in two trials, each the most serious of its kind in this century. The first was the Austin Friars crash which brought Clarence Hatry fourteen years penal servitude, and the second was the 'Fire Trial', as it was known, at which Leopold Harris was found guilty of planned arson for enormous gain in the City of London.

In 1929 the country was in a desperate financial situation and on the verge of the slump which lasted many years. On 20 September 1929 Clarence Hatry and three others were arrested for conspiracy to defraud and a wide range of fraud and forgery, which covered a total loss of some £13,500,000 to banks, brokers and the general public. All had trusted this brilliant financier, but under enormous temptation he and his colleagues had descended to the gutter of crime. In passing sentence, Mr Justice Avory described their crimes as 'the most appalling frauds that have ever disfigured the commercial reputation of this country'. Hatry had successfully created Steel Industries of Great Britain. He then attempted the same for the light steel industry. The capital needed was enormous, and had to be created by credit. I forget the exact sequence of events, which moved very rapidly. There was a sudden whisper round the City that all was not well. Credit was withdrawn, the true worth of securities in trustee stocks examined, and almost overnight a crisis involving six figures faced the four men. They fatally agreed to flood the market with forged scrip in the hopes of re-establishing credit and being able subsequently to burn the forged scrip and so to conceal the fact that the great merger had succeeded by way of wholesale crime.

I appeared for the second defendant, Daniels, but, save for a brief clash of arms with H. D. Roome, who prosecuted at the preliminary proceedings in the Guildhall Justice room, I took no part, as I was led at the trial by Sir Henry Curtis-Bennett. All pleaded not guilty, to give the defence time to cross-examine Sir Gilbert Garnsey. He was the brilliant accountant to whom Hatry had, when the attempted forgery had failed, made a full confession, thereafter helping all he could to minimise the damage to cash and credit in the City of London. All defendants then pleaded guilty, my client receiving seven years penal servitude.

The 'Fire Trial', tried by my father, occurred three years later, but was curiously similar. This was the worst arson of the century, and it is difficult to imagine a more heinous offence than fire raising in a crowded city when the fire brigade is always hard pressed to cope with accidental fires. In each case the principal villain was given the maximum sentence. In each case one of the chief accomplices escaped punishment, for in the Fire Trial Capsoni turned King's Evidence and became the leading witness for the prosecution. I defended Priest, one of the seventeen men in the dock, but after a few days he pleaded guilty on my advice, having in fact made a complete confession to the police which it was impossible to deny. I went on holiday on 31 July, the day on which he pleaded, and returned on 18 August when, in sweltering heat, the 33-day trial ended. I referred in my mitigation for Priest to some fact at which my father, with excusable sarcasm, remarked, 'Yes, Mr Humphreys, I am aware of that fact, which emerged in evidence during your no doubt unavoidable absence.' Priest, almost a buffoon in his misguided sense of humour, went about with a photograph of himself in a fireman's helmet. He received three years penal servitude. Leopold Harris, who planned the stuffing of poor quality premises with second-rate goods, high insurance for both premises and goods, and then the successful fire, richly deserved his fourteen-year sentence.

In 1930 I was elected to the Garrick Club. It was ideally situated for me. I could walk there from the Temple, and lunch away from the shop talk which was the chief subject in the Old Bailey Bar Mess. The club was founded in 1831 for 'bringing together the patrons of the drama and its professors, and to offer literary men a rendezvous'. The membership was soon widened, but to this day it is a great honour for an actor to be elected. It is famous for its quality of membership and for its magnificent collection of pictures of past actors and actresses, one whole wall being covered with the works of Zoffany. The favourite is that of a very *décolletée* Nell Gwyn, which faces one on entering the club. It was said that there was a queue when money was needed for cleaning the painting.

When I joined, the dominating figure was that of 'Chuddles', real name I think Chudleigh, who inspected new candidates from his chair in the corner of the entrance hall. I was frightened of his possible disapproval but I seemed to pass muster. The most charming feature of the club was the long table in the coffee room at which one sat where one chose. I came in early one day and sat down next to the only other person at the table. We chatted, and he told me of his first visit to a film studio, 'where they are doing something of mine'. I waited till the next man came in and sat beside me. 'Who's the chap on my right?' I muttered. 'He looks just like H. G. Wells.' 'He *is* H. G. Wells, you fool.'

The list of the famous with whom I lunched or dined is wonderful to recall. Most were connected with the stage, letters or the law. The actors' contingent was strong indeed and, for the reason mentioned, of the highest quality. Gerald du Maurier was for a very new member a trifle remote, but Seymour Hicks was as witty and ebullient in the club as on the stage, and kindly signed my copy of his *Difficulties, an Attempt to Help.* Owen Nares, Felix Aylmer, Donald Wolfit, Cyril Maude and his son, John Maude, later a popular member of the Old Bailey Bench, were frequently there, and I made great friends with Harry Ainley, my hero as Hassan in the exquisite play of that name by James Elroy Flecker. Those connected with the stage included Ashley Dukes, so helpful to the Ballet Guild in the war.

The writers were as strong in fame. Somerset Maugham was not an easy man to know, and A. A. Milne was a very silent person, but Charles Morgan enlivened any conversation. I hardly knew T. S. Eliot, perhaps because I never quite appreciated his poetry as others said I should. Alf Mason, creator of Hanaud and two of the best detective stories ever written, was a friend to everyone.

Lawyers were there in quality if not yet quantity, and when I arrived they included Lord Hewart, the then Lord Chief Justice, Mr Justice Avory, my father, G. D. (Khaki) Roberts, Percival Clarke, who was one of the senior Treasury counsel at the Old Bailey, Melford Stevenson, now a High Court judge, and, as time went on, many more who, alas, brought their 'shop' with them.

Our friend Mrs 'Pan' Harmsworth, whose husband had been my pupil at the Bar, was during the war fulfilling a remarkable role in her house on the Downs near Steyning. She was indeed in the front line of England. Her house was at the same time the H.Q. of a Canadian Division, a depot for girls being dropped in France and returning with news, a dump for ammunition buried in the garden in case of invasion, and the off-duty home of pilots from the airfield at Tangmere. Deeply in trouble, the pilots asked for her help, and Marigold, as I called this six-foot, red-headed Scot, implored me when staying with her to get an urgent message to someone very high in the R.A.F. Their planes just could not cope with the new German bombers coming over the coast in force. The next day I happened to go to the Garrick for lunch and sat down next to Lionel Heald, later Attorney-General. He knew Pan Harmsworth well and I murmured her trouble. 'Who shall I tell?' I asked. 'Me,' he replied. 'I am head of Air Intelligence.' And things got done.

One more story, less serious, and one of a score about a much loved member, Sir Edwin Lutyens, one time President of the Royal Academy. Puck and I were in the Academy looking at scale models of some new building when Lutyens came up, and in his usual loud voice, audible all over the crowded room, asked, 'Have you seen the portrait of the Lord Chief Justice in there?' I said I had. 'Have you seen the hands? Bloody great bunch of bananas!' and he strode away. I trust the famous painter of the portrait was not in the room.

The centenary of the Garrick fell a year after my election, in 1931, and there was a great dinner in the presence of the Prince of Wales, who had asked to come because his ancestor was present at the founding of the club. Lord Buckmaster, in a worthy speech full of good stories, stressed one of the club's most admirable qualities, that of 'equality, where old and young, wise and foolish meet together measured solely by their merits'. So I found it.

In 1932 I was appointed counsel for the Crown in the few cases where the Director of Public Prosecutions had to be represented, either at London Quarter Sessions or in the Court of Criminal Appeal. My foot was now on the bottom rung of this particular ladder, the top of which was my sole ambition at the Bar. The term 'Treasury Counsel' derives from the fact that when it was found necessary to appoint some person with adequate staff to prepare and conduct trials of importance the Treasury Solicitor of the day was given the additional title of Director of Public Prosecutions. The last to hold this double office was Lord Desart, whom I once met with my father. The first full-time Director was Sir Charles Willie Matthews, with beautiful eighteenth-century offices in the Treasury buildings in Whitehall. A descendant of great actors, he was intensely dramatic of speech, and I once heard him at a conference in which my father was engaged explaining to him the outline of the proposed prosecution as if it were a passionate speech to the jury, or an appeal for mercy from the scaffold. His successor, from 1920 to 1930, Sir Archibald Bodkin, was of a cooler mould, but a tremendous worker as his counsel knew, for he was apt for conferences to ignore the clock or the day of the week. Meanwhile the name remained for those appointed to represent the Director at the Old Bailey, and today they are still called Treasury Counsel.

My first case in this office was the most curious I knew. It concerned Brenda Dean Paul, daughter of a baronet, and for years one of the 'smart set' in London society. Through no fault of her own she became one of the earliest and most famous of drug addicts. In 1930 while she was abroad she had an operation for which she was given morphia. She was given too much and fell totally under its influence. In London she tried to obtain treatment as a registered drug addict. She could not resist the craving for more and was arrested for being found in possession of a parcel of morphia. She appealed against her sentence of six months imprisonment, and an astonishing sequence of hearings ensued. She appeared before various chairmen of London Quarter Sessions, represented by various counsel and helped by an eminent doctor who completely changed his mind about her. At the end she was set free. The one constant factor was that all concerned felt pity for the girl, who was at times described as dying of the drug and at others somewhat better after treatment. When she was on remand in Holloway Prison she was given salt and water. She was allowed to be removed to a nursing home on two sureties, but the sureties ran out of funds. As prosecuting counsel I argued that prison might well be in her own interests, while her name rang through the press, with headlines such as 'Drugs – or Madness – and Death' and 'Doctors give up Brenda Dean Paul'. On the appeal she was allowed out of court while doctors wrangled over her, and we lawyers argued a nice point of law as to whether her sureties could be released from their obligations. In the end the appeal was allowed, and in March she sank into oblivion. Seven years later, in 1940, a physical wreck, she was penniless and unable to find work or lodging under her own too well remembered name. She stole from a store, and appeared again at London Sessions. This time I appeared *for* her, at her express request, and my speech in mitigation persuaded the Court to free her into kindly hands, for treatment, a job and a new name, far from London. Thus again she disappeared from public sight, and it was some twenty years later that, as a prematurely aged woman, she called on me at home to help her with some trustee matter. I did what I could. She died soon after.

In 1933 we moved from St George's Way to 37 South Eaton Place. The house-warming party was memorable. About midnight Val Rosing really got into his stride and, with the drawing room windows open, burst into the great arias of *Pagliacci*, with Olga Alexeeva joining in with what she remembered of Nedda's part. The piano, a boudoir grand, had to be brought upstairs round a very narrow bend. Five men tried it and failed. Three from another firm positively walked up with it. I have always been fascinated by real skill in any craftsman. In the General Strike, the workman already mentioned as shovelling coke took a day to teach some of us the knack of it. How much more skill is needed by the expert mechanic or surgeon; or by the maker of jewellery! I used to watch fascinated as my wife, hour after hour, worked on some tiny corner of a ring or at joining the parts of a silver cup. In my view I myself am at best a craftsman of words, particularly when trying to meet the exacting standards of poetry.

What is the relation of craftsmanship to art? I suppose this brings in the subjective factor, that 'beauty lies in the eye of the beholder'. Certainly the eye is able to change with remarkable speed and through a very wide arc. But there is, so I have found, such a thing as absolute Beauty, even as there is absolute Truth above truth and falsehood, and the absolute Good which contains both good and evil, which are indeed as 'thinking makes them, so'. This Beauty I have found in flashes of 'experience', while kneeling at the foot of the most famous Buddhist image in India, or just looking at a tree from a nursing home window. One has suddenly seen what *is*, beyond argument and all description. Nature produces Beauty in the countryside or even in an ordinary garden if we only look for it, and what is nature but a name for a cosmic force beyond the normal mind's achievement?

To these moments of 'no-time', each a breakthrough of the mind, using it in the sense of the Chinese *hsin*, or mind/heart or soul, the Japanese give the name *satori*. It is not to be confused with a 'hunch or merely psychic flash of awareness, and 'I' as we know it has no part in it, which is why 'I' cannot remember, still less explain what happened. But it is unmistakable and unforgettable.

There were times in the early thirties when the Society was in danger of petering out. Sometimes no one came to a Monday meeting, and Puck and I would stand waiting on the doorstep in South Eaton Place. Then we would go upstairs and light incense before the Burmese image of the Buddha, which was the first present given to us, and read aloud from a work such as the *Dhammapada*, *The Light of Asia* or *The Voice of the Silence*, and then meditate. People would come again, and the work for which we lived moved on.

In 1935 my father suggested that I should 'keep a King', that is, apply for permission to attend a Levée. I did so, and was duly summoned to St James's Palace to the last held by King George V. I had to hire my elaborate dress of knee breeches and correct coat, and my sword kept getting in the way, but even the most blasé could not fail to be impressed by this gorgeous and utterly royal ceremony.

The ground floor of St James's Palace was designed for the ceremonial of its period, and the levée – the male equivalent of the presentation at Court for women – came to consist of a long procession past the Throne, where a low bow to the King was returned by the seated monarch. In the anterooms, before the slow march began, was such an array of robes and decorations as would nowhere else be seen. All alike, bishops and judges, admirals and generals, and servants of the Crown of high degree were splendidly arrayed. Lesser mortals wore their approved attire or, failing all else, the velvet coat, knee breeches and sword of a gentleman. All these, however, were dominated by the Gentlemen-at-Arms, in helmets with enormous plumes, who, to the extent that one dare use such a phrase kept order in this motley gathering and marshalled us in such a way that as each in the line drew near the Throne, the right name would be called as he stepped forward for presentation.

Behind George V, already ailing and with only a few months to live, stood the Prince of Wales and his brothers and officials of the Court in their own magnificent robes. As my turn came I stepped to the right before the throne, made my bow, was acknowledged in the same way, which was of necessity a slow pendulum movement of the head, and then I moved into the room which led through others back to the entrance. Here was ceremonial dignity at its finest, such as is perhaps to be seen no more.

7

The English Bar

Members of the English Bar will not need to be told about their profession, but others may like to learn something of its traditions, rules and methods of helping in the administration of justice, which have changed very little in the last fifty years.

Solicitors and barristers (also known as counsel), are members of separate branches of the legal profession. In relation to a criminal trial, the solicitor takes instructions from his client, prepares the defence with appropriate witnesses, adds points of law and grounds of mitigation to be used if found guilty, and sends the brief to counsel of his choosing, discussing the fee with his clerk. The barrister reads the brief and has one or more conferences with his client. When the trial comes on the barrister is in charge, although taking instructions as the need arises.

The barrister, after passing the Bar examination but before being called to the Bar at one of the four Inns of Court, will probably have chosen the speciality he wishes to follow, and looks for chambers specialising in, or at least including, that type of work. We assume here a set of chambers which includes criminal work, and its clerk is a very important person. My clerk, Billy Hollis, and Fred Walden who followed him, built up my practice at the Bar, and I have known famous clerks who actually invited barristers to enter their chambers, of course with the approval of the chambers' head. The newly fledged and very frightened young man or woman will have entered chambers as a pupil of a senior barrister, to whom he is apprenticed for a settled fee for at least twelve months. He is assumed to know a certain amount of law; now he will learn, by following his pupil–master round, the practice of the courts, and the traditions, responsibilities and courtesies of those who work in them.

Nearly all judges have been barristers, and are therefore merciful of inexperience but harsh with any lowering of the standards in which they themselves were brought up. The judges are, in any trial, masters of the law, but are entitled to receive the best possible assistance from the Bar in any argument about it. There is, however, little argument in law at the Criminal Bar, which works on a set of recognised but unwritten principles. When I sat as a judge weeks would go by in my court without a word of law being raised, save by reference to some well-known decision or Act of Parliament on which the counsel concerned wished to rely.

But law can be tricky when the meaning is uncertainly expressed. Roger Casement, in the First World War was, they say, 'hanged by a comma'; and I like the story of the libel action in which Sheridan was concerned, where there were no commas in the passage said to be libellous. Wrote Sheridan, 'I did say you are a liar it is true and I regret it.'

Barristers at the Old Bailey, the principal Criminal Court in the United Kingdom, which copes with the affairs of 8 million people, lunch in their own Bar Mess. Many fathers and sons are colleagues there (even as sons practise before their fathers on the Bench). Some families are interlinked for long periods. The great Sir Edward Clarke led my father in the Oscar Wilde trial; my father led Sir Edward's son, Sir Percival Clarke, who led me when we were both Treasury counsel; and I led the present Edward Clarke, one of the Old Bailey judges, for the defence in a murder trial, and his son is now in my old chambers. This covers four generations and some eighty years.

The great moment in many a criminal trial comes with the cross-examination of the accused. It is, strangely enough, an essentially English procedure. How else can the evidence of a witness be tested save by questions put by counsel for the other side? Sometimes the cross-examination of a witness takes days; at other times it can be short but deadly, as in the famous case of Mrs Barney, who was tried for murder. Sir Patrick Hastings, standing as he always did with his hands behind him under his gown, quietly cross-examined two witnesses without using a note. Before he sat down he had torn the prosecution's case to pieces so effectively that my father, who tried the case, told me afterwards that had 'Pat' made a submission of 'no case' at the close of the prosecution he as the judge might have upheld it. Once at least, one question was sufficient. In cross-examining Ruth Ellis I asked, 'When you fired that revolver at close range into the body of David Blakely, what did you intend to do?' 'It is obvious,' whispered Mrs Ellis. 'I intended to kill him.' I sat down.

On the other hand, one can ask too many questions in cross-examination and lose one's case. On one occasion, during long questioning a police officer said that by the accused's breath, speech and manner of walking to the nearby police station he formed the opinion that he was drunk (this was long before breathalysers). Defending counsel asked one question too many. 'Why are you so *sure* that he was drunk?' 'Because', said the officer, 'when I opened the driving door he fell out!'

I should like someone to write a work on the psychology of evidence. The witness may be simply lying; or he may be wrong but genuinely believe that he is right; or he may be speaking out of a world of fantasy built up of emotionally charged opinions, which may carry conviction while being quite untrue. I began collecting stories to illustrate the difficulties. One which ended in a shout of laughter must suffice. A driver was charged with the 'motor-man-slaughter' of a woman on a pedestrian crossing. He said that he did not see her in time because he was trying to avoid being hit by a bus which swung in a wide sweep out of a narrow turning on his off side. The driver of the bus, the conductor and three passengers were called as witnesses. The final witness for the Crown was a somewhat pompous gentleman, who was driving his car out of the turning behind the bus. 'Now tell me about the bus, Colonel. When it reached the turning, just how was it being driven?' The jury waited, breathless. After a pause came the answer. '*What bus?*'

Alibis can be tricky. If true, what better defence than to prove that at the time of the offence you were a hundred miles away, or at least in a party at home? When I was prosecuting those whose alibis I was sure were untrue, I enjoyed destroying them, and claimed to be the champion 'alibuster'. Once, when two men were charged with breaking into a store in London they claimed that on that Saturday morning they were, with other members of their family, in a solicitor's office in Liverpool. One after another the family filed through the witness box, giving, when allowed, great details of the family transaction being conducted. Last came the solicitor, who said that this was indeed the date of the occasion. 'And your diary?' I asked, as I rose to cross-examine. 'May I see your office diary, in which no doubt you entered this appointment?' He had 'left it behind'. I sat down. The jury convicted.

On another occasion I was myself at fault. I went to much trouble to prove that my client, whom I was defending for robbery, was at home listening to the news at 10 p.m., at which time the robbery was being committed by someone about ten miles away. The jury started to giggle and the judge himself enlightened me. 'For the last six months or more, Mr Humphreys, I think I am right in saying that the one-time ten o'clock news on this channel has been given at 11 p.m.' It had. End of my defence.

The admission of a defendant's bad character is a matter in which a change is slowly taking place. A man's past record cannot be made known to the jury unless he deliberately, by one means or another, 'puts it in', as by attacking the character of a witness for the prosecution. But defending counsel are growing bolder, believing that a jury will not automatically convict on hearing of a bad record. The bravest question which I remember scored a bull's-eye. 'Officer, when anyone commits any sort of offence in this village, do you at once go to my young client, because you know of his record, and accuse him of doing it?' The officer, getting rather red in the face, said 'Yes, Sir'! I forget the result of that case, but I have known a similar defence or something like it to be successful on various occasions since.

Prosecuting counsel, whether briefed by the Solicitor's Department at New Scotland Yard or by the Director of Public Prosecutions, have considerable latitude in their conduct of a case, and I made for myself a rule about character which worked, I think, for justice. If the principal witness for the Crown was of bad character, and the defendant's character equally bad, I thought it fair to use some phrase in opening the case such as, 'Members of the Jury, I shall be calling the man who knows most about this case, but I must warn you that he is not of good character. You may want supporting evidence before you decide to believe him.' Defending counsel would have agreed to go no further than to repeat my words in his address to the jury. Otherwise, the wretched defendant would be at the mercy of a man whose character was even worse than his, and thus be fighting with his hands tied behind his back.

But there is character and character. I once had a conference with a man who wanted a licence for a small restaurant. I got all the information I wanted, and as I closed my papers remarked that I assumed that he had a good character. A long silence ensued. The client looked miserable and the solicitor embarrassed. It was the latter who finally broke the silence. 'One,' he said. 'For what?' said I, assuming a driving offence or something of the kind. 'Murder!' He had done seven years for it when his sentence of death was commuted. But he got his licence.

I have been asked many times whether the standard of advocacy today is as high as that of fifty years ago. This is a large question, and in the Old Bailey, where the number of courts has risen from four to twenty-four it is not easy to generalise. From my own experience I think it is as high, though very different in character. The atmosphere of the trial today is more like a business inquiry, but the standard of justice may be none the worse for the change. The style of advocacy has changed accordingly. That of Marshall-Hall, which I have already described, would I think today cause something akin to laughter, but the points can be made to a modern jury with no less effect for being couched in more colloquial terms.

But cases do seem to take much longer. The delay between crime and trial in any case is thereby increased, and this period is itself an important factor in the administration of justice. There was a time when we at the Old Bailey boasted of the speed with which a case was brought to trial, and the present causes of delay should be examined. One is the system of legal aid which, while admirable in purpose, may have the effect of slowing down the average trial. Why hurry, when the 'refreshers', the fee paid for each day of the trial, are guaranteed for an indefinite number of days? A sound way of counteracting some of this delay is that first advocated by my father: some sort of pleadings, which are part of every civil action, at which counsel on both sides meet in the judge's room and agree matters which will not be in dispute. They may discuss the line which the defence will take, or matters not in dispute, and defending counsel may, on instructions, offer pleas of guilty acceptable to the prosecution and the Court. All this can save perhaps weeks of time in a long trial and the practice should be extended.

But without recourse to a formal appointment, counsel for both sides, I have always strongly maintained, may at any time see the judge on any matter relating to the trial. The result of the conversation may well be a proposition agreeable to all and the saving of a great deal of time.

If, however, defending counsel has a real defence, and does not wish to disclose it, he is always at liberty to save it for the trial. Two examples may suffice. A man was found lying asleep on a ladder under a window, a pane of which had been broken and through which a large quantity of goods had been stolen. He was 'a stale drunk', and in his pocket was a large screwdriver. He pleaded not guilty, and in support of his story called four reputable witnesses to say that there had been a party at his house to celebrate, in two days of heavy drinking, two birthdays, one marriage and a new baby. The accused had finally staggered out for fresh air and sleep, lain down where it was at least dry, on the ladder, and gone to sleep until arrested. And the screwdriver? During the party he had been in the loft mending a leak in the cistern. And the total evidence for the defence was so impressive that the jury rapidly acquitted. Was counsel going to reveal that in advance, for the police to check it all and perhaps shake it? 'Not bloody likely', as the lady said in Pygmalion.

In the second case, I was defending a young man whom I described as so rich that he was virtually unable to be guilty of an intent to defraud. He was the son of an Indian rajah, worth in his own right some £6 million. He was very young, and staying in London with a friend who, having an account at Austin Reed's, had bought himself a new suit by simply signing for it. The accused, who, at home, could have a new car or yacht for the asking, also wanted a new suit, so he just signed his friend's name and got a suit. It was unusual for him to have to bother to sign anything at all. The judge quite rightly held that this was admirable evidence in mitigation but not an answer to the charge. But I was not going to spoil my story by revealing that suggestion in advance.

One of my strangest cases suggested the words with which I longed to open this chapter: 'The first time I entered Buckingham Palace was through a half-open window.' It was almost true, though

I had been to many a garden party with my mother when deputising for my father if he happened to be on Circuit. A young man wished to show that he could enter Buckingham Palace despite its guard of sentries and plain-clothes police. He went in through an office window on the ground floor of the south side. As it was a summer's night, the window had been left open. He took a small clock from the office mantelpiece and departed. I was prosecuting, and wanted to see just what he had done. So with a collection of police and palace officials I went to the window and, saying nothing, suddenly climbed in. The 'collection' followed me. I went into the hall outside the office where I found a large pair of doors leading into the main corridor round the inside of the palace. These doors, too, were open, and no one challenged me. However, the young man, having boasted to friends of his exploit, did it again. This time he climbed along the wall of what is now the art gallery, and jumped down into the main garden of the palace, where he was promptly arrested. His sentence of twelve months was received with equanimity.

Defending counsel may be pleased with an acquittal, and counsel for the prosecution will not be troubled thereby if he has done his own job properly. But there will be few compliments paid or gratitude expressed for obtaining an acquittal, and any student of psychology knows why. The accused, on being acquitted, fills his mind with the thought, 'How disgraceful that I was ever accused, and my "spout" should have got me off much sooner!'

In forty-five years at the Bar I remember but few compliments. The first came from a fellow barrister who was later a High Court judge. 'I hate the man like poison', he remarked, when I defeated him in a magistrates' court, 'but by God he's good.' The second came from a man whom I had recently prosecuted, and with success. He now wanted me to defend him. 'If he's good enough to get me two years,' he said to his solicitor, 'I want him for the defence this time!' But apart from a family of Sikhs who filled my chambers with flowers when I successfully defended a young member of the family, and the young lady who on acquittal leapt into my arms in public in the hall of Kingston Assizes, I think the most charming compliment came from a man whom I had successfully defended for receiving stolen goods on three occasions. When he was arrested a fourth time he was told that I could not defend him because I was in Japan.

'Then I shall plead guilty,' he said, and did. Was he guilty on the previous occasions? I do not know, and it was not for me to inquire, or even to form an opinion.

An acquittal is the end of the trial, irrevocably, and that man is not guilty. It is a practice for defending counsel to rise to his feet when such a verdict is given, and ask that his client be released from the dock. 'Certainly,' said Sir Gerald Dodson, then Recorder of London, on one occasion. 'When he has recovered from his surprise.'

Appeals from verdicts of guilty to the Court of Appeal are usually on points of law, but nowadays more vaguely on the ground that, all in all, the trial was unsatisfactory, which is in my view right. Appeals to the House of Lords in criminal cases are rare, and I was only concerned in one. The Attorney-General, leading me in the appeal of one Davies in what was known as the Clapham Common murder, patiently divided a vast mass of previous cases into two lines of argument concerning the right direction for the judge to give to the jury about the evidence of an alleged accomplice. I listened, and when my turn came to address their Lordships, asked, as I had nothing to add to the legal argument, to be allowed to remind them of the facts about which their judgment would have to revolve. They consented, and so, for the fourth time, after a double trial at the Old Bailey and a hearing in the Court of Criminal Appeal, I 'opened' the case for the Crown from the same, now rather dog-eared note. But the fascination of the appeal for me was the delightfully English compromise between a hearing 'in the House of Lords' and the fact that no one who was not a peer could in fact enter. We counsel were all crowded into a small pen, half in and half out of the Chambers facing the Lord Chancellor some thirty feet away, with law books piled about our feet, and papers everywhere. Nothing more inconvenient could be devised, but, like so many of our comic compromises, it worked. The appeal was rightly dismissed.

8
1935–6

I have noticed, when trying to make my memory obey the rules of chronology, that events come in groups, covering about a year. Such for me was 1912, 1924, and now 1936 (astrologers please note). In 1935–6 came the last case tried in the House of Lords, the Abdication, the World Congress of Faiths, the visit of Dr D. T. Suzuki, and the Chinese Exhibition.

In 1936 crimes were either felonies or misdemeanours, and 'killing by dangerous driving' was felony. A peer charged with felony could only be tried by his 'peers', his fellow members of the House of Lords, and it says much for their Lordships' behaviour that there had been no such trial since 1901, when the then Lord Russell had been found guilty of the felony of bigamy. However, in August 1935, Edward Southwell Russell, Baron de Clifford, driving his car on the Kingston bypass, hit a car coming in the opposite direction and killed the driver. On a Coroner's Inquisition Lord de Clifford was committed to take his trial at the Central Criminal Court, but being a peer he could not be tried for felony there. I was therefore instructed to apply for the indictment to be transferred to the House of Lords, which being done, that august building was prepared for this unusual event. The Royal Gallery, a magnificent room of about the same size as the Chamber itself, was built up into a court, with a throne, a chair for the Lord High Steward, and seats for four High Court judges below it. Along the walls were seats for some hundred peers, and chairs and tables in the well of the court for counsel, officials, and the dock. Some hundreds of peeresses and privileged visitors were seated at the back. As all concerned with the trial wore their fullest robes, the scene was at once immensely colourful and profoundly impressive.

The Lord Chancellor of the day was not, as such, the presiding judge. It needed a Commission signed by the King to appoint him 'High Steward of Our United Kingdom' for the purpose of this trial, and a staff of office was presented to him for the occasion. Then a Writ of *Certiorari* ordering the trial to be held was read, followed by the Return, sending the Indictment and the Inquisition back to the King, then Caption of Indictment, of five hundred words or so, and then the Indictment itself, of about fifty words, and the Caption to the Inquisition, and then finally the Inquisition, each of these of five hundred words or so. And after all that the trial began with the Arraignment, a reading of the Indictment to the accused and his plea thereto. Lord de Clifford pleaded not guilty. 'How will you be tried?' asked the Clerk of the Parliaments. 'By God and my Peers,' answered Lord de Clifford. 'God send your Lordship a good deliverance,' said the Clerk, and all settled down for the trial.

So far, to my slightly frivolous mind the proceedings seemed like a blend of the Voice of Sinai and Alice in Wonderland; but a trial is a trial and we set to work. Counsel for the Crown were the Attorney-General, Sir Thomas Inskip, the Solicitor General, Sir Donald Somervell, Eustace Fulton, who was the senior Treasury counsel, and myself, junior Treasury counsel. Lord de Clifford was represented by Sir Henry Curtis-Bennett and Ryder Richardson. A charming personal touch was the appearance, in the person of the barrister's clerk sitting in front of Ryder Richardson, of his wife, looking very businesslike in a black skirt, white silk blouse and with a large note-book in front of her. As it needed a ticket to gain admission and his wife wished to come, that was that!

At last the Attorney-General rose to open the case for the Crown. I had made him a beautifully typed note with all that he could require, but he preferred a series of what looked like the backs of envelopes, and managed to make two important mistakes of fact in his opening, even omitting the brief statement by the accused to the police at the time, which some might have thought to be almost the main item of evidence against him. It had been agreed in a

brief conference before the trial began that as there were eight
witnesses each of the four counsel would call two, which we did.
As it was later held that there was insufficient evidence against
the accused to warrant the defence being called upon there
is no point in even summarising the evidence here, which was
much like any other trial for 'motor-manslaughter', as it was then
called.

At the close of the case for the Crown, Sir Henry, who I think had
no such thought in mind, noticed a signal from one of the four judges
who sat below the President to advise on law. It seemed to be an
invitation to Sir Henry to rise and submit that there was no case to
answer. It was a brilliant effort, as one would expect from one of the
finest defending counsel of our era. The Court, meaning the President, the judges and the whole body of peers, as being all alike concerned in law as well as fact, returned to their own Chamber to
consider the submission, and the Court was adjourned until the
afternoon.

When the Court was reassembled the President gave its collective
answer to Sir Henry's submission, to the effect that it was well
founded. Addressing his fellow peers he said, 'My Lords, the
question for your Lordships is: Is the prisoner Guilty of the felony
whereof he stands indicted, or Not Guilty?' The Clerk of the Parliaments rose and called every peer by name. Each, placing his right
hand on his breast answered, 'Not Guilty, upon my honour.' And so
the prisoner was acquitted.

The Commission of High Steward was then formally dissolved. He
was handed the White Staff of his office and broke it in two, and
the House adjourned with its dignity unimpaired. At the trial
of Lord Russell, thirty-five years earlier, the tragedy of a conviction
ended on a note of farce. It seems that the staff then used was of some
substance. Lord Halsbury, being already eighty years of age, was
unable to break it and, although he put it across his knee and panted
mightily, in the end he had to be helped, that tradition might be
satisfied.

With Lord de Clifford's trial an ancient precedent was followed for
the last time. Soon afterwards an Act was passed to remove the need
of a trial by his peers for felony, and not so long after this the distinction between misdemeanour and felony was itself abolished. But
the justice done was justice according to law and of the quality we

look for in this country, and not in vain, from the humblest Bench of magistrates to the highest court in the land.

After a steady decline in health, George V died in January 1936, and his eldest son came to the Throne as Edward VIII. Here was opportunity for the English genius for dignified, dramatic ceremony. My father was invited to take me with him to the lying-in-state in Westminster Hall, and from the side we watched the unending slow procession as it passed the draped coffin with the crown upon it. The wintry light in the historic hall fell upon four silent figures who stood facing outwards at each corner of the catafalque. These were his sons, for at times the new King took his place with his brother George, later to be George VI, and the Dukes of Gloucester and Kent. The silence was complete save for the soft shuffling of the feet of those who came in thousands to pay tribute to their King of twenty five years.

The procession from the Abbey to Paddington Station for the service at Windsor passed up the East Carriage Drive of Hyde Park, and there in the enormous crowd I stood with Puck and Alan Watts and his father. A few paces behind the gun-carriage walked the new King, about whose private life and plans much troubled speculation was already gathering. We did not see the incident when a small corner of the crown itself fell off, and was quickly picked up by a following soldier, but for those concerned with omens it was an omen indeed.

And so for 1936 we had a new King, loved for his charm, his human touch and his wide range of personal knowledge about the affairs of the Empire and the State.

About this time Henry Dicks, my friend of Cambridge days, asked me to join the Council of the Tavistock Clinic, where he was for many years a senior consultant. I was profoundly impressed with the quality of its membership. I was once asked to take the chair, and although I have been chairman of many committees and councils in my day I never knew another in which all concerned, without egotism or rancour of debate, enabled one to get through a long agenda with speed and efficiency. There is much indeed to be said for training the thought-machine to think clearly, and to keep invading emotion at least under control!

It was also through Henry Dicks that I had the pleasure of meeting Carl Jung, when he took me to the first of his series of lectures at the Institute of Medical Psychology. I had deeply studied much of his writing and at this time held the view that although he had enormously advanced our knowledge of the mechanism of the mind his books give little evidence of his having pierced the ceiling which lies above that mechanism and is the floor, so to speak, of the abode of Spirit above. But much more of his work was published after this date, and I gained the impression that he was revealing to the world only part of his own spiritual discoveries. Now we have Laurens van der Post's *Jung and the Story of our Time*, and even allowing for the element of hero-worship in the author's mind, the revelations of Jung's inner thought and spiritual experience herein described lift him to the level of one of the really great minds of this century.

In *Psychology and Religion* (1938) Jung wrote of man as 'an ineffable totality', and that it is 'impossible to define the extension and the ultimate character of psychic existence'. This must be so, for to define is to limit, and the man of religion has no limit if man consists of Spirit functioning in the complex machine which Jung analysed and described. But if man is in truth a religious animal one can understand Jung's remark that among his patients over the age of thirty-five 'there was not one whose problem in the last resort was not that of finding a religious outlook on life'. What, then, did religion mean for Jung? It may be enough to remember his answer on television when asked about the existence of God: '*I know.*' Be it so, for argument must here be silent. Surely true religion, a 'binding back to the source of being', will never be found in the mechanism of thought/feeling. In 1931, in the face of ridicule from several members of his own profession, Jung had given us his commentary on Richard Wilhelm's translation of *The Secret of the Golden Flower*. Perhaps he thought that in this he had gone far enough to tell the West of Eastern spiritual achievement. He was clearly right in deploring any attempt to import ready-made religion from the East, and expect it to be absorbed by the West either in its conscious or collectively unconscious aspects. Wisdom is clearly beyond geography, but its forms may be right or wrong for a particular civilisation. Eric Graham Howe took the process of transmission a stage further in some of his books, such as *Invisible Anatomy* and *Mysterious Marriage*, but the present need is not for the grafting of already matured forms of thought on to the Western search for reality, but for the awakening of a newly lifted consciousness which finds the one wisdom on its own plane, and then creates a locally acceptable series of forms for its expression. At least, such is my own view, and I have expressed it in my classes and writings of some forty years.

It is not easy to understand the astonishing success of the Chinese Exhibition at the Royal Academy of 1935–6. There were, of course, many educated people with a taste for Eastern art, some with their own substantial collections; but no one reckoned that for month after month there would be long queues of people waiting to get into Burlington House. Puck and I went many times, often to look again at something of exceptional beauty, be it early Chou bronze, T'ang Buddhist images or Sung paintings. Here was Buddhism in craftsmanship, setting forth an utterly 'different conception of the universe and man's place in it', as Laurence Binyon pointed out in his introduction to the Commemorative Catalogue. 'Each living thing is seen in relation to an infinite whole, and acquires a significance from that relationship.' The writer notes, too, what the Buddhist would call *sunyata* or emptiness in visible form. The empty spaces in the finest Chinese pictures have enormous meaning! These are not something left over; they have an integral, positive function. Thus we loved them, day after day. We looked at the Nanking blue and tried to remember it enough to compare it with what we had at home. In vain, for each piece in a single cabinet was of world rank in value, whereas a favourite little vase which I brought back from Japan was cheerfully described by a knowledgeable friend as 'Woolworth'. However, one learnt from the three thousand exhibits, or as many of them as the weary eye and mind could take in.

Why was there this love of Chinese art by the public at large? It far exceeded that for Indian art, which was exhibited many years later, and the Chinese Exhibition lacked the dramatic value of the Tutankhamun exhibition of recent years. Perhaps Alan Watts, who reviewed the exhibition in our *Buddhism in England*, was right when he found a picture called 'Bamboos and Rocks', dated AD 1350, so beautiful that he could say nothing about it. The finest Chinese picture is not complete, and in its incompleteness leaves the beholder power to move on where the artist left off, with a flame of greater life now burning within.

Whether I spoke on these lines when in April 1936 I opened an exhibition of Tibetan Art at the Berkeley Galleries I do not remember. I find it embarrassing to talk to a shop full of people anxious to begin buying, so I was reasonably short, especially as Puck and I had thoughtfully put 'sold' tickets on what we regarded as the two best articles on sale.

For hundreds of years the religions of the world, with the sole exception of Buddhism and Taoism, have fought one another to the point of deliberate extermination. The thought that they might have a common purpose, though couched in differing phraseology, was absent. The first modern attempt to assemble representatives of a large number of these religions on one platform, where they might discuss their relative forms of approach to reality, was the Parliament of Religions held in Chicago in 1893. In July 1936, Sir Francis Younghusband, famed for his march to Lhasa in 1904, convened 'The World Congress of Faiths' in London and, in a fortnight's hard work, it hammered out with remarkable good will the common ground of at least seven religions. The result may be read in a large volume, *Faiths and Fellowship*, published in the following year.

In fact, as my personal diary of the Buddhist Society shows, an attempt had been made in London as early as 1928 to arrange such a congress, although on a smaller scale, convened by a group of three such movements under what I consider to be the better title of 'Fellowship of Faiths'. I spoke for Buddhism, but do not remember why the venture was not continued, although Sir Francis had then been present and had spoken for Christianity.

The English, or those of them concerned with any religion at all, are firmly entrenched in the dogmas and ritual of some form of Christianity, and take hardly to the suggestion that others, particularly those from 'foreign parts', may be as right as they in matters of religion. Indeed, when I represented Buddhism at a convention of various faiths held in the twenties, there was real surprise in the audience that a Christian, a Jew, a Muhammedan, a Hindu and a Buddhist could sit side by side without tearing one another's hair out! But once the seeker for spiritual progress grasps some rendering of the source of our Wisdom, as I personally found in *The Secret Doctrine*, religions become so many languages in which to teach and discuss some aspect of it. I had an example of this in practice. About 1947 Father Dumoulin, author of the best history of Zen Buddhism, called at the Society on his way to the U.S. from Japan. We were alone in the library, and he prowled round the room during our interview as though seeking some point of attack. After a while I murmured with a smile, 'Father, why not drop your Christianity?' An incredulous grunt was the reply. 'And I will drop my Buddhism,' I added. 'Let us begin our meeting again – in *Parabrahman*' (which is the Supreme in Indian Sanskrit terminology). He laughed and relaxed and from then we could talk to our mutual interest.

The purpose of the 1936 World Congress of Faiths was specific, and well described by Sir Francis in his Foreword to the above-mentioned volume: 'The organisers had no intention of maintaining that all religions were "the same", nor of seeking the lowest common denominator and building on that. Not breadth without depth did they seek, but only that breadth which comes from deepening depth.' This aim was carried out in a series of twenty discussions, each opened by a well-known speaker and then made free for all points of view. In addition there was a public meeting at the Queen's Hall on 9 July on the topic of 'The Supreme Spiritual Ideal'. I was asked, a week or two in advance, to stand by in case Dr D. T. Suzuki, advertised as one of the speakers, was unable to reach England in time. How grateful I am to the Lords of Karma, if such there be, that he succeeded, for I should certainly have spoken in capital letters, so to speak, to match the grandeur of the theme. Dr Suzuki did nothing of the sort, and all who have later discussed with me that memorable evening have made the same remark, that they remembered only his speech. Professor Malalasekera of Ceylon and Sir Sarvepalli Radhakrishnan, later President of India, made fine contributions, but Dr Suzuki, as the man of Zen, was as fascinating as he was unique in his approach to the occasion.

He seemed to be dozing as he sat on the platform, and was roused, when his turn came, by the chairman. He confessed that the phrase 'the supreme spiritual ideal' meant nothing to him. 'How can a humble person like myself speak about such a grand thing before such a grand assembly of people?' And he described a Japanese straw-thatched house where, with its large windows, 'one side of the house is taken away and the house opens right into the garden'. Slowly he developed his theme, that house and garden are one, that house and occupants are one, that 'nature, you and I are one'. Little by little he drew down the highly-coloured abstractions of his fellow speakers, and replaced them with humble, concrete, daily things, implying rather than stating that here would truth be found. And so he enfolded his great audience into a sense of oneness with each item of the garden, the trees, the fish, the water in the pool, and never used a single abstract term. As though bewildered with them he analysed the three components of the theme, the Supreme Spiritual Ideal. He confessed himself puzzled by them, for to him the spiritual-material is one. He ended with Joshu's famous story of the bridge, which was but a plank over a stream yet all the world passed over it. Then he thanked his audience for their kindness in listening to him. 'The kindness must be mutual, and in this mutuality of kindness do we not seize a little glimpse of what we call Spiritual World fellowship?' And he quietly sat down.

Even Sir Francis, in an introduction to a later edition of Woodward's *Some Sayings of the Buddha*, when searching for an analogue for the supreme charm of Buddha, as distinct from his words, remembered Dr Suzuki and this Queen's Hall speech: 'He had studied the teachings of Buddha. He had taught the teachings of Buddha. But he had gone much further than this. He had saturated his whole life with the teachings of Buddha, and in his own way expressed those teachings so that everyone who saw or heard him was drawn to him and disposed towards Buddhism.' He too was infused with the spiritual power of that small, frail, elderly professor with his lovely, memorable smile.

Here was my first taste of Zen itself, and from a master of it who became for me the most spiritual human being I have met in this present incarnation.

On 20 July he visited the Society. Dr Malalasekera was there and Miss Constant Lounsbery, founder of Les Amis du Bouddhisme in Paris, and Ch'u Ta-Kao, a young Chinese who walked in one day and offered to do for us the first translation of the *Tao Tê Ching* by a Chinese into English. It was for us a historic meeting, illumined by another glimpse of Zen. A German Buddhist, after Dr Suzuki's brief talk, asked a question which was part thesis, part argument, part alternative solutions to itself, and took at least three minutes. He ended, and our visitor, with his usual adorable smile replied quite simply, 'Yes, yes!' which, as the saying goes, brought the house down.

He came again, and according to my diary, 'he went right through the field of Mahayana and in an hour and a half we learnt more than in years from books'. He came once more to say farewell, and we bombarded him with questions for two hours. I did not see him again until 1946 when I found him in his war retreat in Kamakura.

The World Congress, gradually changing its title as an organisation to the truer Fellowship of Faiths, is still doing excellent work, leading the way in a coming together in mutual interest of faiths of widely different form, so that the spirit which all seek, and whence all came, may be the better found in the face of the world's materialism.

In December 1936 Sir Henry Curtis-Bennett K.C. died, and I learnt a lesson from what ensued. Day by day he would come into the Bar Mess of the Old Bailey behind a cloud of smoke from his large cigar, and regale us at the coffee table with his wit and reminiscence. Then he came no more. Just three months later someone asked of another, a propos of some story, 'Do you remember Harry Curtis-Bennett?' 'Yes,' said the other, after a brief pause, 'he often used to come up here.' But he had to think for a moment. The wave had closed over, and in case we imagine that when we are gone more than a handful of people will even remember our existence, we had better think again. We shall not long be missed.

In December 1936 the crisis over the Throne had been reached, and the King was called upon to make a desperate and cruel decision. We heard of the great names involved, and how the parties for and against abdication were lined up in implacable opposition. There were even mutterings of the possibility of strike leading to such rioting as might be called civil war. 'Will he go, or stay?' we of the public asked ourselves, seeing clearly the enormous difficulties which would arise should he stay. Seldom in history has a man had to choose between the sovereignty of an empire – for he had much to say and do in its affairs – and the woman he loved. He chose, and the nation felt his agony as they listened on 11 December to the most dramatic broadcast of modern times. I knew well his great friend, Sir Walter Monckton, and asked him to give the King the following lines, which seem to express the views of most to whom I have shown them.

Edward

I know not the inward story which the unborn years will tell,
But whether he served us badly or whether he served us well,
I know, for these eyes have seen it, that even if Edward failed,
A light went out in England on the night when Edward sailed.

His reign was short but I for one am proud to possess pieces of
china and glass and a gold medal commemorating that which never
happened, his Coronation in Westminster Abbey on 12 May 1937

9
1937–9

The thirties were glorious years for building the home truly beautiful, not just collecting – as with stamps or Poole pottery – but choosing carefully the articles of use and ornament which a large house needs. Collecting calls for knowledge, a natural flair for good workmanship and design, and agreed principles on what is wanted and what merely clutters up the home. We were not concerned with technicalities or dates or even mendings; still less with money value in case of later sale. We wanted things which had been lovingly wrought, as Puck's own silver was wrought, whether chair or image or vase, whether a hundred or two thousand years old.

Once we called at the shop of Mr K. K. Chow near the old British Museum station. It was near closing time, and we sat on the floor handling lovely Chinese bronze and jade. Then with a sigh we had to admit that we could not afford the prices and rose to leave. 'No,' he said; 'please have a cup of the tea sent me from my estates in China.' We sipped and loved it and again rose to go. 'And please take these,' he said, handing Puck the piece of 'mutton-fat' jade she had loved so much, and me the Wei dynasty bronze dagger I coveted, as I thought, in vain. 'I am tired of people who come and talk to me of nothing but rarity and value. They have no love of beauty as you have. Please take these. I shall retire soon and go back to China.' And so we left, all but in tears, and bowing profoundly.

But we bought lavishly, within or just beyond our means of furniture, from Wolsey Brothers near St James's Park station and from Kyle's in the Pantiles at Tunbridge Wells, where we went frequently to stay with Puck's mother. The knowledge of the antique furniture dealers is impressive. Once we bought in Petworth an early seventeenth-century court cupboard with four carved doors. We boasted of our find to the elder Wolsey brother. 'You bought it?' he exclaimed in horror. 'But the doors, man the doors! They were carved later, fifty years later!' He knew the piece and had refused to buy it, to our advantage.

Any article of furniture can be interesting. Our waste-paper baskets range from an Australian hardwood mortar, almost too heavy to lift, to a copper Irish still, a leather bucket of Nelson's time and a modest bread-bin of the eighteenth century. For the floor we invested in Persian rugs, brought to us in a taxi on Saturday mornings by a Mr Behar. We haggled fiercely and laughingly the whole morning, while he all but sobbed about his starving children, and implored us to take two rugs rather than one, at a reduced price. When at last the bargain was made we were embraced before we separated, all of us well content with the morning's work.

My pictures were unconventional, save those by Harry Jonas, Norman Lloyd and my wife, and those of some of my ancestors. One of the latter was a portrait of my great-great-uncle Charles who defended R. E. Corder, the murderer of Maria Martin in the Red Barn. I proudly possess a gallery of signed photographs of King Edward VIII, Winston Churchill, Dr D. T. Suzuki, and my father, all of which were given me, and a signed photograph of H. P. Blavatsky. The rest are Tibetan tankas; prints of famous pictures, such as the self-portrait by Leonardo da Vinci, which was incredibly difficult to obtain; a commissioned painting of the 'Japanese Alps' by Take Sato, with whom I stayed in Japan beside them; and small rugs, far better displayed on the wall than on the floor, from China, Persia and Tibet.

I have made a speciality of collecting artists' first drafts or sketches rather than their finished work; of Gilbert Bayes the sculptor, for example, picked up from the floor of his studio after he had used it to mark the clay before he modelled it; of Augustus John, a drawing of his first wife found for me when I implored him for a drawing of robes of which he seemed such a superb master.

But we spent most time in Sparks and Moss and Bluett, learning to feel the right surface of porcelain with the eyes shut; and with Captain Spink, whom we knew at Tunbridge Wells, and with whom we haggled hard, to the horror of the assistants. I was cross when one of these experts, coming to my house, said of a Chinese plate, which had been clearly marked on the back a long time ago as 'once containing food given by ancestors of the Humphreys family to Charles II when concealed in the Boscobel Oak', that it was eighteenth-century. I do hate debunkers. . . .

But whether we bought our treasures in England or Peking or were given them, we loved them, at any time considerably and even more when acquired unexpectedly, as was the case with a fine Japanese Kannon, the Goddess of Mercy, used as a doorstop in a shop in Baker Street; and with an even finer figure lying in the garden of W. W. Winkworth, who, we were told, 'only collected Japanese netsuke'. The Buddhists say one should not be attached to possessions. I try to obey.

And the cost? One night when Puck and I were doing accounts I suddenly asked her, 'Are *you* interested in these accounts?' 'Not in the least,' she replied. 'Hooray,' I said and we put them in the fire, and kept no more. As we had one bank account the situation was that much easier.

Puck and I from early days suffered from balletomania, to name the splendid disease enjoyed by balletomanes, and derived originally from Arnold Haskell's *Balletomania*. Night after night when the ballet season was on we would return home, exhausted and still panting, from two or three hours of ecstasy and the yelling and clapping which followed every ballet.

From a heavy armful of programmes, I have tried to extract a story of twenty years' visits to the ballet in London – in vain, partly as a result of the curious fact that many programmes bear no mention of the year in which they were used, and partly because when the craze really gripped London there were at times four separate companies playing simultaneously. Puck and I went to them all: de Basil at Covent Garden, Markova/Dolin at the King's Theatre, Hammersmith, Robert Helpmann/Margot Fonteyn at Sadlers Wells. 'Mim' Rambert was everywhere, criticising the poor *port de bras* in the rival national-to-be company of Ninette de Valois. Our major attachment, however, was to the de Basil Company, with its three amazing young women who hit the headlines overnight in 1933: Baronova, Toumanova and Riabouchinska. Baronova was the all-rounder, the finest Queen of Shemakhan in *Coq D'Or*, and catch-ing the eye, rather naughtily perhaps, from a corner of the stage in *Le Beau Danube*. Toumanova was the more aloof, the same virginal type as Margot Fonteyn. I remember her holding court under the great chandelier in the foyer at Covent Garden during an interval, coping with the mighty of the land as indeed a queen might have been trained to do – and she then about eighteen! Riabouchinska was more of the fairy, though with a great sense of fun, and many will remember the night when the news ran through the theatre that she and Lichine, then in each others' arms in *Jeux d'Enfants*, had become engaged. One night, when Danilova was in one of her Russian tantrums and refused to appear, Riabouchinska came on, almost unrehearsed, to dance in *La Boutique Fantasque*, and when carried off on a bier of staves nearly fell off with laughing. Only the *cognoscenti* in the audience noticed the skill with which others whis-pered or gestured to her what to do.

All in all I remember Danilova as the finest Odette/Odile, and Markova, English by birth, as the finest Giselle. The name of the company changed from de Basil to Blum and after the war to the Marquis de Cuevas. Dancers moved from one company to another, and although new ballets were produced in all of them, there was a hard core of classics common to all which are still, and rightly, being produced.

Massine's attempts to put classical symphonies to dance notation were bold. In his first, *Les Présages*, to Tchaikovsky's Fifth Symphony, he produced, in the opening bars of the second movement as danced by Lichine and Baronova, one of the most profound moments in ballet. The yearning love cry of the music was somehow translated into the movement of two bodies. The Seventh Symphony of Beethoven barely succeeded, and only Massine would have dared it. Personally, though in a minority, I loved *Choreartium*, Brahms's Fourth Symphony, if only for the unforgettable slow second move-ment in which Verchinina led the line of slow-moving girls.

One further word on this period of ballet, to me of more than sensuous pleasure. In *Le Beau Danube* there comes a moment while the stage is full of dancers whirling round him when Massine, as the Hussar, stops and stands quite still. From that moment one's eyes were riveted, not on the other dancers but on him. Again and again I saw this 'still centre of the turning world' and its symbolic value.

Then, as the others spun off-stage and he was utterly alone, there came a sudden fling of the arm to summon his still invisible partner, and the very gods of the waltz blended all their powers into that immortal melody. Or thus do I remember it, a step nearer to that no-thing-ness to be studied more deeply after my visit to Japan.

Of music and the theatre one can but call to memory the occasions still fresh after forty years: Lady Diana Manners in *The Miracle*, with Massine as the Spielman, and that exquisite dancer, Tilly Losch; John Gielgud as the finest Hamlet I ever saw; Robert Speight as Becket in *Murder in the Cathedral*; George Robey as an admirable Falstaff when he could remember his lines; Anna May Wong in *The Circle of Chalk*, the cast of which included Laurence Olivier, and a company of Japanese actors who could leap from a gallery, turning a somersault, and come up with a naked sword at the opponent's throat. After that I worked harder at my kendo, even with a bamboo sword!

Apart from serious drama, opera and ballet, and as deeply satisfying as any, were Noel Coward's series of revues. For sustained quality, for elegance, to use an old-fashioned term, for sheer beauty in décor and costume and splendour of total production, there has been nothing like them since. Would that they could be rescued from the silence of the past to delight us again on television. For where today is the man who could write, compose and produce such a mountain of delight?

Music is equally a catalogue of high points of memory: John Foulds's 'A World Requiem' at the Albert Hall on 11 November 1923, and thereafter for many Armistice nights (some of us had listened as he composed it at the piano in his home in St John's Wood); or Menuhin, still a boy, holding eight thousand people breathless and spellbound in the Albert Hall. To my eyes the people faded out and nothing remained but that bow, rising and falling, and music as though it sounded in heaven.

In 1936 Toscanini came to London to conduct a concert at the Queen's Hall. All the music-loving world tried to get in, for it was, I think, his first appearance in London. Puck and I suggested to four friends that they should dine early with us, and dress for dinner. We would then sit round the radio as though listening at the Queen's Hall. We dined and then I broke the news. 'There's room in the car for six,' I said. 'I got tickets a month ago.' The great man first conducted the National Anthem. We looked at one another and Alan Watts said, 'I've never heard that gorgeous hymn before.' Such was the impact on me, too, for whom Toscanini was in a class of his own.

For the last Act of *Tristan and Isolde* we went again and again to hear Flagstad, even greater, because more human to my ear, than Frieda Leider. Basil Cameron was a frequent visitor to our house, and once, before conducting at a Prom, asked to be left alone for a while with the score of Beethoven's Seventh Symphony because he had thought of another way of improving his rendering of some phrase. And in the summer of 1939 we saw such a *La Bohème* as made us never want to see it again, with Gigli skipping about in Act One like a schoolboy and we, as usual, crying at Mimi's death at the end.

The Albert Hall has seen some wonderful occasions, but on 5 October 1938 a wildly enthusiastic audience celebrated the silver jubilee of the Proms, when sixteen of the leading singers in the country joined to sing for Henry Wood 'A Serenade to Music', composed by Vaughan Williams to words taken from Shakespeare's '*The Merchant of Venice*', beginning 'How sweet the moonlight sleeps upon this bank'. Here was a compliment indeed, our leading composer presenting a symposium of solos and what amounted to a choir of our leading singers, with Sir Henry himself conducting the B.B.C. Symphony Orchestra. This short work will surely rank high in the landscape of English music. It may have been at the same concert that we heard Rachmaninov play his own second piano concerto, and we wondered how a modern pianist, hearing the record of it, could play it otherwise.

As a barrister I was concerned in this period with three cases of unusual interest.

In April 1939 two brothers named Orsborne left Grimsby with a motor trawler belonging to the Marstrand Fishing Company. They certainly took it, and they certainly took it all the way to South America, changing the name to *The Girl Pat*, and on the journey changing their own names too. The issue in the case was whether this was theft or a permitted spree, and therefore not 'against the will of the owners'. The two men were extradited from Georgetown to England, and rightly convicted at the Old Bailey. The interest for me, and I was led for the defence by a one-time pupil–master,

John Flowers Q.C., was in the romance of the voyage, whether criminal or not. After calling at Dakar they had food for a day and water for eight days, but they made the trip across the South Atlantic with no better chart or map than his small child's atlas which the skipper just happened to have in his pocket when they sailed. Seamen, amateur or professional, will appreciate what this meant, and I am proud to have this one thumbed page of the South Atlantic framed and before me as I write. They made no money out of the trip but, as the long story of the voyage unfolded, they seemed to me to have added to the adventures of British seamanship.

The second trial, generally referred to as the Mrs Casserley case, was in fact the prosecution of Edward Chaplin for the murder of Mrs Casserley's husband by beating him on the head in his own sitting-room. The law in this case, as in a score of others, was clear but the evidence was circumstantial. It was a question of piecing together items to constitute proof in the absence of the direct evidence of anyone present on that occasion. As junior to George McClure I was allowed to accompany Sir Bernard Spilsbury, the most famous pathologist in our lifetime, to the room where the attack took place, and to watch him at work. I was Watson watching the Great Man using his enormous knowledge to unravel by minute signs what had happened.

In the room where Casserley died, I watched a fascinating analysis of the events of weeks before. It concerned bloodspots on the wall. Some showed drops of blood going upwards. Here a bloodstained weapon had been raised and the drops flung on the wall. Other blood drops pointed down. Here the weapon had come down again, as in a blow, to fling more drops on the wall. A close examination made clear this double action, of hitting someone again and again with a weapon already bloodstained. Those were facts, but on the total evidence the verdict was manslaughter and not murder. Mrs Casserley was charged with 'misprision of felony', meaning the concealment of a felony known to have been committed. She pleaded guilty and was discharged. My father tried the case and I was in trouble over the indictment, for which I was responsible. In it I had reintroduced this charge of 'misprision of felony', even as in the war I reintroduced the old crime of 'public mischief'. His Lordship, in sentencing Mrs Casserley to one day's imprisonment, remarked that

Lord Westbury in 1866 had described this law as long redundant. I did not revive it again!

Spilsbury was indeed a great man, and the perfect witness, so impersonal and unbiased that defending counsel grumbled at the way in which juries regarded his evidence as conclusive. He came to public notice during the Crippen trial in 1910, and had steadily risen in his practice as a pathologist. His life was taken up with interminable inquests, and his forensic skill became unrivalled. Because I have heard him referred to as a witness for the prosecution, pure and simple, let me relate one single example which disproves this. In a case of an alleged abortion–manslaughter, by the then usual method of a bowl of water, soap and a knitting-needle, as a desperate hope defending counsel suggested to him another way in which the injuries to the woman's body *might* have been caused. Sir Bernard, as always when considering a point, put his head slightly on one side and after a while said 'yes'. The judge thought he had not heard aright. 'You say "yes", Sir Bernard?' 'Yes, my Lord,' said Spilsbury, and being released from the witness box was out of court immediately, carrying as always his black bag. The judge turned to counsel for the Crown. 'In view of that answer,' he asked, 'can you rightly continue with the charge against the accused?' 'No, my Lord,' I replied, and the jury was discharged. By that time Spilsbury, already on the way to another inquest, had no doubt put the matter out of his mind. He had given a considered opinion, and the consequence of it was of no concern to him.

The third case, also tried by my father, is of interest as one of the first of the I.R.A. trials, which today we are inclined to regard as modern. Mason, the leader, was sentenced to seventeen years penal servitude, and was described by the police as the 'C.O. of the I.R.A. in Great Britain'. The offence was conspiracy to cause explosions and arson, and the haul of material in various parts of the country was enormous. Their violently-worded poster, which I have before me, was provocative in the extreme. The moment of drama came when one of the men refused to plead either guilty or not guilty, denying the right of the Court to try him. Instead, he flung himself down in the dock. 'Enter a plea of not guilty', said my father, 'and let him lie there if he pleases.' He did for a while, and then finding an oak floor very uncomfortable, and the trial proceeding, took his seat.

I was reminded of this remark from the Bench some thirty years later when a man in the dock before me produced a razor blade and slashed his wrists. I had reached the point of my summing up when I was reminding the jury of the enormous strength of the evidence against him, and the prisoner was waiting for that moment. 'Let him be taken down to the cells and medical assistance sought,' I remarked in, I hope, the same almost casual voice, and after a brief interval for cleaning up the dock the trial went on in his absence.

Holidays were for us an important part of the year, and we travelled widely by car. In England we plunged into very amateur archaeology, naughtily helping ourselves to artefacts from a newly opened trench at Verulamium (there were hundreds more), or to a kerbstone on the Ermine Way through Lincoln. Following Roman roads straight on, where later roads had deviated, was great fun, sometimes involving a stretch over smooth turf where the farmers had most carefully never ploughed, until the straight road appeared again. We felt the force of Glastonbury, helped by Mrs Maltwood's newly published map of *King Arthur's Round Table of the Zodiac*, which is once more in the public eye. For Whitsun we hired a camping punt on the Thames, and slowly and in blissful silence made our few miles a day, only going ashore to shop or visit the local for a well earned pint. At night we lay under the stars, and at dawn might see a heron on the bank, looking in the morning mist like a Japanese print. Save for the occasional river steamer from Oxford we had the world to ourselves, and I know no more perfectly restful holiday. For weekends we used the Queen's Hotel at Brighton, with bedrooms overlooking the beach so that we could hear the sound of the sea at night. From this hotel we went for the only deliberate walk we ever took, eight miles east along the cliff to Peacehaven (and we took a bus back). Since then I have never walked or taken any deliberate exercise, save that involved in gentle gardening, or a brisk walk from the Old Bailey to the Temple or to the Garrick Club and back for lunch. Maybe I keep fit by a vast output of mental exercise, with a mind which works all out from 8 a.m. to 10 p.m. when – seldom later – we would turn out the light.

We took the car for several visits to Ireland, staying with Mr Justice Mcnaghten at the Giant's Causeway, or with Puck's relations in and around Dublin, or in the south-west corner near Killarney where we revelled in what I regard as the most beautiful

light in the world. I never believed 'Irish' stories until I was involved
in two of them. On one occasion we asked at the station at Avoca for
two singles to Dublin. 'You will be wanting two returns,' said the
official in the booking office. 'I do not,' I explained. 'I am not coming
back and I want two singles.' 'But the return fare is cheaper,' he
said. And it actually was cheaper than a single. Or again, when
stopped by an officer in the middle of a vast bogland on the way to
the border and Belfast, we were asked for our identity papers, then
needed. I cursed, and rummaged in the suitcase in the boot for them.
I produced my AA wallet and began to look. 'Och,' he remarked, 'I
see you have a lot of papers there. Be on with yer.' We went. But how
logical!

But, apart from trips into Belgium, Luxembourg and Andorra, we
spent most of our time in France. We had all the Michelin maps, and
chose yellow, second class roads whenever possible to avoid the
traffic and to see the land in peace. But it was long before I could
cure Puck of the habit when going south of trying to stand on her
head in the car to read the map. She would, however, from the map
find the ideal place for lunch, off the main road, facing south, with a
stream near by to cool the beer and for washing up. We bathed
wherever there was enough water, in small lakes which were never
without one fisherman, or small rivers where the village children had
cleared the weeds. We never did more than about two hundred miles
a day, and after arrival had time for a walk round the town of our
choosing. Our goal in those days would be one of the small coast
towns of Bandol or Agay, with few visitors, where it was warm and
cheap. So cheap for the English that once, just before the war, we
had nearly a month abroad on £60 all told. In the winter we could
afford to go skiing in Davos or the Engadine.

In one of our earliest trips abroad with a car we found our way to
Chartres Cathedral, and although in the next thirty years we visited
a large proportion of the cathedrals of France and Belgium, that of
Chartres is to my mind the noblest building, in terms of architecture,
and spiritual inspiration, in Europe. I have noticed friends whom I
took with me through that great West door fall back at the impact of
its total beauty, 'the leaping columns of pure line', the flood of light
in coloured splendour from the hundred windows, the sense of an
immemorial centre of power surging from beneath one, flowing from
above. It calls for perpetual music, and I always link Vaughan

Williams's 'Fantasia on a Theme of Tallis' with that other beauty of the eye. We began to distinguish those cathedrals and churches built in the phenomenal period between 1100 and 1250. This burst of genius in planning, engineering, sculpture and glass, is indeed mysterious, for it faded rapidly. I agree with Louis Charpentier in *The Mysteries of Chartres* that the secret of the windows is a secret still. As he says, 'this glass does not react to light like ordinary glass. It seems to be transformed into a precious stone that does not so much let the light pass as itself become luminous.'

Bourges, although its glass is a little later, is a better place to examine it, for the windows are lower; one can almost touch them. In each the setting sun throws pools of living colour on the grey stone floor. In this amazing hundred and fifty years it is reckoned that at least a hundred and fifty cathedrals and other Gothic buildings were put in hand, including those of Paris, Rheims, Amiens, Sens and Rouen. How could so much labour be made available; where did the money come from? We do not know; we can only enter quietly, bathe the heart in the beauty of it, and the spirit in the rise of consciousness which for us at least gave inward vision, to remain with us always.

But in 1939 all this came to an abrupt halt. We had taken evening dress with us to Le Trayas, being honoured with an invitation to dine with the Duke of Windsor in his villa on the other side of Nice. But alas, war clouds were gathering and he was packing to come home. At least when we called he signed for us his portrait and a copy of *The Windsor Tapestry*. Then we too raced for home.

10
The Second World War

Looking back on the five years of the Second World War, I see it as a kind of capsule in the lives of all concerned. During that period most of us in London found that our manner of living, place of sleeping, food, amusements, type of work, and even our views on life and death were profoundly altered. Far more important – and of lasting value – was our attitude of mind, the very purpose for which we got up in the morning, did what we did, and went to bed, often for a very disturbed night. It was simply to win the war, and the whole nation's physical, mental and emotional energy was directed to this end. Of course we grumbled and complained at the vast upheaval in our lives. Were we not English, and is it not our custom and right to complain? But we worked, very long hours and often for very little money, with the certainty that soon, or if not soon then later, we should win the war! We did not fear the Germans; we laughed at them, as our publications, cartoons, stage and radio jokes make plain, and Lord Haw-haw was the biggest joke of all. Many of us had to live double lives, acting a 'cover story' to conceal our real and secret occupation. Some, unwillingly, carried about with them secrets of enormous importance. And they kept them, and the people at large kept them. Juries in spy trials, where much had to be revealed, were still chosen from the usual register. They were told to keep their mouths shut and trusted to do so, and they did. When the landing in France in 1944 was imminent, the harbour at Shoreham was filled with small craft laden with war material. Each was covered with a tarpaulin, but a gale blew most of them away. Not a word was said by the thousands passing by; the landing was still a shock to the Germans.

We all have a hundred war stories; I will confine myself to those which illustrate some point I wish to make. I used to pick up four people every morning from a bus stop if I could help them on their way, and on one occasion a girl from Dulwich was telling the others what a terrible night it had been, with 'half the street blown away and I can't say how many killed'. What worried her? 'Coo,' she said, 'and I'm going to be late for the office.' If that is a fair sample of a nation's state of mind that nation cannot be beaten. We were not beaten and we never thought we should be.

Indeed, by 1943 we knew with total certainty that we should soon destroy the enemy and live our normal lives again. I go further, with a suggestion I hesitated to make at the time because I thought it was my own incredible belief. Now I find from friends' conversation that my memory is right. We were surprisingly happy – happy, I suggest, as a result of the removal of so many of the squabbles, neighbours' squabbles, and of much of the trade rivalry which embitters those involved. The usual bickering, as the outsider sees it, of local and party politics was stilled, for we learnt to think for and work for a larger unit than ourselves. In Buddhist terms the basic cause of suffering, which is personal, self-centred desire, was for the time being collectively removed.

We were not plunged straight into war. After the declaration on 3 September 1939 nothing warlike happened in London until the extensive bombing of the Surrey Docks on the night of 7 September 1940, the fires of which enabled one to read a paper in Knightsbridge. But there were preparations for war, not merely by the Government in terms of battle, but in civilian life. For this was to be, as we all knew, total war. We were all issued with gas masks which we carried, but fortunately never had to use. We had ration cards and petrol ration coupons, and we watched the barrage balloons go up in plots of waste land. Those sleeping in London built air-raid shelters in the basements of their premises, and concrete shelters were built in the streets for those unable to do so. There was a widespread call-up of those of use to the Services, and the rest of us learnt the meaning of almost total 'black-out'. Soon there was fire fighting and 'heavy rescue', death in the night and all the horrors of front-line war. We were ready for it all.

Puck went back as a captain into the FANYs and worked as Finance Officer in an underground room at its headquarters in Knightsbridge for seven thousand girls on secret assignment, largely to be dropped in France. I was told to stay at the Old Bailey. There would be plenty of work to do and less than half the normal Bar to do it. Our joint reaction to the war was, as we saw it, right. Trained in Theosophical principles, Puck and I saw the vast cycles of the Life-force which periodically brings a universe into being and then dissolves it; we saw the minor cycles of continents and civilisations as they rise and fall on earth. And the cycles smaller still of the history of any nation or group of nations in any period of the earth's evolution. Here was yet another burst of collective personal ambition causing indescribable misery to innumerable individuals, each of whom, none the less, was involved by reason of his own particular *karma*, the mass causes from past lives which brought him inevitably, justly, rightly, to that precise situation. Like all others we knew extreme uncertainty; we never knew, any of us, if our home would still exist when we returned at night. We two were fortunate in having conquered the fear of death, which is very different from being indifferent to whether one dies or not. The Buddhist is trained on the rhythm of 'coming to be, ceasing to be'. He knows that the cause of death is birth, that all that is born must die; only the date is seldom known precisely. For us it was 'ALL RIGHT', whatever happened. We accepted the situation, and then proceeded to 'Walk On'!

Puck had her secret work; I had my secret trials at the Old Bailey and in courts martial where, as part of my war work, I would defend some service man charged with a serious offence. After receiving all relevant papers, I would be directed to the offender's barracks, have my conference, do what I could at the trial, and then hand over every scrap of paper to be burnt.

Throughout the war, including the first period of bombing of 1940–1 and the second of 1944–5 and in the interval between, the administration of public justice went on as carefully and unhurriedly as before. The first bombing was mostly at night, but the second was by night and day with periods of an alert and consequent all clear, and when the V2s began to arrive there could be no warning at all. In many courts the overhead skylight made it dangerous to continue a public trial, so they continued underground. One morning at the West London Magistrates' Court, for example, I sat in the basement on a pile of *Times* newspapers, while the magistrate sat with his clerk behind a kitchen table. The prisoner and other officials sat or stood as they could. More dramatic was an occasion when a series of alerts so disturbed the work of the Court of Criminal Appeal that my father, sitting as President that day, inquired if there was a room underground to which the Court might adjourn. 'Only the boiler room,' he was told after due inquiry. 'Very well,' said my father, 'then the Court will reassemble in the boiler room in fifteen minutes.' It did, and three judges in their scarlet and ermine robes on kitchen chairs behind a kitchen table, and counsel, with only a chair for law books and their papers, carried on. And the subject of the point of law? A matter of Licensing law, which might affect the hours of opening of the public houses of a licensing division in Essex.

Even with a diminished population there were crimes, both old and new. There were breaches of wartime legislation about rationing and prices. One famous firm in the East End had 'inadvertently' made an enormous illegal profit. In the dock at the Guildhall Justice room were six of its directors, charged with heavily overselling their quota under the Limitation of Supplies Order. After sentence I remember well the six of them literally dancing round the yard outside and hugging one another as they shouted, 'It's only a fine.' The fine was £217,000.

Life was difficult for all of us, and the Bar had its own problems. We had a ration of petrol which had to suffice to take us all over London, to two and even three courts in a day, and we had to cope with the bombing of our chambers. Mine in the Temple were damaged eleven times, and on one occasion my clerk, meeting me at the Middlesex Guildhall in Parliament Square, was unable to tell me if there was any mail for me that morning. 'I don't know, Sir,' he said. 'I haven't been able to get in yet.' Once indeed, as I could not myself get in, I had a conference in the solicitor's offices, or what remained of them, an occasion so contrary to all Bar etiquette that only a war could permit it.

In one's travels about London from court to court one never knew when a street would be barred by a bombed house newly sprawling across it, or by a time bomb which might explode at any moment. Surely the bravery of those men who quietly defused unexploded bombs ranked very high in human virtue. I thoroughly approved an incident I watched once when I was driving east down the White-chapel Road, and had stopped at lights next to a police constable on traffic duty. A few moments later, as he continued to hold up the traffic, a lorry, apparently empty but with two men in it, came roaring through the crossroads. As it passed, the police officer drew himself up and gave a full salute. I asked him why, and he said, 'There are two brave men in that lorry with a live bomb which at any moment may go off. They are taking it out to the Hackney Marshes to dump it.'

The Buddhist Society too carried on. *Wesak*, the annual equivalent of Christmas Day, was held in May as usual. The Burmese Bhikkhu, U Thittila, later for a while Librarian of the Society and today the doyen of the Sangha in Burma, was one of the speakers. Others were the Sinhalese Buddhist President of the Theosophical Society, who happened to be in London, Clare Cameron, then editor of *Buddhism in England*, and Moyine Al-Arab of Egypt. Then I tried to express the Buddhist attitude to war. It was difficult to avoid histrionics, but I stressed the principle that this, as all other events, provided opportunity for the application of our beliefs, and I ended: 'Meanwhile, as we live and have our being in the dark night of war, we can console ourselves, when courage wavers, with the wisdom of three words – "It will pass".' This was superficial Buddhism. Much truer was the notice which Puck and I hung up in our air-raid shelter at South Eaton Place, and about which we would, when each all clear was sounded, repeat with a grin, 'This too will pass'!

At the end of 1940, the fire of London which caused such enormous damage everywhere burnt out at our printers nearly the whole of our stock of books and the standing type for them. Worse still, it was found that we were uninsured. We found new printers, reset the books and carried on. I wrote hard during the war years, producing *Karma and Rebirth*, and *Studies in the Middle Way*, and a quantity of verse. The then Poet Laureate, John Masefield, a subscriber to *Buddhism in England*, wrote of *Peace and War*, 'Each section of the book contains good, original work of much feeling.' And he mentioned those he liked best.

The members of the Society acted as they thought right. Some suffered as conscientious objectors; others fought, and splendidly. At

Dunkirk, Vasa Lindwall stripped and dived from the ship on which he was serving as an R.N.V.R. officer, but wore the captain's cap on his head to show that he was 'in uniform' if made a prisoner. Being bilingual, he was able to assemble the disorganised French troops, and get the maximum number on board the rescue ships for England. Captain John Hardy, D.S.O., R.N., did better still. While in command of the *Carnarvon Castle*, a lightly-armed peacetime liner, in the South Atlantic, he spotted and attacked a German cruiser which was raiding shipping. Although his ship received twelve hits during the engagement, he successfully chased the cruiser away and it was not seen again in the area.

I like the story, not mentioned in the later Admiralty reports, of John Hardy's behaviour on the bridge during the fight. 'He was bounding up and down, shouting abuse at the cruiser and actually shooting at it with a revolver.' This very distinguished sailor survived to found a Buddhist centre in Lausanne.

On White Lotus Day, 8 May 1941, which was the fiftieth anniversary of the death of H. P. Blavatsky, I was asked to take the chair at a joint meeting of many Theosophical Societies and Groups. The most interesting speakers were, of course, those who had known H.P.B. personally, such as Miss Esther Bright and John Watkins, founder of the famous shop of that name which specialised not only in Far Eastern but also in Theosophical literature. It was a noteworthy meeting in that so many of the speakers were Buddhists, as were H.P.B. and H. S. Olcott. I suggested to a number of those present after the meeting that a standing joint committee of all Theosophical organisations be formed to perpetuate the spirit of the meeting, but unfortunately the idea was never put into practice.

Later on in the war the Buddhist Society was reorganised. Clare Cameron found us premises in Great Russell Street and we took the opportunity to make timely changes. The name of Lodge was dropped and we became the Buddhist Society; *Buddhism in England* became henceforth *The Middle Way*, with a new cover designed by Puck, and the library, now consisting of a thousand books or more, was reorganised, and a new book-plate was devised. Meetings began again and continued through the later bombing, and soon were full to capacity. In a second reconstruction just after the war we employed our first assistant, Joan Pope, who remained as General Secretary for the next nineteen years. A Council was slowly formed to establish the running on more democratic lines of what was now becoming a national organisation, and when I left the country in the following year the assistance of the then Hon. Treasurer, Jack Austin was of the greatest value to Puck.

At midnight on 16 April 1941, according to our journals' laconic report, 'Mr Humphreys was standing on his doorstep fire-watching. The explosion (a land-mine), which destroyed some twenty houses, flung Mr Humphreys back into the house and then passed on to wreck the mews at the back of the house, leaving Mr Humphreys lying in the wreckage of the hall with only a bruise or two. The house was very severely blasted, and nearly classed as uninhabitable, but hard work by the builders, and by Mr and Mrs Humphreys, who were living underground, has saved the building, and meetings reopened there on the 19th May.'

Had the front door behind me been shut I should have been crushed against it and killed instantly. Puck was not at home at the time, but when she returned we agreed that we must not leave the house empty. Looters were always on the look-out after a raid, so, although we had to fetch water in a bucket from down the road and use a friend's house for a bath, we stayed. When our maid, Annie, arrived at the house in the morning, she looked round, made 'tut tut' noises and proceeded to wash the china in the kitchen cupboard, which like all else in the house was under a layer of soot.

What splendid philosophy! Just get on with the next-thing-to-be-done! I have developed it consistently since. But as looting was in the air I did some myself. The house next door was totally abandoned, so I went in. I found a good rug, three inches under soot, and curtain fittings, both useful to my charwoman whose own house had been destroyed. I took these and threw them out from the back into my own garden, giggling to myself as I heard the heavy feet of a patrolling policeman passing the house outside.

The first period of bombings ended on 10 May 1941, the day on which the House of Commons and the Queen's Hall were destroyed. There would be no more bombings for three years, though we knew it not at the time.

A year after being nearly bombed out we grew tired of the smell of the ruins about us, and sought a new home. We called at a house-agent in St John's Wood and were solemnly told, 'Here is a list of houses for sale, but if you like the look of any other please ring at the door. You will probably find that it also is for sale'! We chose our present home for its big sitting-room, useful for parties of all kinds, and bought a long lease for a few hundred pounds. The garden would be the right size for Puck in the peacetime we felt to be round the corner. There was a surface well older than any house in the area, and in due course Puck built a rockery from two lorry loads of the ruins of Inner Temple Hall.

During the doodle-bug period we dug a pond for fish and water-lilies, lying flat in the hole when the doodles (flying bombs) came over. The water has not been changed for thirty years, so the authors of volumes on fish-pools in the garden may think again.

We learnt the art of compost from the best source of all, Sir Albert Howard, who had imported the technical craft from India, where it was known as the Indore method. He would take a pinch of the soil and smell it, as would a connoisseur with a glass of wine. 'Good,' he would say, and we were satisfied. I bought two hives of bees, and it was pleasant indeed to harvest over a hundredweight of honey a year to help the ration of our younger friends. Bees are lovely companions, and it was a perpetual delight to watch the 'matron' bees grooming a young bee for her first flight and then giving her a push to go. Bees, however, are dangerous neighbours for babies left unattended in prams in the hot weather, for if one bee stings a score will follow, and a baby can die as a result. So, soon after the war, when a baby next door was habitually left but a few yards from the hives in our garden, we reluctantly sold them.

In 1942 I was appointed Recorder of Deal, a royal appointment in which I acted as Chairman of the Borough Quarter Sessions, with a jury, for cases beyond the scope of the local magistrates but not so grave as to warrant trial at assizes. On the day I took my seat I thought I was a very brave Recorder. There was an explosion which shook the Guildhall where I sat. I remembered that Deal had been shelled continuously, from across the Channel. There was another explosion. Nobody present took the least notice. After a third I nearly gave myself a medal, but after the Court rose I asked the Mayor about the shelling and its result that morning. 'Oh, that,' he answered, 'they are just blowing up stray mines on the beach'! But a week later the train I usually took for my return to London was destroyed in the station, and many were killed.

Incidentally, my sitting as Recorder produced one possibly unique occasion. I dined with my father and mother at Ealing one evening, and we found that each of us had been sitting that day as chairman of our respective courts, the Court of Criminal Appeal, Quarter Sessions at Deal and the Ealing Bench of Magistrates.

By the time the second bombing started I had become a fire-fighting street captain, with a splendid uniform and helmet. But the H.Q. post for the area happened to be outside the door of my wine-cellar, and I was told not to move. I made my rounds, however, on a bicycle bought for the purpose, as we were supposed not to use the telephone, and had great fun instructing groups how to approach and extinguish a sizzling fire-bomb, not having the least idea beyond common sense to hand on to them. Fortunately I had the assistance of a group of five men from an R.A.F. unit in an empty block of flats near by. When there was an alert they came straight to my H.Q. to await my orders. As it happened no bombs fell in my area, but we worked out on a map just how to get as quickly as possible from one sub-centre to another, by leaving ladders in strategic positions and other devices.

Compassion

I knew the bombing. I was there.
I felt the terror, saw the red blood spilled;
Heard thunder in the flame-lit air,
And running feet that stumbled and were stilled.
I knew the bombing everywhere;
I watched the laws of love and hate fulfilled.
Of all the agony too wide aware
I suffered and was blinded and was killed.

I loved, and loving lived in hell,
I that am whole and still unharmed and well.

Throughout the war I had an additional interest, that of the Ballet Guild and its associated activities. Founded on 10 May 1941, it was the brain-child of Deryck Lynham, who wanted it to be a 'non-profit-making Organisation to encourage and develop the Ballet'. The Guild, limited to a hundred interested persons, soon wrapped round itself, as it were, first the Ballet Guild Club, whose members paid a subscription to pay for the running of the Guild, and then the Ballet Guild School, founded by Molly Lake and Travis Kemp, which had its premises in Loudon Road, St John's Wood. Then a library was formed, and it became the best collection of books on the ballet in London at the time. All three concerns were used for the company of young dancers and for the quintet, later an orchestra, created by Leighton Lucas.

My own part was to be a 'front man', to use the criminal slang of the Old Bailey, to be chairman of the Ballet Guild's Council and make speeches at the performances given in public for war charities. Theatres were generously lent us but the majority of performances were given at the Rudolf Steiner Hall, near Baker Street, and the Garrick Theatre in Charing Cross Road.

I was asked by the owner of the Arts Theatre Club, Harold Rubin, to become its chairman while he went on war work, and the Guild put on a series of Lunchtime Ballets, which were a great success, the press being very polite about the quality of the dancing and the range of new ballets performed. Important people helped us throughout; Arnold Haskell, Anton Dolin, and Ashley Dukes and his wife, 'Mim' Rambert. Philip Richardson, Editor of *The Dancing Times*, gave much publicity to the work, and Cyril Beaumont was a tower of strength in his knowledge of past ballets, and publicity for those being newly created.

Considering that the management work was all unpaid and that funds were negligible, it is remarkable how many performances were given. And many of the newly created ballets were adopted by professional companies after the war. Our proudest moment was on 28 June 1941, when we, alone in remembering its centenary, gave a performance of *Giselle* at the Rudolf Steiner Hall with Helene Wolska in the name part. Our most embarrassing moment was when, beneath the stage of the Garrick Theatre, I had a fight with the representative of the firm who had hired us the panatrope, or long-playing record machine, for which we had not paid a promised deposit. He insisted on turning it off. I said, as we could hear, that it was at that moment playing overhead the National Anthem, at the beginning of the performance. I won, without using judo, and the instrument played on! The sum due was paid.

I learnt to my satisfaction how to live in a dual mental capacity, embracing the world of beauty and that of needful usefulness. One night during a performance of *Giselle* the cross on the grave in the corner of the stage was insecurely fastened, and a large and hairy stage-hand's arm was desperately holding it still. I lay beside him and helped, yet still admired the dancing, and still my heart was in that woodland glade. My 'finest hour' however was at a performance in aid of the Free French in 1944. After the performance I brought the French Ambassador in front of the curtain to thank the audience for their attendance, and was suddenly inspired. In ringing tones I told the crowded theatre that the war was nearly over and – I can hear my booming fervour now – 'in one year from tonight we shall perform this set of ballets again – in Paris!' We *did*, under the auspices of Ensa!

Unfortunately, Deryck Lynham's schemes could not continue after the war without much more capital. In addition to this a vast change was taking place in the lives of all who had given their help for our charity, and in place of help a fierce competition would grow up between the professional companies. We founded The London Archives of the Dance as a Trust to equate with the French equivalent, Les Archives Internationales de la Danse in Paris, handed over whatever else was needed to Molly Lake and Travis Kemp to use for their own professional company, and, with much regret but with the memory of enormous pleasure and work well done, bowed ourselves out.

In June 1944 I had Geoffrey Burton and his wife, my old friend Rene, to dine and asked him about a telephone call I would make to him next day. 'Not tomorrow,' he said. 'I have to go down to the coast to see off some bits and pieces of mine.' These were the Mulberry Harbours, of his own design, made ready for D-Day. And so, after a period of flying bombs in England and much hard fighting abroad, came the Armistice, very different from that of 1918. Puck and I, with Hilda Leyel and Diana Moore, old friends who were dining at my house, drove in my open car through the West End on the way to Mrs Leyel's flat in Lincoln's Inn. The streets were crowded but with very little noise, no rowdiness and no hysteria. People were crying but with quiet relief from the strain of five long years of war. And then? Within months, within weeks, the old Adam asserted itself, and every kind of claim and blame and quarrel burst out anew. Had we learnt nothing in five years of war? At times one thought, as the selfish strife began again, we had learnt very little. As the Buddhists would say, the cause of suffering is selfish desire, and will not be resolved until that folly, based on false belief, is dead.

You Had to Go

You had to go. It mattered not
That even as you came to birth
Your father's body, face to earth,
Lay shattered in a Flanders field,
His laughing eyes with darkness sealed.
He never saw the son that he begot.

You heard the guns of battle cease
You saw the birth of fretful peace
As through the aftermath of woe
I weaned you in a mist of tears
And watched you grow.
And as you climbed the ascending years
In sunlit joys and shadowed fears,
Swift to engage
In any foolish wild emprise,
I saw within your eager eyes
The light they say that loved to show
Within your father's at your age.
His life in yours again must flow.
I understand. You had to go.

Life was a gay adventure, death
But the ending of a song.
And while the heart held laughter, body breath,
The road was never sad, nor journey long.
No moral problem dimmed your day;

Your right was right, your wrong forgiveless wrong,
And truth and wisdom never dared betray
The cause of England, viewed in the English way.
You gave your life to healing, to the art
That, born of books, yet lies in part
Within the eye that sees the part made whole.
You hated pain, and man's insensate lust
And all that dragged his freedom in the dust,
Assuming for your knightly goal
Damnation to the unjust.
So did your father long ago.
I said no word. I knew you had to go.

Too soon the marching, feet of war
Made echo at my closed door,
Yet haply died away.
But you, with eyes of longing raised
To sunlit wombs of horror, praised
The freedom of the air.
And all too soon on tunic gay
You proudly flew the wings of grey
And called upon me to display
The joy I could not share.
Your father would have had it so.
And I? I knew you had to go.

Yet when those feet, returning, spoke
Of duty to fulfil,
The half-forgotten horror woke
In agony of will.
And I, who should have set aside
In English pride
The tears that bade you stay –
I said but foolish things, and cried
When you too went away.
I saw your father's sudden smile
The night you said goodbye.
You lightly said, 'It's only for a while,'
Believing it, and I,

Hating the sullen need of things,
This parting, and the noisy wings
That filled the autumn sky –
I simply said, 'Let's hope it will be so,'
And bade you go.

11
War Trials in Japan

Once the international trials at Nuremburg had been opened it was inevitable after the defeat of Japan that similar trials would be held in Tokyo. Trials for specific atrocities were held elsewhere in the areas where they had occurred, but the forty men arrested in Japan in September 1945 at the order of General McArthur were to be considered in the light of the international offences as formulated at Nuremburg. The nations concerned each chose a judge to sit on the International Tribunal, and sent a team of lawyers to prosecute. It says a great deal for General McArthur that he saw at once the need to provide adequate defence counsel for those prisoners chosen for prosecution. The American Bar, too, in the face of enormous difficulties of interpretation and the utterly different mentality of their clients, patiently and in some cases successfully carried out an unpopular task.

I was asked to go out as junior to Comyns Carr, K.C., with Rex Davies as my junior, and gladly accepted. Here once more was a combination of my two major activities, law and Buddhism, for I saw at once that in my circuit of the globe I could meet the leading Buddhists of many countries, and help to draw them together into collective action in the interests, if not of world peace, then of a little less world war.

Before I left I asked Mrs Phyllis Naylor, widow of my old friend R. H. Naylor, who had herself become an astrologer of international standing, what would happen on my travels. She told me over the phone, with my 'map' in front of her, and I wrote it down. I should be planning to leave Japan about July and my return home would be 'romantic and memorable'. That Comyns Carr, about whom I had given particulars, would be the real leader at the Trial, that the value of the trip to me would be Buddhist contacts and inner awakening; that I should write a valuable book at the end of it; and that my health would be good save for a brief spell in November, wherever I then was – every word came true.

We flew the Atlantic, in those days oxygen being needed if the plane exceeded 12,000 feet, as it sometimes did. We landed in New York at 4 a.m. to find it in moonlight under snow, and were told that it then looked and sounded at its best! There I contacted Mrs Ruth Sasaki, a founder of the Zen Institute of New York, who later played a large part in Buddhism in Japan. I had meals with her such as I had forgotten existed, for the Americans it seemed had never heard of the word rationing. We made plans for my hoped-for Buddhist work in Japan. Then our team flew on to Washington to see what had already been done in relation to the trial. The answer from the Attorney-General was 'Nothing', but we gathered that his Deputy Attorney-General, Joseph Keenan, had been appointed Chief Prosecutor. He proved, unfortunately, quite unequal to the position, and at an early stage the direction and control of the whole prosecution, with the covert approval of the American team of lawyers, rested on the shoulders of Comyns Carr.

We stayed for a night at Topeka in the Middle West, where I learnt the meaning of 'twenty-five under'. I had gone for a walk in the evening to escape from a very hot hotel and heard a voice in the darkness call, 'Say, stranger, them ears o' yourn!' I covered them quickly. And so to San Francisco, where I called at a Japanese temple of the Buddhist Hongwanji school. We then flew to Honolulu, where I met again our old friend Ernest Hunt, an Englishman who had rescued the Japanese population from almost forcible conversion to Christianity by providing them with Buddhist schools. With him I visited Pearl Harbour, where some two thousand American sailors had been killed in the bombing by Japanese aircraft on 7 December 1941, when Japan and the U.S. were officially at peace. It is indeed a magnificent natural harbour, and I understood what a death trap it would be for any ship attacked without warning. On a later stop at Kuajalein we lunched with the American Governor, who told us that if we went for a swim we should bear in mind that a hundred yards from the shore the depth fell to six miles! Thence to Guam, a really beautiful Pacific isle, where numerous Japanese were still living in the deep jungle, refusing to surrender. Here our clothing, still that of a wintry London, was absurd, but when we landed the next day in Tokyo we stepped into six inches of snow.

Seventy per cent of Tokyo-Yokohama, once the largest city in the world, had been destroyed. It was at once fascinating and horrible to see a car moving along a road at least half a mile away with nothing in between to impede one's view of it. Apart from a line of concrete buildings parallel with the famous Ginza, all that remained were the magnificent Canadian Legation, the gift of a rich citizen before the war, and the British, American and Russian Embassies. Tokyo's destruction had been gradual in a sense, being the result of prolonged bombing by the Americans. In contrast, the sudden and total obliteration of Hiroshima by the first atom bomb had, we soon learnt, done far more damage to the Japanese morale. The impossible as it seemed to them had happened. They had been totally defeated. The effect on the Japanese mind has been variously described, but they certainly behaved extremely well in defeat. Our girl secretaries were allowed to walk home at night unescorted, and the young G.I.s would borrow a jeep and go off into the country villages and there make friends with the children by giving them chocolate, and with the parents by giving them cigarettes, soap, and their ration of food. The attitude of the people at large to the trial was more complex. Viscount Kano, a noted expert on Japanese art, told me of the tremendous relief of being free of the military clique which had held the nation virtually prisoner for so long in its efforts to dominate the whole Pacific area in its 'Co-prosperity Sphere'. 'Yes,' he said, 'the Japanese people would have enjoyed the benefits of victory, but still they would have been slaves to that clique or some other'. I wondered whether their wholehearted support of the trial of the war leaders might not be some sort of national judo, 'to win by defeat.' 'Why this delay?' I was asked. 'Why not a brick wall and firing squad tomorrow morning?'

Meanwhile the Japanese people clearly loved 'King Mac', as General McArthur was called, who began his 'reign' by sending for vast quantities of food from the U.S., on the grounds that he would not treat with a starving people. That he should have succeeded as brilliantly as he did in winning the Pacific war and then in assisting an utterly beaten people to return to their own prosperity is remarkable enough; but that he should have done it without the active assistance of – and indeed almost in face of opposition from – his own government surely places him very high among the world's leading generals.

The United Kingdom, Canadian, Australian and New Zealand group of prosecutors, under the leadership of Comyns Carr, settled down to work in the Canadian Legation. The choice of Carr to lead the U.K. team, and later as it turned out, the whole prosecution, was a brilliant move by the English Attorney-General, Sir Hartley Shawcross. He was courteous to all yet firm in decision, a tremendous worker, and possessed of a first-class brain which could contain and organise the whole field of law, procedure, and allocation of work. He was able to smooth out those squabbles which become inevitable when men of eleven nations, far from home, set to work on a large joint enterprise. He was indeed one of the few great men whom the two years' trial produced. He at once formed an Executive Committee, with various sub-committees, to consider the four problems involved. Who of the forty men in custody should be prosecuted; and for what offences? What law should be applied in the conduct of the trial, and what evidence should be admitted? It was the task of the committee to decide the first question, and I was deputed to collate the evidence and make the initial choice for submission to the committee. The indictment was left to Carr and it took him two months to prepare. The law was for the Court, and was settled as that of basic English common law. It was agreed by all concerned that all evidence relevant to the issues should be admitted, leaving the Tribunal to decide its weight.

Should the Emperor himself be prosecuted? The Australian prosecutor, Judge Mansfield, soon to be Carr's main assistant, came with instructions to demand it. The rest of us regarded the suggestion as the height of folly. It was the Emperor who had insisted on surrender after the destruction of Hiroshima, thus saving an enormous number of further casualties. It was he who maintained the good behaviour of his people while under submission. It was he who probably saved the country from Communism and approved the new constitution drafted by the Supreme Command of the Allied Powers which, with its fully democratic principles, and provision of a sound foundation for future development, was clearly in advance of current Japanese thought. He was omitted from the indictment and was of the greatest help to General McArthur in the years to come.

We paid a call at the British Embassy on Lieutenant-General Gairdner, and it was while dining with him later that we had our most noticeable earthquake. There are one or two a week in Japan, but few cause any damage. In this case the pictures swung out from the wall and back with a thump, and that was all.

As the weeks went by, more and more defendants were added to the list, and I protested. I thought that fifteen would be quite enough to establish the principles involved, but I was overruled, and the trial, of twenty-six men, was consequently nearly doubled in length. More prosecutors, too, arrived from various parts of the world, mostly in modest groups of three or four. The Russians, when they did arrive, on the strength of a few weeks involvement in the war, numbered forty-seven. Whereas the rest of the prosecutors' offices were open to any visitor in search of a document or even a gossip, the Russian door was closed and any inquiry was met with what we all agreed was fear. They were just plainly frightened people, of one another, and of their brilliant leader Mr Galunsky, who was a very distinguished lawyer in his own country. He in turn was totally under the orders, coming almost daily, of some command at home. If that was Communism in action, as distinct from Communism as a theory of government, we were as sorry for them as they were frightened for themselves. The Russian judge, who had his own interpreter in court, found at the end of the trial that all the defendants were guilty of everything, or so I was told.

By the middle of February the list of defendants was complete, and by Easter so was the enormous indictment of 20,000 words. So Carr and I had our first look at Japan. We went by the excellent train service to Kyoto and there I met at last the Rev. Sohaku Ogata, the abbot of a small sub-temple of Shokukuji (the suffix 'ji' means temple). His English was perfect and he had for many years received and helped all English and Americans coming to Kyoto in search of Buddhism. With him as guide we toured the city and visited many of its most famous sights. We went to Nara, to the hills around, and to a Noh play, but soon I slipped away for an hour with Ogata to begin my work for Buddhism, and we made plans for many more weekends.

On 3 May the trial began, and it was profoundly impressive. Eleven judges faced the twenty-six defendants in a blaze of television lights which forced many of us to wear dark glasses. As the weeks went by the heat became so intolerable that the Americans fixed up a system of air-conditioning. Until it became better regulated, this meant a move from our office temperature of 93° to a court-room one of 70°. Interpretation soon dominated the trial and settled its length and procedure. Commander Denzel Carr, in charge of interpretation, found it necessary to have a large committee of translators in the well of the court. Again and again they held up the proceedings while the English equivalent of a technical term was carefully debated. Soon it was decided that all the evidence against any man must be fully typed out, with supporting documents, and in the hands of his counsel many days before it could be needed. And so the trial became, after some weeks of general principles, a long series of separate trials of each of the defendants, about whom the evidence for the prosecution and often for the defence was well known months before it was reached.

It was permitted to interrogate the prisoners in Sugamo prison under proper control, and out of curiosity I attended some of the interviews. So far from fiercely defending their behaviour, many insisted on talking for hours of their part in the 'war crimes' with which they were charged, and some even boasted of their own part in the outbreak of the war.

My new task as given me by Carr was to prepare a time-map of the whole Pacific theatre of war, filling in the hour at Greenwich time when the Japanese suddenly attacked places, such as Shanghai, Hong Kong, Thailand, and, the gravest offence of all, Pearl Harbour. How to prove the exact time of these attacks in relation to any pretence of a declaration of war? As I later wrote in *Via Tokyo*, 'The hair of the wig of an Old Bailey judge would rise in horror if told that a photostat of a newspaper report of an alleged official communiqué was evidence of the fact that Japanese troops invaded Thailand at a certain time on a certain date.' But that was the best I could do and it was admitted in evidence.

.   .   .   .   .

I was in Japan on the day of my parents' golden wedding, and had great difficulty finding something gold to send them. In the end the young Prince Tokugawa, scion of the one-time Regents of Japan, produced for me a Japanese gold sake cup, engraved with the *mon* (crest) of the Empress Meiji, who had given it to his ancestor, then Lord Chamberlain, at the 'opening' of the country in 1868. To be sure of its arriving in time I sent it by ordinary mail, but the large number of books I acquired from Dr Suzuki and others, and the *objets d'art* of all materials, needed more heroic measure. I packed them in a series of cases, with a list of contents and a blank cheque for the English customs, and sent them back in the cabin of the captain of whatever British warship was then sailing home! My drawing-room when I got back looked like a museum of Japanese art.

My 'fratting' with the Japanese was early frowned upon, but I ignored the frowns, dined with the Foreign Minister, Mr Yoshida, who later became Prime Minister; with Viscount Kano, and soon with a number of Japanese professors of Buddhism convened to form the Tokyo committee to translate, consider, and if possible approve my 'Twelve Principles of Buddhism'. Some of our weekends were spent in Tokyo but most at the hotels which the Americans had taken over for rest-camps at famous beauty spots within reach of Tokyo. Such was the hot-water spa which we visited at Atami. There I realised what splendid specimens of humanity formed the American Eighth Army. It was delightful to watch these godlike men being dried after a boiling hot soak by their Japanese girl friends, who could hardly reach to their shoulders, and one could not complain of the morals of hitherto well-behaved girls when the result of being 'kind' to a large American was probably cash enough for food for her whole family.

12
Buddhist Work in Japan

At last, a month after my arrival, I found time and opportunity to visit Dr Suzuki, known everywhere to his friends as Sensei, a generic term for teacher. I found him at Kamakura, in his little house in the grounds of Engakuji, the temple founded in 1280 to commemorate the fallen on both sides in the Mongolian invasion. It was a lovely spot indeed after the noise and superficial importance of the trial. Dr Suzuki's American wife had planted English flowers to blend with the bushes, rocks and water of a Japanese garden, and the whole, with its wild profusion of magnolia, azalea and blood-red wild camellia, was heaven indeed. My first arrival was unexpectedly dramatic. I climbed up the long path through the cryptomerias with a bag of offerings which to the Japanese were of great value – cigarettes to use for cash, toothpaste, soap and food of all kinds. The old man saw me as I passed his window, and, as I took off my shoes and entered the room where he sat writing at his low table, he turned his head and raised his sleeve up to his face. I thought the shock was too much for him, but then, as I noted in my diary, 'his funny old wrinkled face just unfolded into a gorgeous smile'. At seventy-seven he seemed remarkably hale and hearty.

His old servant, Okano, took my bag and vanished, returning with the materials for Japanese ceremonial tea, which Sensei made, and offered me the bowl. I sipped and he asked my opinion. 'Like spinach soup!' I answered, and for the first time I really saw a man fall over with laughter. Then I saw Okano had piled my gifts up in the *tokonoma*, the shrine which is in the corner of every living-room, which held only a vase and at most two flowers before a picture chosen to match. We had a wonderful dinner and made plans.

I told him of my Twelve Principles, and he told me of his lectures to the Emperor on Buddhism. It was said that they had been arranged by the American missionaries so that *they* might then give him a lecture on Christianity. Later I took down his translation of them, and the Buddhist Society published them in London as *The Essence of Buddhism*. He had built himself a house on the slope of the hill opposite and it was at last ready. I was to be the first to sleep there and he took me over to make me at home. It was exquisite, in that chastity of taste, as I call it, of the Japanese house of tradition. With a few cushions, a low table, and cupboards with sliding doors all round the walls, what more is needed? For beauty there was the *tokonoma*, and I was utterly content. He went off down the winding path with Okano, each holding over the shoulder a lantern of a candle in its paper shade. I had to remind myself that this was 1946, and not the untouched Middle Ages.

Dr Suzuki had had to face the difficulty inherent in any attempt to teach Zen Buddhism. For the Indian sage, Bodhidharma, who founded the school in China about AD 500 had traditionally laid down its principles with fierce simplicity:

> A special transmission outside the Scriptures
> No dependence upon words and letters;
> Direct pointing to the heart of man;
> Seeing into its nature and becoming Buddha.

Truth or Reality – for Zen in the sense of ZEN amounts to no less – can never be found in the field of duality, of 'this' versus 'that'. Nor can it be defined, for all words limit. It is in my view best regarded as a state of consciousness raised above the level of thought to that of immediate awareness of reality itself, a plane of which the West has some awareness in the word 'intuition'. It is a faculty, power or, as I think of it, a wavelength of perception as different from thought as thought is from feeling or the physical plane. But if the scriptures themselves will not produce an awareness of this flame, or spark, or spirit, which is the life of Reality within, how shall it be taught, or how shall the way to awaken it in oneself be taught? True, Zen is a word corrupted from the Chinese *Ch'an*, which means something like

My Father, the Right Hon. Sir Travers Humphreys.

Myself when young.

My Mother, Lady Zoe Marguerite Humphrey

Miss Aileen Faulkner, later to be my wife.

On our honeymoon at Davos, 1927
Photo: The Sawbwa of Mongmit.

A Member of the Bar.

The towers of Chartres Cathedral, for me the most beautiful building in Europe.

H. P. Blavatsky, founder with Col. H. S. Olcott of the Theosophical Society in 1875 and author of *The Secret Doctrine.*

With Elsie Benjamin, co-Founder of the Mahatma Letters Trust, and Boris de Zirkoff, a great-nephew of H. P. Blavatsky and Editor of *The Complete Works of H. P. Blavatsky.* In front of us is the brass-bound wooden box made for A. P. Sinnett to contain the Letters of the Mahatmas M. and K. H. sent him between 1880–84.

The Anagarika Dharmapala of Ceylon. The greatest Buddhist missionary of modern times. Founder of the British Maha Bodhi Society.

A. C. March, a Founding Member of the Buddhist Society and the creator of its Journal, now *The Middle Way*.

The Daibutsu at Kamakura, Japan, 52 ft high, of plated bronze. This figure was erected in 1252.

Kyoto 1946. *L. to R. seated:* Dr. D. T. Suzuki; Abbot Daiko Yamasaki, the Abbot of Shokoku-ji; myself with the son of the Rev. Sohaku Ogata, Abbot of the sub-temple, Chotoko-in where I stayed in Kyoto.

The International Tribunal of the Far East in session, Tokyo 1946. The Judges of eleven nations are listening to the evidence. *Photo:* American Press.

As Recorder of Deal at the presentation of the Freedom of the Borough to
· Mr Winston Churchill on his appointment as Lord Warden of the Cinque
Ports, 1951.

At Agra, 1956, with portion of a very long friend.

A Tibetan esoteric ritual performed for the first time in public at the World Fellowship of Buddhists' Conference in Kathmandu, November 1956. The *mandala* or picture is built up of coloured sand, and the ritual includes chanting, hand-movements and a bell. Only the Navaho Indians in Mexico use such pictures in coloured sand.

As Master of the Saddlers' Company, with *R.* my th[e]
Wardens and *L.* the Beadle and Clerk, after
Company's annual Divine Service.

The Master's Cup of the Saddlers' Company.
Made by Puck of hammered silver in the basement of our home and presented by me to the
Company on relinquishing office as Master, July
1957.

THE SOUND OF ONE HAND

A wood-block print by Hasuko (Puck Humphreys), illustrating the Zen koan 'The sound of one hand clapping'.

The visit of their Majesties the King and Queen of Thailand to the Society on September 14, 1966. *L. to R. standing:* The Librarian, Miss Pat Wilkinson; the Editor of *The Middle Way*, Miss Muriel Daw; the Vice-President, Mr Tom Harris; Mrs Humphreys; the General Secretary, Mrs K. Phelps; myself; the Treasurer, Miss Florence Stacey and Mrs Carlo Robins.

H.M. the Queen receiving the traditional plum cake from the High Steward of Guildford, the Earl of Onslow, on the balcony of the Guildhall. As Recorder of Guildford I had just made the loyal Address of Welcome on the occasion of the 700th anniversary of the Borough. No one knows the origin of the Plum Cake ritual.

Alan Watts, Dr. D. T. Suzuki and Dr. Irmgard Schloegl at the Rembrandt Hotel in London, 1958.

The Visit of H.H. the Dalai Lama to the Society in November 1973. *Standing L. to R:* the General Secretary, Mr Burt Taylor; Mrs Carlo Robins; Dr Edward Conze; myself; the Vice-President, Col. Roger Günter Jones.

Puck and myself beside the Society's Shrine, in the Library of its headquarters, on the occasion of the 40th anniversary of the Buddhist Society.

meditation. But how to teach meditation save by words? Some minds, after lives of effort, reach again this level of Truth by awakening 'enlightenment' or *satori*, comparable with, though incomparably lower than that of the All-Enlightened One. Such a mighty break-through came to Dr Suzuki, as we persuaded him to tell us, in 1896, but he wanted to help others to attain it, and gave his life to that end. Hence in words he taught the futility of words, in some thirty volumes in Japanese and a dozen in English.

The inadequacy of words becomes all the more acute when a reader of a different race has to grasp the subtle distinctions of an idea which is alien to his way of thinking. An example occurred when I was taking down from Dr Suzuki his translation of his lectures to the Emperor. 'You mean', I asked, after some discussion on a difficult point, 'that all is God but there is no God?' 'No', he replied, 'I mean', and he gave the whole sentence without emphasis on any word, 'I mean that all is God and there is no God.' I saw where I had blun-dered. His 'and' for my 'but' raised doctrine to the level of Zen, which knows no opposites. I was rebuked, and took a long step forward on my way to Zen. R. H. Blyth is making the same subtle point in his translation of the Case XVII of the collection of stories known as *Mumonkan*. A famous master rebuked an Emperor to the effect that oneself and the Buddha are not *two* identical things but two *identical* things. Here is Zen made as easy as it can be!

Meanwhile the time had come for me to be – I am tempted to say – confirmed. I was invited to spend the night with the monks in meditation at Sojiji, a large Zen temple at the back of Yokohama. The two committees working on my Twelve Principles in Tokyo and Kyoto were nearly ready; I must be ready too. I arrived apprehensive of what awaited me and was shown to the Abbot's reception room. To my delight Dr Suzuki had come from Kamakura, and he and the famous Dr Tachibana taught me much at a typically Japanese temple dinner. Then, as I had to be up early, I was 'put to bed', the young monks giggling as they produced a hot-water bottle. True, a temple has no heating and there was late snow outside. At 4 a.m. I was roused and we went across to the Zendo, the meditation hall. I was shaken by the gongs and clappers which made me jump at intervals, and I little knew that I should later produce the same effect on those attending my Zen class in London at the Buddhist Society. The chanting, with an almost African rhythm, fascinated me, as did the rapid weaving movement in the small space before the altar, which was almost a form of dance. So the remainder of the night passed and I deeply appreciated the honour done me by all concerned.

Back in the office I found that as soon as my time-map was complete I should have little to do. I should be able to enjoy the wide range of Japanese art and culture available. I went to the Kabuki Theatre, but although I appreciated the acting, singing and dancing I was admittedly defeated by the music, as I was later by that in Hong Kong. But then I am equally defeated by modern music in Europe. I was taken to the principal school of classical dancing, then run by Mme Fujikage, a famous dancer in her day, and shown her method of teaching. Then the old lady, excited by my technical interest, suddenly announced that she would dance for me. Here was an exhibition of very great art indeed. In her working black kimono, on an empty, sunlit stage, and with only a fan as a prop, she danced, to the music of one samisen, a famous dance of a young man whose beloved dies, leaving him with the baby. In her superb acting she peopled the stage with the young man, the baby and sympathetic friends. Here, as I wrote at the time, was the mime of Ruth Draper, the self mastery of Pavlova and the personality of a one-time favourite of the Japanese stage.

I saw the Tea ceremony many times and was privileged to take part in it, although the true training is a matter of years. I appreciated the technical perfection of a Japanese garden, which is not planted but built, and in such harmony of rock and water, soil and bush that it can be admired three hundred years later. Here one stands on 'the moon-gazing' stone, or the 'cherry-blossom' stone, and one's eyes are guided round this living work of art. One can spend an hour being taken round a garden only a hundred feet square.

Of the martial arts I had personal knowledge. I was invited by Tateno, my old kendo teacher in London, to visit the Kodokan, the headquarters of this Japanese form of fencing. The noise was terrific as a dozen pairs of youngsters bashed at one another, landing their blows on armour and their opponents' swords. An exhibition of really high-class judo was more impressive, for, although we had had distinguished visitors at the Budokwai in London, these competitors were of the seventh and eighth dan of black belt, and one was said to be the only tenth-dan man in Japan. The Western equivalent would be bouts between world-champion boxers.

On Empire Day, for we then had an Empire, the British took the floor. A religious service was held on the site of the burnt out English church; the formal opening took place of our own Empire Building near that of S.C.A.P. (headquarters of the American army); and there was a great party at the Embassy. A few weeks later the massed pipers of the Scots Guards and Gurkhas with drums and bugles beat the retreat on the vast parade ground. For an hour they marched and counter-marched before a vast audience of Japanese and American troops. The Americans later admitted that they had never seen anything like it. The timing was perfect, and as the sun went down behind us we watched the slow lowering of the flags, and the whole massed bands and the Guards departed into the distance till the sound died out into the setting sun. I was not the only one crying with the breath-taking perfection of it all, yet not unmindful of the irony that this was carried out before the palace of the defeated Emperor.

With Langdon Warner, the curator of the Fogg Museum at Harvard, I discussed and compared the art and the mental make-up of the Chinese and the Japanese. I was shown in one temple, for example, a genuine painting by Wu Tao-tsu, who is regarded as China's greatest artist, although none of his work survives in China. And at a lunch party in Kamakura our host produced from layers of silk, and hung up for his guests' delight, an early Sesshu, the most famous artist of Japan. After much sake I developed the thesis that the Japanese personality is delicate, chaste and refined, while the inner individuality is the cult of the sword and a longing for conquest. The Chinese, on the other hand, are as a nation inwardly female, gentle, introvert, absorbing alien nations and, as someone put it, 'spitting them out when done with'. But the individual Chinese personality is cheerfully extrovert, noisy, loving bright colours and far from delicate or refined. I once murmured to a fellow guest at a lunch party in Hong Kong, 'At the end of this meal they won't wash the table cloth; they'll burn it.' But then most of my meals in Japan were in temples, where the lunch or dinner would be served at a tiny table in front of one, and at the end not a crumb remained.

I saw a wide variety of temples, and at each enjoyed a cup of tea with the abbot. Each temple grew its own tea, and I came to appreciate the subtle differences in flavour between them. I had been advised to carry about with me an album in which I would ask that something be included. The writer would thoughtfully prepare his brush and ink while he worked out his contribution and the precise placing of it, with his seal, on the page. I soon learnt to read something of character from the different entries of, for example, an abbot, an artist, or the retired geisha who kept a restaurant where I lunched with my Japanese publisher.

As I had completed my work at the War Ministry of collecting and preparing evidence for the case against Admiral Nagano, I now had time to prepare the offering of my Twelve Principles to the assembled schools of Japanese Buddhism. In fact the idea of such a list was not new. In 1891 Colonel H. S. Olcott, founding President of the Theosophical Society, had drafted 'a common platform upon which all Buddhists can agree' and in presenting it to the Japanese had in particular the help of Captain Brinkley, for many years *The Times* correspondent in Tokyo. Strangely enough, his son, Major Jack Brinkley, who being bilingual was helping in the interpretation at the trial, was able to help me actively in securing the adoption of a modern equivalent. My own list, however, was far wider than Olcott's 'Fourteen Fundamental Principles', which were largely confined to the Canon of the Southern or Theravada school. Meanwhile the weekend of Midsummer, chosen for the final meeting in Kyoto, was approaching. Two weeks before I had hurried to a hospital in Kyoto to visit Dr Suzuki, who was recovering from pneumonia, though still unable to talk. He pointed to a cupboard in his room and someone brought him his favourite obi, the dark blue cotton sash which held together his kimono. This he gave me. Words were not needed. I knew where I stood in his regard.

There was one hurdle yet to be surmounted, of importance to all concerned – that of the difference between Shin, or Pure Land Buddhism, and Zen. The former is *tariki*, implying salvation by another; Zen is *jiriki*, concerned with no such help. Rival pundits were unhappy about my making no mention of either, for to me they were different means to the same end, enlightenment. Prince Otani, the hereditary Lord Abbot of the Western branch of the Shin, or Pure Land sect, in Kyoto, was in the chair on this occasion. He listened, then suddenly said in his excellent English, 'I agree with Mr Humphreys that *tariki* and *jiriki* are alike methods of self-salvation.' And that was that.

On 22 June I arrived at Kyoto after a hot night in the train, and in the afternoon went with Ogata to the superb building in the grounds of the Nishi-Hongwanji Temple which had once been part of the palace of Hideyoshi, 'the Napoleon of Japan' in the seventeenth century. Thirty-two Japanese came, representing seventeen schools or sects of Buddhism. As I remarked in my diary, 'I felt the day was electric and made the most of it.' In fact I found myself in a strangely exalted mood, at peace with all existence, assured and poised within. I made a brief speech, and one or two questions were asked, which I answered through Ogata. Then suddenly Ogata said to me in English, 'They agree.' I felt no triumph, which helped me to believe that my continuing experience was genuine – for it lacked any sense of 'I'. A committee of seven was formed to discuss details of promulgation, and after the inevitable but welcome cup of tea the meeting broke up.

I spent the Sunday with Dr Suzuki, who was packing up his Kyoto house, and shamelessly helped myself to books to take back to London, and accepted lovely presents for Puck. On the Monday, Midsummer Day, I was invited to speak at Otani University, where Dr Suzuki acquired his doctorate. I spoke on Buddhism in England and Dr Suzuki himself interpreted. Then to lunch at Myoshinji, a famous temple of Rinzai Zen in Kyoto. Ogata had told me that there was to be a big meeting, the first for many years, of the abbots and Zen masters of the Rinzai School from all over Japan. I had asked if I might be allowed to sit in a corner with him and have some of it whispered to me in translation. He said that he would ask the Lord Abbot, Zengan Goto himself. The reply should have shattered me, but in my strange persisting mood of inward peace I was unaffected by the trivialities of emotion. 'You are invited to give the first lecture!' I bowed my acceptance and in due course talked to the large audience for an hour on Buddhism in the West and the potential place of Buddhism in the future of mankind. There followed questions, and the tireless Ogata gave me the question and returned the answer with uncanny speed. Then came a final question which I felt was testing me and may even have been planned. 'Would the lecturer be good enough to say what he means by Zen?' My diary records:

'Like a flash I leapt for it and could not miss. "The oak tree in the courtyard!"' There was a yell of laughter, a thunder of applause and we swept out on it. Then a photograph of the whole crowd, with me on Goto's right. He was still chuckling.

This was really the climax of my stay in Japan. I had nothing more to do at the trial, and my work was nearly finished. I suggested to Carr that I should ask the Attorney-General in London if I might start for home. He agreed and permission was duly granted. I thought of Phyllis Naylor and her estimate that I should be ready for home in July. There was, however, no hurry, and I went for a week-end to the village of Shibu, on the eastern side of the 'Japanese Alps', where my artist friend, Take Sato lived. He had taught Puck woodblock cutting and printing while in London before the war, and had given her her Japanese artist's name of Hasuko. His village was the traditional Japan, and the hotel where we stayed had gorgeous views of the mountains. I commissioned paintings from him for London and we called on the local temples and the village worthies.

By August I was ready to go, and was given a ticket home marked 'Priority Two', which greatly reduced delay. But I had the firm intention of seeing everything possible of the Buddhist world until I actually wanted to move on. I said goodbye to Carr and my other colleagues. I attended a final committee meeting in Tokyo of those responsible for the Twelve Principles, and received from the Abbot Goto a gold brocade *rakusa*, the kind of apron worn by the Rinzai school over the kimono. I was seen off at the station by a group of distinguished professors and sat back in the train to think things over. At the Trial I had done all required of me, but I had never actually appeared in court. This was partly because so many others were longing for the chance to be seen on television by 'the old folks at home', and partly because I did not want to emphasise to my Japanese friends that I was after all in Japan to prosecute a group of Japanese. As for Buddhism, I had renewed old contacts, made a hundred new ones, and proffered and had accepted a useful contribution to the future of Buddhism in Japan. Inwardly, I had consolidated and developed old beliefs, 'seen' now in the Zen sense, truths which before I had but known intellectually, and wound about my heart the spiritual strength and vision of a very wonderful and to me supremely valued friend.

As it turned out, the adoption of Twelve Principles became my major Buddhist activity in Japan, and their later presentation to the Sanghas and leading Buddhists of Thailand, Burma and Ceylon was, apart from sightseeing and the meeting with Buddhist friends, my major interest in those countries. It is only reasonable, therefore, that they should appear as an appendix to this book. After a weekend of meditation in a Zen monastery in Kyoto, I wrote the poem 'Zen-do'. Before I left Japan, in September 1946, Dr D. T. Suzuki, the greatest authority on Zen in modern times, wrote to me. In his letter he referred to this poem: 'It is fine, and beautifully it illustrates the Zen spirit of Eternal Now, and All in One and One in All. You are a good poet.' I can only bow in silence before such praise.

Zen-do

Silence, and a far-sounding bell.
No words, which broken-winged presume,
Themselves of caged flight, to tell
The beyond of our imagining.
Two slow-descending points illume
The graven stillness. In each cell,
The locked unmoving body, shines
The white flame of a thought awing,
And only the riven heart confines
The ambit of our travelling.

There's no remembrance here, no leaping thought
With eager feet pursuing the unknown.
Desire, and all the fretful folly wrought
Of earth's incessant fancy, sleeps. Alone
The flame which lights the manifold is one.
The universe, contracted and confined,
Dwells in the compass of a bounded mat.
The pale flame in the passion-voided mind
Purges the difference of this and that.
No purpose here, nor time-ascending vow
To stain the moment absolute of Now.

The many and the one. The mind ascends
Twin-footed to the ladder's end, and finds
Unmeasured union. But nothing ends,
And though the sun-flame all consuming blends

The many millioned candles of our minds
In larger union, there's one, and I
That hold it so, and these regardant twain
Impatient cry for larger unity,
And the wheel, contentless, turns and swings again.

The pale candle, reason, droops and dies
And to the low-lit pentagon of sense
Comes beauty, veil-less, naked of the lies
Which foul with argument our dull pretence
Of knowing, and with fingers of delight
Fondles the tentacles of touch and sight.

And here, with eyes of laughter, is the face
Of love, young love, still rosy warm and fair
With the unestimated bold embrace
Of life, and a wild flower in her hair.
Then reason wakens, rude to her caress,
And proves upon the square of reckoning
That all is gilt illusion, love no less;
And I am sick of a wild thought, to fling
To rot in some unmeasurable pit
All sound of beauty and the touch of it.

Now let the unravished heart arise, and find
Communicable light. If all is one,
And all diversity the spawn of mind,
Then madly was this mocking wheel begun.
If in the falling water of the hills
I hear but loved illusion; if the sun
By day on proffered breast and thigh instils
No cherished warming, night no benison,
Then life is but a lie that's told too long,
And love is dead, and in the heart no song.

I will not have it so. Be still my heart.
I will arise, and splendid grasp the whole,
And binding it about yet hold each part
Unutterably so; approve the soul

And substance of the rose, and lightly bring
Eternal glory to the littlest thing.
And each, the part and whole, shall singing dwell
In each inseverable. Not one but two,
The sound of wholeness, and the sounding bell.
And every leaf which unreported grew,
And some time in some other planet fell
Is still the abundant absolute, and grows
Unlabelled on the divine slopes of hell,
Nor cares that it is hemlock or the rose.

I sought for truth, and waking now I find
That there is neither truth nor waking mind.
Yet each exists, supreme, immaculate,
Uniquely one, alone companionate.
At last I know, who feel the risen sun.
Awake, my heart! For two is two, and one!

I rose, and passed into the morning, where
The garden rose in stillness, and the light
Gave benediction to the silvering air.
The flowing hills passed onward, and the night
Her velvet fallen, moved upon their flow,
And suddenly and utterly, 'twas day.
I knelt, the flowers about me, kneeling low
Where the starlit dew, night's holy water, lay
And all about my wakened eyes was new
And soft the dawn wind, and the dew was dew.
I rose and moved upon the way
And in my heart a song;
And what the singing heart shall say
Has never yet been wrong.
And this I know, and sing I must
Of all that I have found;
That every grain of dust is dust
And the wheels of a cart go round.

13
The Long Journey Home

I was in Japan for seven months, and when I left the trial was settling down to what would obviously be a very long endurance. In fact it continued until November 1947. Here I am concerned only with my short part in it and I have therefore said little of the indictment, the law argued, and nothing of the result. These are presumably available for those interested.

I flew with a modest suitcase to Hong Kong, where I found the one friend needed to make life fully interesting in a foreign town. This was Peter Sin, a solicitor, who took me to a party at a Chinese house where, within an hour, I was on easy terms with the Attorney-General, the Chief Justice and a dozen other interesting Chinese people. There were no Buddhist activities to be found in Hong Kong, but I managed to thumb a lift to Shanghai in a plane taking some V.I.P. politicians from London to visit the trial in Japan.

I was eager to see Peking but it was not easy to reach it. I flew to Shanghai and there managed to persuade the American Air Force to sell me a seat on one of their planes. Peking was at that time under American control. The bored official responsible for the allocation of billets wanted reasons why I should have a hotel room. I gave a vague performance of being sponsored by the British Foreign Office (every British passport says so!) and of being a close friend of General McArthur. I implied that it was very nice of me to let him look after me. I got my room in the Central Hotel. At the British Embassy, where I went to deliver letters from Shanghai, I met Henry Vetch, the owner of the French book shop in the Peking Hotel. He in turn had a young

Chinese friend who wanted to improve his English. What more could I want than a powerful friend and a daily guide-companion? I went everywhere by rickshaw, with Vetch, when he was with me, on a bicycle beside me. He showed me the dilapidated but fascinating 'Forbidden City'. We went to the Summer Palace, and to the huge covered market where we dined exquisitely. I was horrified at the bound feet of the older generation of women as they hobbled by.

Buddhist activity was not easy to find, but I was taken by my Chinese student friend to a Ch'an temple where the Abbot was bright and intelligent, and the temple fully alive. I was taken by Mr Vetch to a dealer in early Chinese bronze, Mr P. C. Huang, where my mouth watered at shelves of what are today almost price-less treasures. I spent about £25 in every American dollar I had been able to buy, and carried the resulting collection home in my suit-case. Today it is worth at least a hundred times what I paid for it, but at the time I remember most the charming smile with which, when I was handling an adorable small porcelain rabbit of the Sung dynasty, and had no money left to pay for it, he pressed it into my hands as a gift.

For me the greatest sight in Peking was the Altar of Heaven, where once a year the Emperor communed with Heaven. Nowhere in the world is there an altar of such sublime simplicity. It is made of carved white marble and is designed in multiples of nine. Its three tiers represent Man, Earth and Heaven and one mounts to each by a series of nine steps. At the top there is nothing, nothing but a circle of white marble fifty feet across, which is for the Chinese the centre of the world. Here is the perfect and ultimate altar – a plain white circle and above it the sky. Standing in that circle one understands so much that is beyond all words, the simple relationship of man and heaven, and of the unity which lies beyond their apparent duality.

Back in Hong Kong, I asked for news of a party of colleagues from Japan who were on their way to Singapore to collect evidence. I was shocked to hear that their plane had crashed on leaving the air-field and that all nineteen had been killed, including the third member of our British team, Rex Davies. I attended the mass funeral, and wondered sadly at the intricate workings of Karma. As we took off for Thailand, my fellow passengers and I were silent as our plane climbed out of the dangerous, hill-surrounded airfield where the crash had occurred.

In Bangkok I found myself in a land of Theravada Buddhism, historically earlier than the Mahayana Buddhism I had come to know in Japan. Indeed, as I looked out of my hotel window at dawn I saw a group of yellow-robed monks begging for food on their morning round, and knew that I was again on Buddhist soil. Thailand is the only Buddhist kingdom, and as it happened the late King was lying in state in the Throne Hall of the Palace. I was greatly impressed by the magnificence of the hall and its unique decoration. The dazzling design of coloured porcelain was achieved by smashing a vast number of plates and saucers and arranging the pieces in the desired way.

As in Hong Kong, I soon found the one friend needed, a London acquaintance, Sukit Nimmanhaeminde, who took me everywhere. I was invited to the Buddhist Association of Thailand and was made its first foreign member. At a lunch in my honour I could not forget a dish described to me as 'fried sliced lotus-root, flavoured with roast snake'. I survived that, to be taken straight to the Supreme Patriarch, the head of the Buddhist Sangha who is in fact appointed by the King, and a committee of senior monks. Here I had to defend my Twelve Principles in semi-public, seated at the foot of the huge Buddha image in the largest of the many temples. I was cross-examined, which is how I would put it, on the doctrine of *anatta*, 'no self', meaning in fact that there is no permanent self in man which makes him separate from any other man – no personal immortal soul. Perspiring, I was acquitted and the Principles were approved!

In the few days available on this trip I was honoured with a special performance of the Classical School of Dancing, and marvelled again at the many ways of teaching a pupil. I moved about the city, sometimes in a large car kindly lent me by the British Embassy, sometimes in a tricycle-rickshaw. The rickshaw man had to work hard to surmount the innumerable small bridges over the canals which crisscrossed the city. Now, as I found on a later visit, they are mostly filled in in the interests of traffic. What a very lovely country this was at that time, with the Sangha free from politics, and, although too bound by its own regulations, at least keeping the people genuinely Buddhist in feeling.

.   .   .   .   .

In Rangoon I found my Cambridge friend U Kyaw Min, and was also greeted by the oldest friend in the East of Buddhism in the West, U Kyaw Hla of Mandalay. He had worked hard for the original Buddhist Society of Great Britain and Ireland, and subsequently for our own society. I stayed with U So Nyun, the Mayor of Rangoon, and through him met an English Bhikku the Lama Dorje Prajnananda, who had first entered the order in Tibet. He became a first-class correspondent with us on all things Burmese, and was profoundly respected throughout Burma. Ironically, the Burmese Thera who became in time the doyen of the Sangha was at that moment acting as librarian at the Buddhist Society in London. At the outbreak of war, he had been a student in London, so he took off his robe and acted as a stretcher-bearer for the Red Cross, joining in this decision the Society of Friends, who were also practical in the application of their beliefs. I was deeply honoured to be shown over the Shwe Dagon by a group of the trustees who control it. Here was the traditional Buddhist *stupa* (reliquary) on a vast scale, allied with great beauty of detail, retaining, in spite of its enormous size, an intimate atmosphere of veneration. I, or rather the Society, was honoured further by a meeting at the Town Hall. A Burmese judge was in the chair, and after flattering speeches I received an Address of Welcome in a chased bowl of Burmese silver, and some £1500, the result of 'a quick whip round' organised by U Kyaw Min and U Kyaw Hla. I promised to use this money in England to promote the publication of further works on the Dhamma, as Buddhism is known in the East, and duly did so.

When I presented the Twelve Principles to the Burmese Sangha, my reception was not so enthusiastic. Where, demanded the chairman of the committee convened to consider them, is the doctrine of the unity of life expressly set out in the Pali Canon? There was a fierce argument on the correctness of the translation, and a blind adherence to the very letter of the scriptures. The ensuing argument on Buddhist principles led me, a mere Western layman, to the sad conclusion that their understanding of many Buddhist principles was low indeed. Many leading Burmans had already approved the Principles, and the attitude of the Sangha was disappointing. When my friend Kyaw Min murmured that we might as well escape and go to the races I sadly but cordially agreed.

. . . . .

And so to Calcutta, the only city in the world that, on several visits, I disliked. I was received by the Venerable Jinaratana, General Secretary of the Maha Bodhi Society at its vihara and temple, and told the truth of recent events. India, still then a geographical entity, had not recovered from the vast and wholesale slaughter engendered by Hindu-Muhammadan religious hatred, which has stained for ever the record of that great civilisation. I was told that the English Press had showed no appreciation of the figures involved, and the local estimate was that some 40,000 Hindus and Muhammadans had murdered one another in cold blood during the course of a few days. A body of men from one side would break into the house of a member of the rival religion and hack to pieces every living thing within its walls, and the gutters literally ran with blood. Once, I remember, I was having my hair cut on the platform at the Howrah station when I heard a ghastly scream. When I went out, there was a pool of blood with sand thrown on it. In this atmosphere I was proud to hear of the behaviour of the Venerable Jinaratana, who had stood at the entrance to the temple, and as a Buddhist welcomed in both Hindus and Mohammadans of either sex who were fleeing for their lives. More, he collected funds for the relief of the vast suffering which the murders caused.

I told him I wanted to go on pilgrimage to Buddha Gaya, where the Buddha attained Enlightenment, and to Sarnath, 'the deer park near Benares' where he preached his First Sermon. So we left, I feeling that I was reliving *Kim,* and we travelled by night to Gaya. The thera impressed the occupants of our second-class carriage with my enormous importance, and I spoke equally highly of him. At Buddha Gaya we saw the tree, grown from a cutting of that under which the All-Compassionate One became, as the thousands of his visitors thereafter called him, Buddha, the All-Enlightened One. At Sarnath we saw the site, beautifully excavated and cared for by the British officials, where the First Sermon was preached, and were shown the new Buddhist temple in which, before I left, the resident bhikkhu chanted a blessing for me. At Gaya I received the greatest compliment paid me in the East. For the Annual Congress of the Society a president is elected for the year, and I was asked to serve from a date a month ahead. It would, incidentally, involve my sitting cross-legged on the neck of a temple elephant, holding above my head the casket which contains, if proof is possible, actual ashes from the Buddha's cremation. Under the full moon the long procession would circumambulate the compound to the chanting of a large array of bhikkus and the accompaniment of drums and trumpets. Unfortunately I had to refuse the honour because I had no time to stay for what would have been for me a tremendous occasion.

Back in Calcutta I lectured to a large audience at the Maha Bodhi Society's Temple and then left for Adyar, the Theosophical Headquarters near Madras. I chose to go by train. I needed the rest and as I lay in my sleeping berth I watched India go slowly by. At Madras I was to my embarrassment offered the choice of staying with an English judge, or Mr Govinda Menon, the Indian prosecutor at the Tokyo Trial, or Mr Jinarajadasa, the Buddhist President of the Theosophical Society. I chose, of course, the Theosophist, and was driven at once to Adyar.

The Theosophical Society had acquired a large estate on the Adyar river near Madras. Here they had built up a magnificent library. I visited 'the Roof' where H. P. Blavatsky and Colonel Olcott had toiled at *The Theosophist* and with the expert help of a range of Indian pandits built up the movement throughout India. During my week's stay I made a thorough tour of Adyar. I visited its dancing school run by Rukmini Devi; I talked with interesting students scattered in buildings about the compound; and I had many enjoyable swims in the Indian Ocean where, against all advice to beware of sharks and currents, I refreshed myself in body and mind. I went to Conjeeveram, the birthplace of Bodhidharma who founded the Ch'an school in China about AD 500 and saw the inside of a Hindu temple. How different from the chaste and clean simplicity of a Buddhist temple, and yet I find the Indians as a whole to be the most spiritually minded race on earth.

I moved on to Ceylon, where the indispensable local friend was Mr Arthur de Zoysa, almost a founding member of the Society in London. He drove me through magnificent scenery of genuine jungle to my host, Mr Sri Nissanka, K.C. We stayed with him for the night and then toured the Buddhist sights available in the time. Of special Buddhist interest was Mihintale, the hill where Mahinda, the son of the Emperor Asoka, had first taught Buddhism in Ceylon in the third century BC. Thence to Anuradhapura, once the capital of Ceylon, where we saw the oldest tree in the world, a cutting of the original Bo-tree of Buddha Gaya. It is mentioned so often in the Island's history that there can be no question of its historical authenticity. We went to Kandy where we visited the Temple of the Tooth, and handled its treasures of almost frightening value. A single jewelled dish was made of 14 lb of pure gold. In Colombo I was received by many old Buddhist friends, such as Dr Malalasekera, with whom I had sat on a Wesak (Buddha Day) platform in London in 1926, and I was made welcome by several of the principal Buddhist Societies. I was shown the local dancing and encouraged its principal, Chitra Sena, to bring his excellent troupe to London. I gave a broadcast on Buddhism and was prepared for a large meeting at the Town Hall, as in Rangoon. Here, however, I met disaster. A small but highly vocal group of Bhikkhus, openly Communist, managed to break up the meeting, but in a substitute though smaller meeting at my host's house I dictated to the Press my views on allowing politics of any kind to contaminate the Sangha!

I had not forgotten the Twelve Principles. I met a large and sympathetic committee, who not only approved the idea of them, but made small but helpful suggestions for improving the wording.

I went next to Bombay where I met more Theosophical friends, and then to Karachi where I met another of the rare men of great spiritual stature who have shown me what any human being, given the will and long self-development, can become. This was Mr Jamshed Nasserwanji, nine times mayor of Karachi, a self-made millionaire and outwardly a really big businessman. Inwardly he was a saint, a true Theosophist in heart and act, and the people worshipped him. At a small party which I attended he brought into the room an aura of peace and inner enlightenment. In my diary I wrote, 'He took my joined hands of salute in his and held them to his forehead. We talked for about ten minutes and then he was gone, giving the same salutation and blessing to each of those present, and a light faded out when he went. If ever a man was truly Christ-like it was he.' So a tycoon can be a godlike man as well!

From Karachi I took a flying boat to Cairo, and in due course landed with a lovely splash on the Nile. In the customs office I had a chance to apply my understanding of acceptance. I was asked for my visa to enter Egypt, and I said I had none as they had not been invented when I left Japan. They said that in that case I must go back to India. I said certainly, but as I had no money left they would have to give me a ticket. Long pause, and a request to wait awhile. I waited, and in half an hour was given a visa for five piastres. I proceeded into the city. There I found the needful friend in Mr Moyine Al-Arab who, with his English wife, had been our friends in London. With him I visited many mosques – carefully, in the order of building – from the exquisitely simple earliest to the gaudy and horribly rich mosque on the Citadel. With him, too, I visited the Great Pyramid on camel-back at sunset after the tourists had departed. As night fell we sat on one of the stones at the base of the vast structure and discussed the universe. In the Cairo museum I saw the whole collection of treasures from Tutankhamun's tomb, and was deeply affected by the family pictures on some of the furniture.

It was time to take the plane for England. 'Drained of emotion,' as I wrote in *Via Tokyo*, 'I reached for my diary, and made, as a final entry: "11.40 England and so, all gulpy, HOME." '

Back with Puck at my side I picked up the controls of my London life. The Society now had a full-time General Secretary in the person of Miss Joan Pope, and she remained, for the next nineteen years, a skilled assistant and intimate friend. There was no immediate pressure of work at the Old Bailey, so for a while I turned within, and took stock of my inner travelling while the body had been busily travelling round the world.

Unlike most who search for an inner way to Reality I had found what I wanted by the time I was twenty-one. For a total Plan of the universe, consonant with all known exoteric knowledge but revealing infinitely more, I had *The Secret Doctrine* and its parallel source, the *Mahatma Letters*. For a 'finger pointing' to the way along which to turn reasonable belief into intuitive experience I had the writings of Dr D. T. Suzuki, and I had the example of five or six great men. More, Puck and I early and independently found the *dharma* – the 'thing-to-be-done' – of this life, and early set to work to do it. The process of my inner development in Japan seemed to be one of extension/expansion, a steady lift of consciousness to the plane of a higher self; sometimes, as in midsummer in Japan, with a sense of sustained operation at that level. The extension was, as one must use analogy, up to the Self, out to mankind and all other forms of life, and inwards to the centre.

These lifts of consciousness helped me to remove the belief that the difference between nations was any greater than that between me and my neighbours at home, even as the war had removed the fear of death and any remaining belief in an Almighty yet personal God.

I understood better the cosmic law of Harmony, the living and I believe intelligent law of Karma. I saw how it worked in cycles vast and small under the control, it seemed, of forces, living laws, whether called gods, angels, archetypes or what you will. I saw how it was the karma of the Japanese to be bombed, and of the Hindus and Mohammadans to kill one another as the wildest animal would not do. I saw, looking back, the genesis of the two world wars which I had witnessed, and why, for that matter, I had gone as I did to Japan. Above all I saw that man is indeed one, in his individual causing and the individual and collective result. In my travels I did not only look at a dozen nations; I lived with them as a member of the family, in Japan, Burma, India, Ceylon; and our suffering, as our joys, were one. I remember, when dining with my kendo teacher, Tateno, in Japan, that we talked of our being bombed, the Japanese by the Americans and we in London by the Germans, as though these events were thunderstorms. The results were equally caused.

'Coming to be, ceasing to be', say the Buddhists as we revolve on the wheel of becoming, all that we know and can conceive being part of the vast, unthinkable totality which is the womb of this and all other universes. In this belief and feeling I saw the horror of hate. Let us hate if we must what makes men vile, but never, by all that exists of holiness, a fellow being, large or small, or anything that lives.

I began to 'type' myself, though without much interest in the result. I saw that I am, in Hindu terms, a Karma yogin, a man of action, consumed with all of me in the Next-Thing-to-be-Done, and prefer- ably done now and here and well. If I had not yet reached Wisdom/ Compassion as the ultimate pair of values, save as a noble thought, I was on the way to it. Here, then, was a new set of values, a wider vision of what Puck and I had tried to do and now would begin to do still better.

The Bodhisattva

Waste not your praise on those now passionless.
In them the self is slow consumed in deeds
That flow responsive, eager, to the needs
Of man's totality. Such beings bless
All life by their own being. Here's no sense
Of sacrifice, no loss when fond belief
In severed self is minimal. No leaf
Upon the tree of life seeks recompense
From other, nor would loudly claim the sun
For personal possession. Deep at rest
In endless toil, life's weal their only quest,
These are content with duty gently done.
The mind the master of its thought; the sword
Of will the sheathéd power of the Void,
Here's human worth with gold of heaven alloyed.

The Bodhisattva, careless of reward,
The incarnation of compassion, moves
With laughing eyes yet heart attuned to woe
And with a thousand skilled devices proves
His inmost being's individed flow,
A love so deep he knows not that he loves.

14
Interests Old and New

I woke from these introvert reflections to a variety of duties and interests pulling me in as many directions. The Law came first and I resumed my practice at the Old Bailey. I was pleased to be appointed Deputy Chairman of Kent Quarter Sessions, under the Chairman, Tristram Beresford, K.C. This gave me experience in sitting with a jury, and marched well with visits to Deal as its Recorder. As luck would have it, 'Chimp' Beresford lived at Deal and, when Puck and I stayed there, he gave us magnificent meals of his own cooking.

I reported to the Buddhist Society the highlights of my journey round the Buddhist world, and handed over the cheque for £1500 collected in Rangoon. I told them how surprised and impressed I had been with the interest and knowledge shown by Eastern Buddhist countries in our work in the West. I also told them about the immense honour accorded me as a leader of Western Buddhism; of how committees had readily been formed in Tokyo and Kyoto to translate and consider the Twelve Principles, and of the meetings convened for me by the Sangha and Buddhist organisations on my way home. There were those who sneered at my success in Japan, suggesting that the Japanese were merely fawning on a member of the conquering nations who might be of help to them. But in Burma, we British were on the point of being 'thrown out'!

I made my first appearances on television at this time and during one of them I broke a record. I went to sleep. Four of us, including a bishop, were to talk about religion. It was very hot in the studio and the lights made one sweat so much that one was made up and powdered against such a contingency. I dozed off, and sweated even more on waking in case I had been addressed by the interviewer. I had not, but later was congratulated by an effusive friend on my power of 'keeping so still, as if in meditation, while the others were bouncing up and down and trying to get a word in edgeways'. So I escaped detection; but what of the bishop who went off to another meeting, with a bright yellow bald head which no one had had the time to help him clean?

Some years later when trying out a new idea of television interviews with the famous dead, I had to join Equity. I took the name of Temple Gardener, to the amusement of the Press. In the first episode I cross-examined Paul Daneman on why, as Richard III, he murdered the Princes in the Tower. Alas, the idea fizzled out, but I have had some good fun on television since.

I went round the bookshops in London which usually stocked works on Buddhism, and found the relevant shelves all but empty. We set to work to fill those shelves with our own publications and, by stimulating other publishers to produce new works and new editions of old ones, in five years or so we had succeeded. My own books helped, with profit to all concerned. *Via Tokyo* had been in the hands of Hutchinson for many months so I wrote them a somewhat fierce letter, asking for the date of publication. I was surprised to have a phone call at 8.30 one morning: 'Is that Humphreys? Hutchinson here.' It was the great Walter himself, and he addressed me in that way, even though we did not know each other, because he was a barrister himself. He said my letter was at the top of a sackful of letters which he read in bed each morning and that he would publish *Via Tokyo* at once, and so he did. Puck designed a delightful dust-jacket made up from colour photographs of my travels. Then, as the subject was seething in my mind, I turned to a book on *Zen Buddhism*. I planned it so carefully that in writing it I made no deviation from my initial plan. The format was the most pleasant I have known and the wrapper by Puck matched perfectly. A curious quirk in my character appeared, however, on the evening before publication. Heinemann were to publish the book, and their managing director, A. S. Frere, whom I knew well at the Garrick Club, telephoned to say that we had omitted something. My heart sank. 'A contract!' he explained. I said, as a highly unconventional lawyer, that he was to draft one and I would sign it. I did, but have not yet read it. I would rather trust a friend than attempt to interpret legal verbiage. A larger and, as it turned out, extremely successful venture was with Penguin Books. One of their directors, Mr Glover, invited me to write for them a work on the whole field of Buddhism. He rejected a revised version of my *What is Buddhism?*, first written in question and answer form in 1928; he wanted something new. I set to work and in precisely twelve months produced *Buddhism*, which has now, I am told, sold over half a million copies.

Before I left Japan Dr Suzuki had asked me to be his agent in London for those of his works published in Europe, and through Rider and Co. I have kept them all in print. We ourselves published, as *The Essence of Buddhism*, his translation of the two lectures to the Emperor, the manuscript of which I had brought back from Japan. Later I made a collection of his talks and articles in this country, called *Studies in Zen*.

In 1949 the Society celebrated its silver jubilee. A great reception was held at India House, where the High Commissioner of the day, Mr Krishna Menon, was our host. *Zen Buddhism* was published, and at a large meeting at the Caxton Hall the Thai Ambassador presented to us for our shrine room a complete Buddhist shrine, the figure being a small replica of a famous Buddha-image in Thailand, and the table and its furniture of teak lacquered in gold and scarlet. Puck and I felt that by now the Society really was established and, as I remarked to her, I was becoming known! I was waiting in a traffic block in Smithfield Market when a large policeman's helmet came through the window of the car and a voice inquired, 'Excuse me, Sir, could you tell me a good book on Buddhism?' And a teller in my Bank asked me, when I was cashing a cheque, whether he should start with basic Buddhism or Zen? Of such is fame.

But there was trouble in the Poetry Society, then housed in its eighteenth-century premises in Portman Square. Founded by the Chevalier Galloway Kyle twenty years earlier, the society had built up a very fine membership and library. The time came for Kyle to retire and his successor was the unwitting cause of immediate trouble. While running competitions in the *Poetry Review* I had twice presented the prize to a Mrs Muriel Spark. She was now elected as General Secretary and editor of the *Review*. This young, extremely attractive Scot, who possessed charm, ebullience and office efficiency, proved to be, through no fault of her own, more of a Chinese cracker than a new broom. Soon, indeed, she was staying with Puck and me as almost a refugee from the storm in Portman Square. How the storm died down I do not remember, but Sparklet, as we knew her, went on to become a famous novelist. Some years later I also resigned. The form of verse then published in the *Poetry Review* ceased to appeal to Puck or me; we preferred memorable lines of beauty in form and craftsmanship. We shared the same views on verse, prose and poetry. We agreed that poetry must sing, whether it be a love-lyric, or battle-hymn, or a dirge. Historically verse is far older than prose and was always sung to some instrument. One has only to read the Psalms to see that there is no sharp line between prose and verse; but as I said in a lecture to the Poetry Society in 1943, 'verse usually has metre, rhythm, rhyme (unless blank, which has laws of its own), uses poetic words, has a definite form however tenuous, and at least some meaning to the heart or mind. Compared with prose it is more succinct, emotional and dramatic.' Writing poetry needs, save for the rare genius, hard work, as does any other craft. But either prose or verse may rise to the level of poetry, which is the addition of an indefinable spark of light or beauty, as from the plane beyond thought. All artists seek it and few of us attain it. Such a spark can light up quite poor verse, while perfect verse, for want of it, may never leave the ground. Poetry must excite the heart, and where it fails it is not poetry. As Roberta Shuttleworth wrote:

> The poet is hindered by these two things,
> The presence of feet and the absence of wings.

I cannot criticise 'modern' poetry for I do not admit that it is poetry. It gives me no pleasure to read; I do not want to learn it and recite it to myself, as I do with those of my own anthology, *Poems I Remember*. Let me be dubbed a classical-romantic diehard and left to enjoy the forty volumes of verse in my library, from Shakespeare to Rupert Brooke, from Tennyson to – yes! – the Muriel Spark of her Poetry Society days. I have written verse for precisely seventy years, from my first poem in 1907 until today, and I am frequently told that I say more and say it far more deeply in a page of verse than in a dozen pages of prose.

I have mentioned Shakespeare, but who was he? In 1950 I found a society, the Shakespearean Authorship Society, with a large library and a most distinguished membership, which exists to find out. Its Hon. Secretary was Mrs M. H. Robins who soon became a leading member of the Buddhist Society, and later for many years editor of *The Middle Way*. For the moment she and her sister, Hilda Amphlett, were concerned to embroil me in one of the most fascinating problems in English history. Was William Shake-speare or Shakespeare, who wrote the plays and poems, the same as the man of Stratford-upon-Avon who signed himself, in the only writing of his which has survived, Shaksper? There is certainly a strong tradition, largely invented it seems by Garrick for his own purposes at Stratford, that this youth who came to London and spent many years in the theatre was the author of the plays. Is there, however, any evidence, as a lawyer regards evidence, that he could even write, beyond his signature?

This was a period full of mysteries. Why was the Earl of Oxford paid £1000 a year from the Privy Purse when virtually exiled from Court? What was the truth of Bacon's fall from grace, of Marlowe's death, or of Leicester's relations with the Queen? As for Shakespeare, if you ask some literary friend 'who was Shakespeare?' you will probably get one of three answers: Why not Shakespeare? Does it matter, when we have the plays and poems? Or, thirdly, well, who did? My reply is that there is virtually no evidence where you would expect a great deal, that the plays gain interest when attributed to a great nobleman, and that surely the real author is entitled to the honour of his achievement. The poet at the heart of this mighty output must have had a sensitive, refined and highly educated mind; a considerable knowledge of law, warfare, naval combat, fencing, hawking and other courtly sport; and much experience of foreign travel and the subtleties of Court etiquette and diplomacy. On the whole I think he was Edward de Vere, the 17th Earl of Oxford, a recognised poet, the inventor apparently of the 'Shakespearean' stanza, and he had his own company of players. But – here's the rub – if he himself wrote plays he would by Court etiquette be forced to use a pseudonym.

Who still believes in Shaksper? Not so many, of those who have troubled to examine the evidence. Some have admitted to me the private doubt which would have no place in professorial lectures, but others have expressed their doubts in public. In history there seems to be no claimant to such greatness about whom there is so little evidence to support the claim, and there are many facts which make it as a theory difficult, if not impossible, to believe; or, in the more formal language of Mr Justice Wilberforce in a High Court action in 1964, 'There are a number of difficulties in the way of the traditional ascription.'

Mark Twain said that all that we *know* about Shakespeare could be written on a postcard. The evidence that he wrote the plays would take up far less room, and Sir John Russell, a fellow lawyer, and I brought it down to two sentences, both of which are consistent with the alternative suggestion, that he was but the mask of some-one of such rank that he could no more use his own name as a play-wright than he could appear in public as a common actor. And against the claim? I think the 'three period' argument, first put for-ward by T. J. Looney in his *Shakespeare Identified* (1920), remains unanswered. In the first Stratford period this youth appears to be of low education and no noticed ability. He comes to London and immediately, it seems, writes the long poem 'Venus and Adonis', which is stuffed with classical allusions, shows a knowledge of passages from Ovid then untranslated, and considerable technical mastery of verse form.

In his subsequent poems and the thirty-five great plays he shows a range of knowledge not to be equalled save by the highest in the land. Then he retires to Stratford and reverts to his previous status. None honours him or visits him; he takes no interest in the publica-tion of his works in London. His death is utterly ignored, although his lesser contemporary, Ben Jonson, was buried in Westminster Abbey. He left no single book, no line of manuscript. Only by accident, until Garrick exhumed him, as it were, did he leave to posterity his actual name.

As a mask, or paid lender of a pseudonym, he will pass, but he calls for no honour at Stratford or anywhere else. As for the descrip-tion of him as the world's greatest poet, I agree with Henry James: 'I am sort of haunted by the conviction that the divine William is the

biggest and most successful fraud ever practised on a patient world.'
The inquiry continues.

Much happened in 1950–1. I became 'No. 1' at the Old Bailey, and
thus achieved my only ambition at the Bar, to succeed my father as
senior Treasury counsel. Of what this entailed more later.

In February 1951 my fiftieth birthday was celebrated with the
publication of my *Buddhism*. Puck made me a silver drinking mug
with, chased on it, a satyr behind a bush observing two young ladies
in the 'altogether' who had clearly indulged in the wine flask in his
hand. Her teacher, G. T. Friend, the engraver of the Stalingrad
Sword, congratulated her on her untaught ability, which he did not
himself possess, of engraving freehand on a curved surface.

In the same summer Basil Cameron, the well-known conductor
who was also a member of the Society, took me to the rehearsal to
test the acoustics of the new Festival Hall. A pistol was fired to
record the success of the slate floor in front of the orchestra, but as
the slate was later covered up I presume the result was a failure. On
the opening night, in the presence of the King and Queen and the
Bishop of London, the new Hall seemed so hallowed that one hardly
noticed the ensuing concert save that Sir Malcolm Sargent introduced what seemed to me the proper rendering of 'Rule Britannia',
with a heavy beat unvarying in tempo from the first note to the
last.

In St John's Wood the Mermaid Theatre was opened in a building
which at one time housed the St John's Wood School. Encouraged
by their friend Mme Kirsten Flagstad, Bernard Miles and his wife
collected a group of distinguished helpers, led by Ivor Novello and
Peter Daubeny. Between them they converted the old building in
the garden of their house into a theatre with an Elizabethan apron
stage. A wonderful cast assembled for the opening season of *Dido and
Aeneas*, including Kirsten Flagstad as Dido, Maggie Teyte as Belinda,
Edith Coates as the sorceress and Thomas Hemsley as Aeneas. They
gave their services free and the whole spirit of the enterprise was one
of gay enthusiasm. The contract signed between the Miles and
Kirsten Flagstad showed the high spirits in which the idea was born,
and has since so very successfully grown up. I particularly liked
Clause 3, which stipulated that Mme Flagstad 'should use only
her best voice, fully supported by the breath throughout the

performance'. But 'she was not to brag about the Vikings'. She would, per contra, 'receive two pints of oatmeal stout per diem . . .'

In the summer my father was seriously ill and, being then 84, decided to retire. He was well enough, however, to attend the Diamond Jubilee Dinner of the Old Bailey Bar Mess, held in the Middle Temple Hall. As chairman of the Mess I took the chair and in my speech could refer to his presence and to the remarkable feature about it. When the Mess was formed in 1891 it was thought that there should be some 'youngster' to represent the younger generation, and 'young Travers', only called to the Bar that year, was elected. Sixty years later, as an original member not only of the Mess but of the Committee he was present at its Diamond Jubilee. Such longevity seems to be a family trait. Puck and I founded the Buddhist Society in 1924, and fifty-three years later I am still its active President.

In Marlborough Place the garden flourished. Wisely, Puck and I divided our several responsibilities. I looked after the well, the fish-ponds, the grass and the compost heaps. Since I knew nothing about gardening, I generously conceded that she could do the rest. I love flowers, singly or in bunches, and today when living alone make friends with them in the garden which Puck made. But I hesitate to pick buds for the house, for the garden is their proper home. I prefer to take full blooms which can spend their last hours in my room before the time comes for honourable cremation. This may be senti-mental. I plead guilty to sentiment but not to sentimentality.

I disliked the Chelsea Flower Show to which Puck once took me, for it gave me a headache to look at such an acreage of flowers. Perhaps I like my pleasures in a glass of wine rather than a bottle, a sonnet rather than an epic, a single aria rather than an hour's opera-tic recitative. Perhaps I dislike all things very large, airplanes, liners or limited companies. They become inhuman and I am interested in humanity.

Every year we held some two or three garden parties for about twenty-five persons. In some ten or twelve years we never had one drop of rain between 2 and 6 p.m., and our reputation became such that neighbours began to make their own arrangements ahead accordingly. The fish, of various breeds, approved, for they were grossly overfed by the visitors.

By now I was president or chairman of many organisations, and prominent in more. They ranged from Buddhism to osteopathy and from herbalism to Shakespeare, but I totally failed to amalgamate any two of them. I was, for example, a member of both the Royal Asiatic Society and the Royal India Society. The former had fine premises, a large library and few activities; the latter, many active members and no facilities for them. They would not even consider joint enterprise. Nor would the new and immature British School of Osteopathy join the original Osteopathic Trusts Ltd with its clinic in Dorset Square, in spite of the efforts of Ben Bathurst, Q.C., now Lord Bledisloe, the first Chairman of the Register of Osteopaths in 1935. I gave up amalgamating.

These were the great days of our travels in France. We would stay in Chassignol, a tiny village in the very centre of France, with our Australian artist friend Normal Lloyd, and soon be on friendly terms with all the villagers. Then we would stay at Aix-en-Provence with Pierre Dupin and his Russian wife. He it was who translated my *Buddhism* for the French edition, and he is now the leader of a Buddhist group in Paris. On the coast we would borrow the villa of our friend Terence Gray, who writes in *The Middle Way* as Wei Wu Wei and has the keenest, purest intellect of any man I know. At Le Trayas we found what then was rare, a hotel actually on the beach, and the main road could be forgotten. Here on the last occasion I had what to others was a hilarious operation. Having stepped on a sea-urchin, I had one of its poisonous spikes deep under a toe-nail. 'Have it out at once', said a French doctor friend then with us, 'or by tonight it will be a case of a major operation in hospital.' Before I could decide he had invoked the aid of two 'anaesthetists', meaning fellow bathers, to sit on me; his wife got eau de cologne as an anti-septic and her best nail-scissors. The doctor cut off half the toe-nail, removed the spike, applied a home-made bandage and said that I could swim the next morning. Drinks all round for the patient, relieved of the weight of the anaesthetists, was cheaper than the hospital, and I was grateful indeed.

Once, on our way home through the Basses-Alpes, we called on a very remarkable old lady, Mme Alexandra David-Neel, whom Puck had seen in Paris in 1912 creating a sensation in male evening dress and a monocle. She became the most famous woman explorer in Tibet and was so deeply versed in Tibetan Buddhism that a hut was specially built for her in the compound of the Kum-bum monastery, and she was listened to by the lamas as a scholar knowing more than they about their school of Tibetan Buddhism. Her books on her journey to Lhasa and aspects of Tibetan life are famous. When we found her in a somewhat dark room in her small house, Tibetan-style, in Digne, she was reading proofs for a new book and she wore no glasses. She was then ninety-five and lived to be a hundred.

Twice on our travels we had the good fortune to visit the caves of Lascaux. We crawled about in other prehistoric caves, but Lascaux is unique. Discovered by accident during the war, it was opened to the public in ignorance of what proved to be a tragic result. For 25,000 years this magnificent art gallery had existed unknown in the heart of France, and then in a year or two the warmth and moisture of the breath of visitors brought life to the sterile cave and a lichen-moss began to cover the paintings. I understand that a replica is being built near by, so that generations to come may appreciate what lies in fact next door. When Puck and I went we were impressed, first, with the simplicity of access. One passed through heavy doors which were closed behind one and there they were, a whole range of powerful animals in glowing colour, a kind of wizard bull, surely with magical significance, and stylised figures of slain men. And all this must have been done, however high up the wall, in torch-light, smoke and all. The grandeur of conception, the power in the animals' posture, and the sheer age of the art makes this surely one of the Wonders of the World.

An adventure at Chartres Cathedral had a more personal and lasting meaning. For Chartres the most important day of the year is the birthday of the Virgin on 15 August, and on one occasion we were there for it. Puck stayed down on the river painting a view of the Cathedral. Carlo Robins and I attended the High Mass. We were separated on either side of the central aisle as the Virgin was brought out of her Shrine and borne down the aisle on the shoulders of four men amid a cloud of incense, the great organ throbbing overhead. Behind the Virgin came the Cardinal, and behind him the Bishop, and behind these the local choir of townsmen in their quiet clothes with berets in their hands. As they passed me I stepped out of my seat and joined them. I too was quietly dressed and as usual in France had my beret in my hand. At the great West door we were handed printed hymns in French, and so I sang and marched, slowly because small children in the care of nuns headed the procession, for a mile or so round the hilltop where successive shrines had had their being for enormous periods of time. Then we returned, still singing splendid hymns, but as we approached the West door again, with a long procession of devout inhabitants of Chartres behind us, I entered an ocean of sight and sound as I shall not in this life know again. The great bells overhead were, for this one occasion, bursting in a wild carillon, and the towers were visibly moving under the strain. The vast crowds were singing in the sunlight as though to wake the angels, and the organ in the darkness as we entered again greeted us with its own imperious and splendid sound. I climbed on to a pedestal to wait for the sermon by the Cardinal, but still the bells were sounding within me, though all about me now the crowd, tight-packed in the cool dark aisles, waited in a silence which transcended sound. Yes, Chartres has been for forty years or more my European spiritual home.

15
Reading and Writing

I have done most things to books except eat them. I have read them and written them, reviewed them and published them, bought them and sold them, introduced them and edited them, lent them and lost them, collected a carefully chosen thousand or so and loved them always. In these circumstances a chapter on the subject may be excusable.

I began reading with the appropriate classics of my generation, the Golliwog books, *The Swiss Family Robinson*, *Grimm's Fairy Tales*, *The Water Babies* and Beatrix Potter. Every year as I reread *The Wind in the Willows*, given to me by my mother in 1908, I find it to contain some most beautiful writing. *Alice* reveals, on periodic reading, a remarkable depth of philosophy, beneath the inspired nonsense. Later came Henty, Ballantyne, Conan Doyle and *Treasure Island*; and so to *Kim*, which I still read every year, and Talbot Mundy's *Om*, in my view one of the finest works of spiritual value in fiction. I have tried for many years to get it back in print.

Kim was not all that I read of Kipling. For all the controversy about his politics, he was a master of English, and took immense trouble to be sure of his facts in the modes of life he described. He is, incidentally, the subject of the most brilliant bilingual pun I know, in French and Hindi, which I found in a Punch review. Speaking of the women in his tales of India, the writer remarked, 'But surely it is a case of "plus ça change, plus c'est la mem-sahib".'

At Cambridge I was led, as already described, into the vast field of Buddhism, and to the dozen works in which Theosophy, as repre-

sented to the world, is set out. Also I found time for books of biography, history and travel, and acquired the habit of keeping handy
in my pocket one of the dozen small volumes which are surely sufficient for our spiritual needs. My Epictetus, Marcus Aurelius, *The
Bhagavad Gita* and *The Voice of the Silence* are well worn. Later I added
the *Tao Te Ching*, and the classics of Buddhism such as the *Dhammapada* and the *Sutra of Hui Neng*. A page from one of these I found more
profitable than letting the mind run fancy-free which, like racing an
engine out of gear, is of no assistance to the car.

Save for collections such as *The Arabian Nights* – Powys Mathers'
translation, far finer than Burton's – I soon abandoned fiction;
Dickens and Scott, and the immortal ladies such as the Brontës and
Jane Austen, passed me by. But I confess to a secret exception known
in my family as the Blood-Bank, a hundred or two chosen detective
stories, or 'Bloods'. I am proud of my 'forgettery', the opposite of
memory, which enables me to read a 'Blood' at least three times in
the course of years. Sherlock Holmes and Father Brown are always
available at bedtime. Other favourites are Dorothy Sayers, followed
by Margery Allingham and Ngaio Marsh, and not quite so hotly by
the best seller of all, Agatha Christie; of the men, I favour Michael
Innes, John Dickson Carr or Carter Dickson (I forget which he was
at the Garrick Club), or 'Bony's' Australian adventures by Arthur
Upfield, or one of Ellery Queen's early series, those with a country's
name such as *The Greek Coffin Mystery*, or the Chinese detective stories
about Judge Dee by Robert van Gulik. These, re-bound in one
magnificent volume, will be with me on my desert island for ham-
mock reading, at the close of a long day spent in finding food for the
body.

Nowadays I buy little for I have enough, and the London Library
in St James' (I detest St James's) Square has served me splendidly
for twenty years. I add to its shelves the works which I write myself,
produce as the European agent for D. T. Suzuki, and those for which
I stimulate a reprint or write a foreword on request.

I have edited books, always an anxious task when the author is not
available. In particular, it took me nearly five years to prepare the
third and definitive edition of *The Mahatma Letters to A. P. Sinnett*, on
behalf of the Mahatma Letters Trust, which owns the copyright.
This necessitated long visits to the British Museum with Mr C.
Jinarajadasa, the Buddhist President of the Theosophical Society,

to check with the original words which did not seem right as they stood. More difficult still was to help reduce the great bulk of H. P. Blavatsky's *The Secret Doctrine* from some 1300 pages to a more convenient 250. A great deal of the original was a painstaking effort to refute the religious or scientific views of current writers, many of whom are since forgotten. Today this makes tedious reading, and present members of the Theosophical movement may be forgiven for wanting 'something simpler'. *An Abridgement of the Secret Doctrine* was therefore published, the pioneer work being carried out by Miss Elizabeth Preston, with whom I discussed the problems involved at the Theosophical Headquarters at Adyar, and I did the actual editing in London. The resulting work, I claim, contains the essential teachings which no student of cosmology or of the occult science of the East can afford to ignore. Would that Western scientists would study not only the wisdom that the East already possesses, but also how it is handled, before attempting rediscovery from their own materialistic foundation. In failing to do so they distort the Wisdom and place the enormous power derived from such knowledge into the hands of those who for the most part promptly apply it to the desires of the self and the destruction of those who oppose them.

In all my work with books I have had the most happy relations with publishers and bookshops, content to make loose arrangements on the telephone without formality. The nearest I came to a difficult moment was at John Murray's celebration of the 100th volume of The Wisdom of the East Series, and I, who had them all, murmured to Sir John Murray that I made the number ninety-nine, as one was a reprint from elsewhere! I was forgiven.

And so to my own collection. I am no bibliophile, and I acquire a book because I want to read it. I keep it only because I think I may want to read it or refer to it again. On the shelves in my library I arrange the books with some regard for appearance, but I do not follow the unique habit of Samuel Pepys, as may be seen in the library of Magdalene College, Cambridge, where all the books have precisely the same height because a sliver of wood of appropriate thickness is placed under each to make it so. At least I know where each book should be and am cross if I cannot find it. I lend, making a note of the loan, but in the matter of books how low are the morals of friends who would be the soul of honour with the loan of fifty pence!

I doubt if I have the entire works of any writer, for surely no one ever wrote so that every word is gold. Poets rightly destroy much as they write, and executors should be allowed to do the same with their discovered trivia.

Mrs C. F. Leyel, the greatest herbalist since Culpeper, and founder of the Society of Herbalists and the shops of Culpeper Ltd, is a near-exception. I have her six volumes on herbs, beginning with *Herbal Delights*. Often at weekends I would lie on the sofa in her large library at Shripney, near Bognor, while she worked away at her desk. Suddenly she would throw at me, 'I want a few lines to begin the chapter on' – whatever the herb was – 'and can't find anything suitable'. She would give me its properties and I would set to work. The brief poems duly appeared. Puck contributed some of the garden drawings for the wrappers.

Of course the largest part of my collection is in the field of Buddhism and Oriental art, and I am told that it forms a valuable library. But I am ceasing to buy. In the present rush to publish anything on Buddhism, in answer no doubt to an existing demand, publishers are producing or reprinting works which, except for a few on Tibetan Buddhism, add little to our knowledge or spiritual experience. The same has applied for many years to Theosophy. Theosophy I must insist is not a pastiche of principles collected from existing religions, but a re-presentation, under a title invented by Ammonius Saccas in the fourth century, of actual records existing in Tibet of the ancient Wisdom, 'the accumulated wisdom of the ages, tested and verified by generations of seers', as one of H. P. Blavatsky's teachers wrote of it to A. P. Sinnett. This presentation may be found, by all interested in the origin and nature of the universe and man, in a mere half a dozen books; those written later are at the best commentary, and at the worst a debasing of what I find to be the highest exposition of the subject extant.

For the rest, my collection is general, with a leaning towards the reign of Charles II, our most brilliant foreign minister, and his true love, Nell Gwynn. It so happens that next to her are the four works which set out the evidence that a woman ruled the Vatican as Pope under the name of John VIII for two years from AD 853. What the two ladies would say of each other I have not inquired.

My shelves of English literature hold few surprises, save that true poetry ends with the Second World War, as I think it largely did. I have few plays: Flecker's *Hassan* which Harry Ainley inscribed for me; *Murder in the Cathedral*, which I regard as T. S. Eliot's greatest contribution to English literature; the score of *The Immortal Hour* of Fiona Macleod, set to music by Rutland Boughton which, after Puck and I had attended eighteen performances, I got the whole cast to sign for me; and *The Lady's not for Burning*, in which I think Christopher Fry rises at times to a quality of writing comparable with Shakespeare (whoever he was).

I write in my books in pencil, to the horror of some, first by way of my own brief index at the end so that I can quickly find the passage I am looking for, and then in the margin so that I can find the comment on the page. Puck and I occasionally used strong but contradictory remarks in books we both read carefully. My 'bosh' might be countered with her 'nothing of the sort', or vice versa. More important additions to every book are, first, my book-plate which I had copied from that of my grandfather. More than once I have founded an after-dinner speech in the City on the story behind the coat of arms it bears. When the arms of the 'building Masters' for insertion in the windows of the rebuilt Saddlers' Hall were being made in St John's Wood, I called on the maker to see how the shields were progressing. He murmured that he was having difficulty with my own as they were not registered at the College of Arms. The best he could find, he said, was a very similar set of a Lord Mayor of London of the early eighteenth century, who bore my name but – embarrassed cough – 'he is described as with descendants extinct'. Be that as it may, as it is full of nags' heads it is most appropriate for a past master of the Saddlers' Company, of which my family have been Masters in their time since 1769. The motto beneath the arms, 'Be always just', is one which I have humbly tried to obey.

A more important entry in some forty of my books is the author's signature, beginning with that of J. B. Priestley whose first book, *Brief Diversions* I reviewed while we were both at the Hall at Cambridge, and rising to that of the Duke of Windsor in *The Windsor Tapestry* in 1939. Winston Churchill signed the first volume of his *Marlborough, His Life and Times* when I swore him in as a Freeman of the Borough of Deal, which contained his castle as Lord Warden of the Cinque Ports. There are many between, including H.H. the Dalai Lama, and Dr Sarvapalli Radhakrishnan, later President of India.

.   .   .   .   .

And so to writing. As I have said, I am no scholar but rather a retailer of the manufacturer's wares or, if the manufacturer is of the rank of teacher, then perhaps a wholesaler of what I understand of the teaching. Legal training helped me to present a clear exposition of what I had to say, and I began early, in the *Cambridge Law Journal*, my College magazine, and reviews in Theosophical and Buddhist journals.

One may calmly decide what book to write next, but poetry is different, and one cannot sit down and decide to write a poem. It is born, and shouts for utterance, at least as to its opening phrase and the feeling or thought behind it. The need for a quiet retreat for the writing of poetry, or even verse, is to me nonsense, for I wrote one of my best sonnets, on the theme of my London garden at dawn, in the car on the way to the Old Bailey and back. The poetic muse is a form of intuitive intervention into the dull ways of thought. It happens, and the result, good or bad, will depend on the strength of the feeling or idea and one's skill in presenting it in terms appropriate.

For actual writing I pencil notes, in an armchair or in bed. Then an improved version of the notes, and then straight on to my ancient typewriter, still with three fingers as I taught myself about sixty years ago.

I have written some three books on law, five on poetry, one being an anthology, *Poems I Remember*, one travel book, *Via Tokyo*, and some fifteen on Buddhism and Oriental philosophy. Looking at the output with an impersonal eye, I am satisfied most with *Via Tokyo, Walk On!, Zen Buddhism, Buddhism, Buddhist Poems* and *The Wisdom of Buddhism*, a kind of Buddhist Bible. Many of these books have been translated into foreign languages, as well as being published in America. The translation fees are acceptable, but what *does* one do with six copies of a favourite work in Portuguese, or Finnish?

Later works have been invariably somewhat repetitive, but *A Western Approach to Zen* is my contribution to Western thought, as distinct from making known, as others have done, what they understand to be the teaching of the All-Enlightened One.

I state the problem at the beginning: Zen Buddhism has arrived in the West. There is no likelihood of Zen roshis, in the full meaning of the term as used in the Rinzai School, arriving in Europe in sufficient numbers to give us expert training, nor of quantities of Western students having the time or money for years of training in Japan.

How, then, should we in the West approach the Zen way of life, and its goal, a wide expansion of the whole field of consciousness?

The book is an attempt to assist the student to develop the intuition, which alone can flood the mind with the light of Zen, or, more accurately, help him to remove the obstacles of thought-attachment, false belief and the claims of the ego which blind us all to the light already there. The latter half of the book is a course in four 'phases' designed to achieve this, and a series of experiments in which members of the Zen class at the Buddhist Society in London recorded their answers to searching questions. How many in the last five years have found my suggestions profitable I know not, but the problem must be faced and solved if Zen Buddhism, as has happened to so many other schools of self-discipline, is not to disintegrate into another set of intellectual doctrines or a witty form of playing the fool.

In my recent *The Search Within* I have tried a different form of approach, but what is the value of any such if one does not strive to *approach* unceasingly and with 'the whole soul's will'?

16
Senior Prosecuting Counsel

The ladder of Treasury Counsel has already been explained. From the first appointment by the Attorney-General as No. 6, it is a process of moving up as vacancies appear, through retirement, a permanent appointment to the Bench or by 'taking silk', which means to become a Queen's Counsel. The Treasury counsel are all 'stuff gownsmen', and a Silk, although he can thereafter defend in any case, is very seldom briefed to prosecute at the Old Bailey.

By tradition the '*No. 1*' was given most of the murder cases, which for me had the advantage that I should not be conducting the long fraud cases in which, knowing much of fraud but little of accountancy, I was never at home. However, I did conduct other cases of exceptional importance, such as the trial of Fuchs under the Official Secrets Act, and the Lewisham train crash in which ninety people were killed. I could also accept defence briefs if I wished, but my time was almost fully occupied with cases of murder.

In any year there was an average of two such cases at each of the twelve sessions of the Old Bailey, and in one session there were actually seven. I had been junior counsel in many more during my practice at the Old Bailey, so in all I must have been concerned in some three hundred murder trials. I have, therefore, some basis for my views on the subject, but none need agree with them.

There are two considerations, the law, which I must explain, however briefly, and the trial. The crime of murder includes three ingredients, each of which has been the subject of numerous cases in the Court of Criminal Appeal and the House of Lords. The killing must be unlawful, by a person of sound memory and discretion, and with malice aforethought, expressed or implied. The crime of manslaughter, unlawful killing, differs from the above, as will be seen by the absence of any need to prove malice. An example is what used to be called 'motor-manslaughter', where killing was unintended.

I must interpolate here one case where the last sentence was in doubt. A dead body was found by the side of an arterial road in Blackheath. It looked as though the man had been run over, and the driver of the car had lost his head, throwing the body on the grass before driving away. The evidence pointed to a man in North London who had had a quarrel with the deceased outside his garage, and in the ensuing blows had killed him. The killer panicked, ran his car out of the garage, drove twice over the dead body and then put it in the boot. He then kept his dental appointment in Harley Street, after which he drove on to Blackheath, where he deposited the body some time during the night.

Was that motor-manslaughter? G. D. ('Khaki') Roberts, Q.C., a notable defending counsel, did his best to attack the allegation that the initial blows were murder and not manslaughter, but his client's confessions to the police were too strong for him, and this remarkably callous murderer was in due course rightly convicted.

On the three ingredients of murder set out above, the defence to the first may be that the killing was in self-defence. In such a case a man may have the right even to kill deliberately. On the second issue, the accused might be insane at the time, or really drunk, or acting under extreme provocation, or with 'diminished responsibility', defences which need not be examined here. But the essence of the crime is malice, meaning to kill, and that being a state of mind which has to be, as it were, reconstructed for the jury, is often a difficult matter to prove.

Let us omit cases of poisoning, which must be deliberate but are very rare. Let us also omit those of the real killer, where a man is tried for murder but the evidence is available for several more cases; those of mercy killing, of joint suicide pacts where the survivor may be tried for the murder of the other, and cases where there is one real killer, but another so close to him in body and purpose that both are held to be murderers. All these I would say amount to less than 20 per cent of the cases of alleged murder before the Courts. Of the remainder, in many cases a plea of guilty to manslaughter is accepted, the evidence of malice being not very strong. In the remaining cases the accused is not very often, in my belief, guilty of 'the worst crime', that of unlawfully killing a fellow human being.

Most such accused had very little schooling and had come from a poor background. Few were of strong moral character; many drank too much, and at the time of the crime were well under the influence of drink, or recovering from it. Few had much, if any, emotional control, and on losing their temper would easily resort to violence. Many were at cracking-point from some slow emotional build-up, as between man and wife, fellow workers or just pub companions. Have we not all of us at some time felt and even muttered through clenched teeth, 'I could *kill* that man'? How much did we mean it? The situation is far worse when the man concerned has never known a true home life. He may have had a drunken father and prostitute mother and received from them only abuse, beating or – almost worse – neglect. To me it is a very powerful factor that such a youth – they are usually fairly young – has never known the real meaning of love. In this sort of situation, especially when killer and killed are both of this type, a quarrel may result in murder. If the murderer, perhaps habitually, carries a gun or at least a knife, of course murder is more likely, and he will repeat the old story, 'I carried it for protection', or 'I drew it to frighten him'.

Here, then, very often is a man not strong enough to control the forces in his mind, for want of training in this profoundly difficult exercise, who suddenly hits with a weapon. The blow may kill, or it may do little damage or it may do none. A miss does no damage, a stab missing the heart will probably heal; a half-inch one way or the other may decide the issue between murder and a far less serious offence, but all the ingredients were there save actual killing.

There are in my belief far worse crimes than such a blow. What of the deliberate professional blackmailer, who slowly ruins many people's lives, homes and happiness, and drains their assets to the dregs? I only once, when a judge, gave a man as much as eight years imprisonment, and that was for this offence. What of the 'house-agent' who, with a flat to let, takes large deposits from a dozen young couples and vanishes with what is often a large proportion of their life savings? What of brutal rape, when two men hold a girl down and a third rapes her? What of the importer of heroin in large quantities and for huge profits, who year by year causes an increasing number of young people to die horribly? I repeat, there are worse crimes than the majority of the murders which for many years I put before a jury for trial.

A trial for murder bears little resemblance to the average detective story. In the latter case the issue is whodunnit? in the former, 'Is it proved that the man in the dock *did*?' The preparation for the trial is normal: inquiries, statements, arrest, interviews, and maybe an identification parade; then committal for trial if the evidence seems good enough to the Magistrate. Then the brief is prepared and comes to counsel and his junior. The latter will draw the indictment; both will read the depositions of witnesses, and the accompanying exhibits, often including a statement from the accused, and the police report, setting out the progress of their inquiries to date. Then there is a conference, attended by both counsel, a representative of the Director of Public Prosecutions, senior police, quite often the pathologist concerned, and maybe a scientific officer to cope with such evidence as fingerprints.

So the trial was planned, or was in my day, though today, I understand, it is far more casual. Its purpose is to place before the jury the evidence on which the Crown submit that they should convict. However, I personally never asked a jury to convict if on the evidence before me I did not believe that the accused was guilty of murder. On many occasions when I was not sure that a verdict of wilful murder was justified I have so used my discretion in cross-examination and my tone in the final speech, that the accused was found guilty of manslaughter only.

Before the trial came on I would see that defending counsel had possession of all evidence which I myself was not using, but thought might be of use to the defence. On one occasion I even called as a witness for the Crown a police officer whose evidence clearly showed that the accused had been seen at some place at a time which gave him an alibi. I was quite sure that the officer was wrong, and he later saw that he had his date wrong. Nevertheless, while telling the jury that I did not rely on his evidence, I called him for what his evidence was worth. As it stood it was relevant and that was enough for me.

The one case in which a verdict of guilty was given which I thought, and still think, wrong, concerned two men who entered a hotel at night and bound and gagged the nightwatchman. As he lay, one of them kicked him and broke his jaw. They left. One might say that at that moment their crime was complete. During the night the injured man managed to crawl towards the door, and in the darkness hit his nose so that it bled hard as he rolled over. He died of suffocation as the blood went down his windpipe. Was that wilful murder by those who had left many hours before? This brings in the Eastern law of Karma, cause and effect. Of course any effect can be traced back through successive causes, but at what point is philosophical subtlety overtaking justice? The judge recommended a reprieve and expected it. The two men were hanged.

I have mentioned the Buddhist belief in the universal Law of Harmony called Karma, that cause and effect are equal and opposite, whether we can trace the process or not. Another Buddhist belief is Dharma, in a sense duty, the next-thing-to-be-rightly-done, and for the right reason. I have often been asked how could I prosecute in a murder trial, knowing, as was true in those days, that the penalty might be execution? In fact the figures show that only about one in ten of those sentenced to death were hanged, but that does not affect the principle. My answer is clear, that it seemed to me my dharma to follow my father to the criminal Bar, where for forty years I was successful and happy. The work involved murder trials which at that time involved the death penalty. If I refused to prosecute in murder trials it would be right to give up my post as Treasury counsel. Indeed, by maintaining my own high standard of the proof of guilt, I was in a position to save a number of lives. Believing this work to be my dharma in this life, I did it.

But the law of Karma affects the situation more profoundly still. If it was my karma to prosecute, it was the karma of the prisoner not only to be prosecuted by me but also to have committed that crime or at least to be on trial for it. The result would be within the ambit of his thinking-feeling-action in lives gone by. And his death, if he were hanged, would be the result of *his* causing, and might, as it were, wipe out the causing in the infinitely complex, infinitely subtle weaving of this cosmic web.

My belief in Karma throughout my adult life had given me, among other boons, an unusual attitude to physical death. A few years ago I missed death from a lorry by what I calculated to be four seconds. I noted as I walked to my car that I had not missed a heart-beat or a breath, save as caused by the leap to safety. We all die; we all come back, according to the law. It may be that these views, sunk into my mind to become part of my total processes of living, also affected my attitude to the future of the men whom I prosecuted.

Very few of the cases in which I was concerned were planned murders. But I do remember one which illustrated the sole weakness in that great pathologist, the late Sir Francis Camps. A man in-decently assaulted a girl who said that when she got home that night she would tell her mother, who she knew would at once go to the police. He made a rendezvous with the girl in a narrow, little-frequented street, bought a cut-throat razor, kept the rendezvous and from behind cut the girl's throat from ear to ear. When cross-examined by defending counsel, Dr Camps answered an almost casual question just too quickly. In cutting the girl's throat arteries, would not the murderer have her blood all over him, and more especially on his sleeves? 'Oh, certainly,' said Dr Camps. Counsel sat down. I tried to save the situation in re-examination. 'You appreciate, Dr Camps, that the man was standing behind her and, so you say, with a hand round her neck wiped the razor across her throat? Would he necessarily get any blood on himself at all?' 'No, no, I see what you mean,' began Dr Camps, but the damage was done. Counsel went to the jury on the admitted fact that this man was seen in a public house in what would be a very few minutes later, and no one saw any blood on him anywhere. He was acquitted, thanks to the brilliance of his counsel and the fact that Dr Camps *would* answer first and think afterwards!

Dr Camps was a pioneer in experiment. A man was charged with literally throwing his father over the balcony of a fourth-floor council flat because he had attacked his mother. The defence was that he fell over when arguing with his son. 'No,' said Dr Camps; 'I got a sack of his weight and threw it over. It landed where the body fell, precisely. He was thrown; he did not fall.' Verdict guilty, but with a reprieve to follow. There was a better example of this habit of 'practical pathology' when I took him with me to Germany to defend a charge of murder at court martial among the British troops stationed there. The Crown said that the injuries on the dead man's head were caused by a helve, the wooden handle of a pickaxe used in drill. I called Dr Camps, who had been allowed to see the body. 'How were the injuries caused?' I asked. 'With an army boot,' was the reply. 'Why do you say that?' 'Because I tried kicking the head o a dead body with an army boot and the marks were precisely the same.' 'And if my client was wearing gym shoes at the time?' 'Then he did not kill that man.' My client was acquitted.

Of the cases when I thought it worth preserving a newspaper cutting there are but a dozen in the nine years in which I was the senior prosecuting counsel. The trial of Donald Hume, who murdered Stanley Setty, cut up his body and then dumped it in parcels from his plane into the Thames, was made the more dramatic still by events which happened daily during its course. On the first day the judge was taken ill and had to be replaced. A reporter was severely handled by the second judge for interviewing Mrs Hume before she gave evidence. There were belated discoveries about cord which might have been used to tie up the parcels, but which the judge held it was too late to put in evidence. The story, as proved in court, seemed deadly. It was only because I was not quite sure that the jury were accepting it that I cross-examined Hume at length to get his admission that he was at least 'an accessory after the fact'. In this case this meant that he knew the parcels contained a murdered man when he took part in their disposal. The jury did disagree on the issue of murder, but Hume was given twelve years on the second indictment, as an accessory. When he came out of prison eight years later he made a confession of murder to the Press, knowing that he was quite safe in doing so. This is not, however, what the police think really happened, and the truth, I believe, is uglier still.

In the trial of Davies in the Clapham Common murder no fewer than six youths had been committed for trial. I offered no evidence against four of them for the good reason that there was none. The jury disagreed on the trial of the remaining two, but at the retrial, when Davies stood alone in the dock, as I had always advised, he was convicted. The sentence of death was commuted, and in due course some writer came to see me in chambers to tell me that he had been commissioned to write a book on the trial. I asked if the basis would be – I could think of nothing else – my gross unfairness, or some nonsense of the kind, and he admitted as much. What he really wanted to know was whether I would sue him for libel if he did so write. I told him that he could say what he had apparently been paid to say, that I should not in that event sue, and that he could get out.

In the much-reported trial of Craig and Bentley for the murder of a police officer, I have only two memories to add; the apparent injustice of hanging only the less guilty youth because the much more guilty happened to be too young for the death penalty; and the sheer drama of murder being conclusively proved by the shouting of five words, 'Let him have it, Chris', when the man who shouted was actually himself under arrest at the time.

These brief phrases fascinate me. Others were spoken in all innocence by a witness at the trial of Mrs Christofi for the murder of her daughter-in-law. Two doors from this house a neighbour at 11.45 at night took his dog into the garden for the usual purposes, and saw what seemed a bonfire at the back garden door of Mrs Christofi's house. He climbed the intervening fence and peered over. He saw what he took to be a dressmaker's model on its back, on fire. 'When I saw that it was all right', he said to the jury, 'I climbed back to my own garden and went to bed.' What he saw was the murdered and naked body of the daughter-in-law over which Mrs Christofi had poured a tin of paraffin in the belief that this alone would ensure complete cremation. 'When I saw that it was all right . . .'!

Sometimes there was drama in the trial itself. Two men had a row and agreed to have it out in a public garden. In a corner they took their coats off but Johnson, the accused, had picked up a brick on the way, and with this he killed his opponent, who was unarmed. In his evidence in the witness box he said that the brick was up his sleeve and that he showed it to Mead, the deceased, before the fight began, but that he had had to use it when the other man was strangling him. In cross-examination I asked him to show how the brick would go in his sleeve. He took it and for the moment I was troubled for he was only about twelve feet from the judge. He could not get the brick up his sleeve, threw it down, shouted that he wished to plead guilty and started back to the dock. The judge gently reasoned with him and the trial continued. He was found guilty, the jury accepting the Crown case that he picked up the brick after the fight began with their jackets off, and deliberately killed Mead.

Of all these trials it is the Towpath murder, as it was called, which I best remember. Whiteway, the accused, was on the towpath of the Thames when two girls appeared on bicycles. He hit them one after the other on the back of the head, hard enough to render them un-conscious but not enough to kill. Then he raped them and threw them, still alive, with their bicycles, into the river. The local police could not have made more blunders. When the whole country was looking for Whiteway, an officer let him go when he was actually in the police station; and another, finding an axe on the floor of the car believed to be that of the Whiteway, took it home to cut firewood. Then Superintendent Hannam of the Yard took over, and with him I had a long view of the neighbourhood. I even found on a tree near the assault axe marks where Whiteway had, it seemed, been practis-ing throwing his axe. The almost impossible defence was brilliantly conducted by Peter Rawlinson. He began by asking me not to men-tion in my opening speech to the jury evidence of which he proposed to challenge the admissibility. I noted what he said and looking woe-fully at my notes remarked, 'I shall have to say to the jury, "Members of the Jury, the charge is murder. He had blood on his boots", and call the first witness.' Little by little, however, the challenged evidence was admitted by the judge, and the verdict became inevitable.

Far more serious to the community than any murder was the offence of Klaus Fuchs, charged with betraying secrets learnt where he worked, with a high reputation as a theoretical physicist, at the Atomic Energy Establishment at Harwell. A convinced Communist, he was yet troubled by the oaths of allegiance and security which he had made before being entrusted with British secrets, for he had be-come very fond of his colleagues and of England, where he had lived and worked so long, so happily. In my opening at Bow Street Magis-trates' Court, I spoke of 'induced schizophrenia'. But the reasons for the crime were of no importance compared with their appalling gravity. I shall not forget the conference at which all the senior persons concerned attended. I asked, 'Just how much has he given them?' The answer, from the head of Harwell was, 'Everything' – which included the details of the H-bomb. At the trial the Attorney-General led me, and Fuchs pleaded guilty, receiving from the Lord Chief Justice the maximum sentence, fourteen years imprisonment.

So much for the prosecution, but in all cases of gravity an experi-enced counsel would be briefed for the defence, even before the days of legal aid, and there were indeed giants in those days. I have written of Sir Edward Marshall-Hall and of Sir Henry Curtis-Bennett. Equally great were Sir Patrick Hastings, who will be long remembered for his defence of Mrs Barney, and Sir Norman Birkett, later a High Court judge, whom my father jokingly called, for his brilliant defence in a famous murder trial at Lewes Assizes, 'public enemy No. 1.' Let me close by mentioning the problem which seems to trouble so many members of the public: 'How can a barrister defend a man whom he knows to be guilty?' The answer is simple, that he does not. If his client confesses in terms to his guilt he cannot go on defending him, but if his instructions, through the solicitor, are that the accused is not guilty he does what he can for his defence, as presented to him. What he personally believes is quite irrelevant to his duty, and should be to his conduct of the case. It is the business of prosecuting counsel to prosecute, fairly and unemotionally, according to the high traditions of the English Bar. The same applies to counsel briefed for the defence, and the two men may be literally changing places in court later the same day.

I Hear He's Died Again

'I hear he's died again. It had to be
Though choice of circumstance was his alone.'

'You mean that we have lived before, that we
His fellow men have met and truly known
The substance of his yesterday?'
                                'His life
Is of the One Life; all you see is wrought
Of feeling, thought and act in needful strife
Of self-becoming, for the Way is nought
But of our choosing, and we meet and part
Obedient to effect.'
                        'The new is strange
To memory.'
                'Of some, and yet the heart,
New-lighted by the Changeless beyond change
Knows that we love and die and live again
In forms of our alone devising. Blind
As yet and bound in self-engendered pain
The foolish man with unawakened mind
Creates himself and strives to rob the Whole
With phantom forms of an immortal soul.'

'Then hands of prayer are raised to heaven in vain?'

'There's only Buddha-Mind or Self or THIS
The Namelessness where death itself is slain.

One Life that dies not; forms that ever die.
Here's hell of loss or fullness of pure bliss
Till, purged of error neither shall remain.'
'So here is grief repeated? Each return
A recognition and a long goodbye?'

'Such is the Wheel whereon we sadly learn.
Such is the Law. We ask but know not why.
Only I know I loved my brother I,
And now I hear that he has died again.'

17
A Year of Destiny

1956 was indeed for me a year of destiny. Between November 1955 and November 1956 I became a Bencher of my Inn, and attended the laying of two foundation stones; my father died; I became Recorder of Guildford and received the queen in that capacity; I became Master of the Saddlers' Company; the Buddhist Society moved to its present premises; I went to Lagos to do a case for the Bank of West Africa; and to Katmandu and New Delhi for the celebration of Buddha Jayanti.

The four Inns of Court are each governed by a body of Benchers, who fill their own vacancies. In November 1955 I was elected Bencher of the Inner Temple. As I was not then a Silk this was presumably by virtue of my position at the Old Bailey. The old Hall had been destroyed by bombs in 1941, and when the Queen laid the foundation stone of the New Hall, I stood at the subsequent reception at the far end of the line which was headed by my father as the oldest Bencher. In the years to come I thoroughly enjoyed my lunches in Hall, after a brisk walk from the Old Bailey, but in terms of committee work I have been a poor addition to the Bench. While I was No. 1 at the Old Bailey I was Chairman of the Bar Mess Committee, and that building ever had for me priority.

As Key Warden of the Saddlers' Company I was present when my father laid the foundation stone of our fourth Hall, for the old one had also been destroyed in the bombing of London. He was not well, and I had asked that the ceremony planned for the spring be brought forward. Indeed, he died the following February at the Onslow Court Hotel.

It is difficult to assess one's father's character and professional prestige, although I saw him regularly, on the Bench, at the Garrick and at our respective homes, and also when he came as a High Court judge to the Old Bailey and I appeared before him. We each respected the other's differing way of life. His was that of a great lawyer, with a wide circle of friends. He spent many of his evenings with his beloved Dickens and must have known many passages by heart. My life, apart from the law, lay in my love of Oriental philosophy, art and poetry. But although we moved in different spheres, we could meet on the basis of mutual affection. He deeply missed my brother, his first-born, and I could respect this; but at least I was following his career as Treasury counsel, and striving to be worthy of the family's motto 'Be always just'. When he retired, Lord Simon, an ex-Lord Chancellor, wrote of him 'There is no judge before whom I should more fear to be tried if I were guilty of some crime which could only be proved by patient and remorseless study of the evidence. But there is no judge before whom I would more willingly go if I were innocent but were needing deliverance from the accumulated weight of prejudice and suspicion.'

He was wedded to the field of criminal law, as I was, but when he became a High Court judge and therefore concerned with civil cases too, he rapidly acquired the needful extra knowledge. He refused elevation to the Court of Appeal, as this would take him out of criminal trials as distinct from argument on law, but he acted as Lord Chief Justice for some years during the illnesses first of Lord Hewart and later of Lord Caldecote. He was made a Privy Councillor in 1946, and in this capacity attended the Accession Council of the present Queen.

On his retirement in 1951, many described him in the Press as one of the greatest criminal judges of the century, and so he seemed to me. Soon afterwards I helped him and my mother sell up the house at Ealing, and they went to live at the Onslow Court Hotel in Queen's Gate, Kensington. My mother died just before Christmas 1953, and for a while my father came to live with Puck and me. But, as he said after a while, my friends and his had different interests, and he went back to the hotel from which he could go almost daily to the Bench or the Garrick Club.

Let me end this passage with words I used when addressing some years later a meeting of the Medico-Legal Society, of which he had been president: 'I think you will agree, those of you who remember him, that he set an immensely high standard of fairness and humanity, and never let the letter of the law interfere with what seemed to be the justice of the case. As far as I am concerned he was more than a beloved parent; he was a wonderful example of an English gentleman.'

In the summer of 1955 Derek Curtis-Bennett, son of Sir Henry, died when Recorder of Guildford, and I applied for the vacancy, Guildford being far easier of access than Deal. A Recorder was one who sat with a jury at least four times a year to try cases in the City or Borough which would otherwise go for trial to County Quarter Sessions. As such he ranked next in order to the Mayor. I thoroughly enjoyed my twelve years of visits to Guildford, but none could equal what was almost my first. Guildford has a unique tradition: whenever the Sovereign enters the Borough he or she must be presented with a plum cake – yes, a Plum Cake, exactly as if this was a page omitted from *Alice in Wonderland*. And so it happened when the Queen and Prince Philip attended the 700th anniversary of its charter. The main road was closed to traffic and filled with residents. The Queen and Prince Philip arrived at the medieval Guildhall, and having been welcomed by the Mayor and myself, appeared on the balcony which overlooks the street. I, with an arm in a sling from a smashed shoulder blade, none the less managed to handle and read a large Address of Welcome, and the Earl of Onslow as High Steward of Guildford then presented the Queen with the eight-pound cake, amid thunderous cheers and laughter. After replying to the address, the Queen left for another appointment.

After lunch the Bishop and I were taken to the local cricket ground to await the return of the Queen, and just before the match started Prince Philip was brought to our table by the Mayor. 'You know the Bishop of Guildford, Sir, I think,' said the Mayor. 'Yes,' said Prince Philip. 'And the Recorder, Sir?' 'Hm,' the Prince remarked, 'a choice of religions, I see!' I was puzzled for the moment, as were the Bishop and the Mayor at this knowledge of my unofficial affairs, but the Prince explained as we sat down that he and the Queen were just back from a visit to Ceylon, and he wanted help on some aspect of the life of a bhikkhu, or Buddhist monk.

I asked Prince Philip what would happen to the cake. Would it go to some hospital? 'Certainly not,' he replied. 'I shall take it home for my young!'

In July, having served in successive years the office of Renter Warden, Quarter Warden, and Key Warden, I was 'freely and lovingly' elected Master of The Worshipful Company of Saddlers of the City of London. I promptly wrote to *The Times* to issue a belligerent challenge, mentioning how proud I was to be elected as Master of the *oldest* of the City's Guilds. There was only one reply, from the Weavers. They too have a document which proves beyond doubt that they are pre-Norman and therefore Saxon in origin, but we Saddlers darkly mutter about an influx of Flemish refugees who were weavers, whereas we were native and indigenous! Be that as it may, there is for me a profound satisfaction in taking an active part in the affairs of an institution which, for one thousand years, and largely on the same site, has helped to create the deep-rooted traditions which have made London, as some of us believe, the greatest city in the world. No other guild of such an age exists in Europe, and The Worshipful Company of Saddlers, one of the smallest and, for its size, one of the richer of the eighty-four Guilds, displays today an increasing concern for the whole craft of saddlery.

The Guilds differ widely in date of origin, from the tenth to the twentieth century; in size from many hundreds of members to the Saddlers' sixty-five Liverymen and twenty-four Members of the Court; in wealth, and in connection with their craft, from none at all to the control over gold and silver wares exercised by the Goldsmiths' Company. But we of the Saddlers still preserve the right to destroy any saddle not 'well and truly wrought', in the London area, and a small committee appointed by the Court makes periodic inspection of the factories and shops concerned.

It was my father who, when 'Peace Master' in 1918, began to draw into the ambit of the Company's work all leading saddlers throughout the country, and today we are forging stronger links with the centre of the trade in Walsall. We are known for our gifts of saddles and bridles at most of the larger equestrian events, and our charity to those of the leather trade generally, and to a wide range of public need, is generous.

None can enter the Saddlers' Company unless at the time of his birth his father was a Freeman of the Company, or he is admitted by 'redemption', as it is called, as being a worthy saddler of high standing, or otherwise suitable, as the son of a daughter of a Saddler. The Company is governed by a Master and three Wardens, elected annually by secret ballot. After the election, as laid down six hundred years ago, the whole Company moves in procession into St Vedast Foster, the ancient church next door, for Divine Service, when the Master reads the Lesson, and the Chaplain, as ordered in a Charter of 1395, preaches the Sermon.

Thus have we conducted our affairs for a thousand years, generous in entertainment as in the care of our own poor members, and accumulating in the course of centuries treasures of all kinds which, in the periodic fires of our history, have been in part destroyed and then replaced with new. It is easy to laugh at our customs, as those of any old institution. At the time I was 'cloathed' with the Livery in 1922, being twenty-one and the son of my father, himself the descendant of a line of Masters from 1769, we solemnly, as our names were called, presented sixpence to the Wardens seated in front of the Master. They were 'collecting the quarterage' for every Quarter Court in accordance with an ordinance of the reign of Elizabeth I. But on leaving we were each given half a crown as an attendance fee.

Some of a younger generation sneer at such 'nonsense', but the eighty-nine men concerned, as the thousands of others in their several Guilds, are united in bonds of family, and of mutual trust and respect which will outlast the destructive fashions of an age. I was a proud man when I took my seat as Master, and was presented with the Jewel, the Purse and the Mace of antiquity. I knew that I was the last of the oldest family in the Company, but there will be Terrys and Sturdys and Lauries and many more to carry on when I am but a name on the boards in the entrance hall.

There is a custom that the Master on leaving the Chair is given a cheque wherewith to buy a piece of plate to hand on to his descendants. I made an exception by presenting the Company with 'The Master's Cup', the last and one of the finest pieces of silver wrought by my wife in her workroom in the basement of our home. It bears the Army of the Company and my own, and is used as a wine cup by each successive Master whenever the Company's plate is on the table.

While I was Master, our principal concern was the furnishing of the rebuilt Hall, and our womenfolk would have been amused to watch a collection of middle-aged gentlemen discussing the place to put the Company's coat of arms on the dinner-service; the covering, if any, for the tables; the glass, the silver, and even 'the needs of the kitchen'.

Here, then, is incarnate tradition, which is much more than a set of habits which, outworn, should be abandoned. A man's long service to his Guild, and obedience to its known and reasonable laws, breeds virtue, a word but little used today as its meaning steadily declines. But here for a thousand years has been the ideal of honesty in trade, of goods well wrought, and sold for a reasonable profit, of loyalty to Crown and City and one's Guild within it. Here was born courage in adversity, and charity of heart and purse to those in need, and between the Guilds a sense of mutual trust and security. These qualities are worth developing, and if need be collectively preserving in the face of the country's enemies without, or the City's enemies within. Long may the Saddlers continue to uphold and serve their motto, 'Hold fast and sit sure'.

In this year, besides coping with my work as Master of the Saddlers and as No. 1 at the Old Bailey, a third activity demanded urgent thought. The Buddhist Society, which had for a short time been housed as a subtenant of London University's China Committee in Gordon Square, had to find new premises. Thanks to the strenuous search made by an architect friend of the Society, Mr Burton-Stibbon, we found our present premises at 58 Eccleston Square, where we have the trees for our skyline and the use of the Square's large garden. A long lease was available for what was then a modest sum and Carlo Robins, an adept at appeals, began to raise the £2000 necessary to repay a short-term loan. We had to fight for our new home, for on the face of it there would be a 'change of user'. I went into battle with all guns firing, as my friends put it, and argued that as many other buildings in the Square were already no longer residential, one whole row of houses being those of the Catholic Truth Mission, I should if necessary invoke the aid of 'our Member' and raise a Question in the House to know the cause of this revolting religious discrimination! I was calmed down by Mrs Naylor, our invaluable astrologer, who said that all would come well in the middle of August, and Puck and I could safely go off to the Haute Savoie. We did, and the news came by telegram that all was settled.

The building, our lease of which lasts for the lives of all of us, has all the rooms we need. The ground floor has a fine library and reading room, with a well-stocked book stall. But it was the creation of the lecture hall on the first floor which pleased my schoolboy mind. A wall with large double doors divided the area in two, and as such it would be difficult to use for lectures. However, Burton-Stibbon and a workman with him agreed that the partition wall was not essential to the structure of Cubitt's splendid building. To prove it, a pickaxe was produced and used, and to my joy the wall began to come down in clouds of dust. By the time I left for a Committee Meeting, I was content to leave behind a first-class lecture hall, capable of holding ninety people if not more. Here famous visitors have been received and great names have lectured to us – lamas, abbots, roshis, foreign royalty, ambassadors, authors and others well known in the field of Buddhism. Next to the lecture hall is a shrine room furnished with the shrine and table given us by the Buddhists of Thailand.

Besides selling books we had steadily added to the list of our own publications, including a translation of the *Tao Te Ching* by Chu Ta-kao, the first by a Chinese into English, a new translation of *The Diamond Sutra* by Arnold Price, and Dr Edward Conze's unique *Selected Sayings from the Perfection of Wisdom*. This, taken from his translation of the *Prajna-paramita*, 'The Wisdom which has gone Beyond', is in the view of many scholars the highest peak yet reached in human thought. His later translation with commentary of the famous Heart Sutra shows his profound grasp of this collection of writings, of which he is the acknowledged master in Europe.

Of the Society's own publications I was the publisher, and this at times put me in an amusing situation. To avoid paying income tax on writings for which I did not wish to be paid, I gave seven of my books on Buddhism by deed to the Society, which therefore now holds the copyright and receives the royalties. But some of these books are now published by other publishers, to produce a wider sale, and I negotiate with them for foreign rights, new editions and the like. Thus, for example, I may deal with George Allen & Unwin in three capacities, as the author of the book, the chairman of the Society holding the copyright, and as the Society's publisher, reporting to the Council my success or failure. But the books get published, and translated, and very widely sold.

I think it was this move to Eccleston Square and the solidity of our new position that enabled Puck and me, as we sat down one evening, in the midst of this confused, exciting year, to assess what we had done. We had created a Centre, and this was the all important term, for Buddhism in Europe. We had collected a group of fellow Buddhists who would 'Publish and make known the fundamental principles of Buddhism . . .' Not those of any one school, nor the ritual and outward forms of any one school, but from a Centre open to every school of Buddhism, with a journal open to comment upon them all, a library including books on all, and a bookstall where they might be bought. Around this Centre other groups, dedicated to a specific school of Buddhism, such as Theravada, Tibetan Buddhism or one of the two Zen schools of Japan, might work in harmony, each obtaining support from the experience, the resources and the national prestige of the central, and in a sense, parent body.

1956 was the year of Buddha Jayanti, the Buddha's victory over *Avidya* (ignorance) achieved some 2500 years ago. True, there are differences between Buddhist countries about the exact date of the Buddha's birth and passing, but it matters not, for it has been well said that of all religions Buddhism is one of the least anchored to a date in time. So we celebrated, and, according to our record, mightily. There was a great meeting at Ceylon House, an exhibition of Tibetan Art, an article in *The Times*, a showing of Buddhist films, a talk on the B.B.C., and a series of public meetings at the Caxton Hall. While all this was going on, five delegates from the Society were preparing to depart for a conference of the World Fellowship of Buddhists in Katmandu, and afterwards for India's celebration of Buddha Jayanti. I did not take Puck as she was not much interested in such events, and both of us knew that it would be very tiring. However, Carlo Robins, then editor of the *Middle Way*, was willing to come, and Colin Wyatt, long a member of the Society and a first-class photographer, and Mr and Mrs Peter Simms, who decided to drive by the then adventurous route through Afghanistan and so down into India. And then, just to show that I liked hard work, I accepted a brief in Lagos to help the Bank of Western Africa at a local inquiry.

I flew to Lagos, wondering how long I should be kept there, but my work proved to be a matter of diplomacy rather than law. Before long I persuaded my clients that there was no further need for my presence, and so returned home. There I packed and prepared for what I felt would be a landmark in the history of Buddhism.

18
Buddha Jayanti in Nepal and India

The purpose of the trip to Nepal and India was, as already indicated, two-fold. First, to attend as delegates from the Buddhist Society the fourth Conference of the World Fellowship of Buddhists, to be held this time in Katmandu. Thereafter we five, with other delegates, would fly to New Delhi, as guests of the Indian Government to attend the Indian 'Symposium of Buddhist Art, Literature and Philosophy', held in conjunction with UNESCO, which was India's celebration of Buddha Jayanti. The World Fellowship of Buddhists was the child of a great man, Dr G. P. Malalasekera of Ceylon, with whom I had sat on a Buddhist platform in London as early as 1926. Scholar, diplomat, born organiser, it was he who convened in Colombo in May 1950 delegates from twenty-nine countries to form a permanent Buddhist organisation with a triple purpose. This was to bring together the schools of Buddhism, widespread in terms of geography and doctrine; to rouse enthusiasm in each to be more active in its own particular field; and to become an organised expression of the power of a united Buddhism in the affairs of the East and thence in those of the world. Since then the Fellowship has held a conference about every two years in some Buddhist centre.

On reaching home from Lagos I found that Carlo Robins, not knowing when I would be back, had preceded me to Bombay. There I found her having dinner in the Taj Hotel, and we made plans for sightseeing on our way to the rendezvous with Colin Wyatt and the Simms in old Delhi. I was happy to be back in India. I find that those of my friends who know both India and the Far East strongly prefer one or the other. I myself loved India at first sight and am happy, as Kim would say, to waggle my toes in the dust. The Indians, if I may use a large generalisation, seem to me a religious-minded people, for whom their religion, whether in its noblest philosophy or most degraded form of bloody ritual, is integral in their lives. Their religion is not mine, for I am not enamoured of any outward observance, whether in a Hindu, Tibetan, Zen or Theravada shrine. My own way aims at that of the laughing 'empty' masters of Ch'an in its early days in China, 'playing the fool', according to pictures of them, but a fool who is a long way nearer divinity than I saw expressed in any form or temple.

Nor were the Indian customs compatible with my own, and when Carlo and I were the guests of Mr and Mrs Rohit Mehta in Benares we appreciated the difference, in food and the manner of eating it, and even the different manner of taking a bath. On one occasion when walking through the crowded streets at night I had my hands behind me and felt something cool and moist and friendly pressed into them. It was a very large white cow which, finding I had nothing to offer, passed on to a vegetable stall where she helped herself.

I had been asked by Mr Chidambaram, a wealthy Indian businessman, whose son I had been able to help in London, to give him my plane schedule for the trip, and as promised he provided a car and chauffeur for us wherever we landed. In such a car the next evening we drove to Sanchi, and, having managed to book rooms in the rest house, set out at once into the soft Indian night to walk, like a million pilgrims before us, round the great Stupa. It stands 150 feet high and bears on its glorious corner gateways some of the finest carving in India. There are many of these stupas, or burial mounds, and from one were taken the relics of Sariputta and Mogallana, two of the Buddha's most famous disciples. But the stupas, built from the first century onwards, have no other Buddhist significance, and although very beautiful of form have little appeal for the heart. We returned at dawn, that magic hour of the tropics, and again absorbed their beauty, and visited the Buddhist monastery beside it; but time was short and so we flew on to Agra.

Agra is not all Taj, as someone put it to me. The Red Fort, built by Akbar in the seventeenth century, contains the lovely Pearl Mosque, and a whole range of palaces and marble buildings.

And it has its own sad memories connected with the Taj. The Emperor Shah Jehan spent twenty years and vast sums of money on building this memorial to his favourite wife, with whom he lived in happiness for seventeen years. Then his son, Aurungzeb, rose in rebellion, murdered all his brothers and imprisoned his father in a cell in the Red Fort. From this cell the ageing Emperor could see the white perfection of his inspired imagining, which others after him have called the noblest monument yet raised to love. As for the Taj itself, I can only advise the visitor to keep silent, to withdraw from his companions, and to see if he can suggest the least improvement in position, height or proportion of any part of the building, or the least detail of the inspired decoration round the tombs within. I tried and failed, and abandoning thought just rested on the grass in silence.

On the following day Carlo and I were driven to New Delhi up the Grank Trunk Road, each of us filling it with word-creations out of *Kim*. We took a picnic lunch and stopped near a village to eat it beside the road. Our driver had vanished but in due course reappeared from the direction of the village carrying two cups of water which he offered us. Which should prevail, good sense, based on all we had heard of the danger of an Indian village well, or good manners? I am glad to say that manners won.

In our hotel in Delhi there was no sign of Colin Wyatt, but he appeared just as Carlo and I met in the hotel garden in the early morning. He had spent the night on the floor of a third-class carriage with, as he said, 'a herd of bhikkhus' also on their way to Katmandu. And so we travelled together, and, having changed into a smaller plane at Patna, met an experience of beauty greater even than the Taj Mahal.

We were allowed into the cockpit to peer over the pilot's shoulder at the most magnificent view in the world. From end to end the sky was filled with the whole range of the Himalayas a hundred miles away and five miles high. Dazzling in their virgin light, Everest and the other peaks challenged man to lift his heart to their immensity. I wrote at the time, 'I feel that I have not lived in vain to have knelt before that sight.'

Nepal was at this time closed to visitors. Katmandu, with its neighbouring cities of Patan and Bhaktapur, lies in a flat valley twenty miles across, the high hills all about them. Each town contains a wide variety of wooden buildings decorated with intricately wrought carving of all kinds, and my camera grew hot with perpetual use. The people, who are Buddhist Newars, were conquered in 1768 by the Hindu Gurkhas, the present rulers of the country. Yet the two races mingle well, and in the famous temple of Swayambunath on a hill 300 feet high outside the capital, there are as many Hindu shrines as Buddhist. Bodnath, on the other hand, with the same all-seeing, enormous eyes painted at each corner of the tower which surmounts the dome, is the most famous Buddhist shrine outside India. Thousands of Tibetans came down over the Hills to worship there, and as I watched some of them I saw in their eyes what devotion means to those who make such pilgrimage.

For a long while the Rana family, as hereditary Prime Ministers, ruled the kingdom, even as the Shoguns in their day ruled Japan. Then they were ousted. Their empty palaces were useful quarters for the three hundred delegates from East and West who assembled for the Buddhist Conference. Transport was the main problem, for in the absence then of a road, each of the sixty cars at our disposal had been brought over the mountains from India in pieces on men's shoulders. The organising genius who handled all our affairs was the Nepali Thera Amritananda who had taken his ordination in Ceylon and returned to Katmandu to open a Buddhist boarding school. He had a distinguished list of leading delegates to accommodate. Dr Malalasekera was President, and from Burma came the Ven U Thittila, once librarian to our Society in London; from Thailand, Princess Poon, now President of the World Fellowship of Buddhists, and from India Dr Ambedkar, fresh from the conversion of millions of India's 'untouchables'. From Japan came the Abbot Daiko of Myoshinji, in Kyoto, where I had spent such a memorable weekend ten years before, and from America Richard Gard, the publisher and authority on Japanese Buddhism.

The King opened the Conference from a high stand on the vast Parade Ground, and speeches followed from leading delegates. Then we broke up into committees to draw up resolutions on different aspects of the work to be done. What happened to all our resolutions I did not inquire. It is all too easy to become gravely cynical.

But there was a wonderful reception by the Queen at the Palace, where we all again made speeches, and there was a great tea party with the King when some of us, when presented, had a favoured few minutes talk with him on the sofa.

During the intervals there was much sightseeing. One day some of us were in the almost empty palace of the ex-Prime Minister, when a servant proudly produced, from an unlocked cupboard, the most amazing crown in the world, for the King's own crown is second to it. This jewelled helmet, literally covered with emeralds, rubies, diamonds and pearls has a heavy fringe around it of enormous uncut emeralds, all but priceless in value and in number at least a hundred. The whole crown is surmounted with a three-foot plume of birds-of-paradise feathers, and must be heavy indeed to wear. Of course we tried it on. . . .

Of more importance was a performance – we were told the first ever given in public – of a Nepalese Buddhist ritual concerned with a sacred drawing made entirely of coloured sand. I am told there is nothing like it except those made by the Navajo Indians of New Mexico. The artist takes the sand in tiny pinches from the appropriate pot and the picture is thus built up. Then the participants in the ritual, wearing strange helmets of beaten bronze, sit round the *mandala* or symbolic picture, facing the shrine of the goddess, which had been brought to the site, and with *mantras* (ritual chanting), *mudras* (accompanying gestures) with a bell and small bronze ritual dagger or *dorje*, celebrate what to them is clearly an esoteric ceremony of profound significance.

In the course of walking about the three towns I was puzzled at what I had been brought up to regard as grossly obscene carvings on the outside wall of many Hindu temples. It may be that the obscenity of pictures and carvings of couples engaged in sexual activity lies in the highly repressed Western mind. Clearly, in terms of fact there would be no more humanity without copulation, and in terms of symbolism, the male/female duality is the most obvious of the pairs of opposites with which every philosophy and region must come to terms. And what better demonstration is there that the two are one than the sight, as in the Tibetan *yab-yum* figures where the deity holds his *shakti* (female counterpart) naked on his lap in copulation? But the Indian carvings, I felt, had a different basis. Alan Watts, in his Introduction to a volume of photographs of the erotic sculpture of the temples of Konarak and Kajuraho, goes some way to explain the practice of covering a beautiful temple with figures in sexual union, but in his *Wandering in Eden* Michael Adam says much more. He points out as a clue to the truth the fact, verifiable from any set of photographs, that the Western eye never looks above the obvious condition of the genitalia. But look at the faces of the pair: 'The figures are sexually active, but they are not obsessed; they are at ease; they are in the world but not of it; they play.' Is the secret, then, that the couples are in love, feel love, although at its physically lowest level, are indeed concerned with the force of love? Here is sex for love's sake, but love must rise above the animal. And here is Adam's second point.

He describes at length how the temple visitor passes from a view of the outside walls, down passages where the figures of dancers and musicians are still sensual but less visibly erotic, to a point where they stand alone. Then there are fewer figures, and just carvings of flowers. Finally, there is a chamber where the noise of the world is absent and near-darkness reigns. And here is nothing, No-thing, No-thingness.

In the West it is far otherwise. No one claims the presence of love in modern pornography. This is the animal let loose, as ugly as it is blatantly obscene. Or do we insult the animals by calling it so? Animals move and copulate according to their being as does man, but surely he should also be moving closer to the God within?

And so, with a final round of parties, and a call for tea at the British Embassy, we left by plane for New Delhi. On the airfield at Patna I found Krishnamurti, whom I had first met at Vienna in 1923. I had had tea with him in London several times thereafter but the chance of a talk with him in the plane on our way to New Delhi was a privilege to be welcomed. I mentioned something which one of his disciples had told me, and he all but snapped at me, 'I have no disciples.' Therein I think lies the enormous strength and the corresponding weakness of this great man. At his innumerable lectures a voice speaks; eyes light up with understanding. But understanding of what? Many have told me they did not know. The message was not to the mind but, as it were, a call from a higher level of consciousness to which unnumbered thousands maybe have been stimulated to follow.

The New Delhi Conference was a great success, and passed for many in a mood of exaltation. The Indians are indeed a religious people, and the Buddha is accepted as one of India's most holy sons.

This was, therefore, not only the celebration of 2,500 years since his Enlightenment but a religious occasion in the history of India.

The Conference was opened with a series of speeches from the high podium on the Ramlila Ground, a great open space about the size of that on the East side of Hyde Park. The U.N. delegates were seated at one side and the W.F.B. delegates on the other, and sitting on the grass as far as the eye could see were thousands of the local population. On the podium were seven people; the President of India, Dr Prasad, whom I did not know before, Dr Radhakrishnan, the famous scholar whom we had known in England when he held the Spalding Professorship at Oxford, and the Prime Minister, Mr Nehru, to whom I had taken a great liking at first sight and found of great help later when I was trying to help the Dalai Lama. With them were four speakers invited from the World Fellowship of Buddhists; U Nu, ex-Prime Minister of Burma, Dr Regamey of Switzerland, a well-known professor of Tibetan Buddhism, the Hon. J. Kuruppu, Minister of Cultural Affairs in Ceylon, and myself. One would have to be hardened indeed not to be lifted by such an occasion. There was a sense of being a conduit for some message to be given. I only remember one phrase of my speech before the massed microphones – probably not original – that 'there is no force on earth more powerful than an idea whose time has come'. I expanded this briefly into the power which a united Buddhism, allied with the spiritual forces of India, might exert in world affairs, and believed every word of it. I spoke into the setting sun, and after a while the vast audience was in shadow. Then night came down on all of us and on a memorable day.

But the Conference was soon dominated by the arrival of His Holiness the Dalai Lama, still King as well as Pontiff of Tibet, accompanied by the Panchen Lama and H.H. the Maharajah of Sikkim, who had brought them from Gangtok. We met them with some five thousand others as they landed in three planes, each with a gorgeously apparelled retinue, and gave them a great welcome. The two young Lamas in their simple robes at once charmed everyone, and they attended many of the meetings. In due course Carlo, Colin, Mrs Freda Bedi, an Englishwoman living and working in New Delhi, and I were presented to His Holiness at a private interview, with Bhante Sangharakshita, the English bhikkhu-lama who was then editor of the *Maha Bodhi Journal*, as our interpreter. We gave him a copy of Dr Conze's *Buddhist Texts through the Ages* signed by all of us, and I got him to sign my copy of *The Voice of the Silence.* He was impressed with a brief account of our work in England, and I was later to see much more of him. The following day we made a similar visit to the Panchen Lama, and I was in turn impressed with his handling of the hundreds of Tibetans who, enduring fatigue and near-starvation, had somehow come down from the hills to receive his blessing.

In a speech to the Conference the Dalai Lama spoke of a prophecy current in Tibet which now made sense to him. It was to the effect that in the course of time the Dharma would move from Tibet to the land of the 'pink-skinned' people. He apologised for the term, but are not the Nordic races of the West pink-skinned? We are not in fact 'white' at all. With the greatly increasing interest in Tibetan Buddhism now manifest in Europe and the U.S.A., is it absurd to see some meaning in this prophecy? And so we met daily with old friends and new. This was the time for making contacts, surely the most important outcome of any conference.

The last night was for me the most memorable of all. The President gave a farewell reception at Government House, the magnificent assembly of buildings designed by Sir Edwin Lutyens to be the Viceroy's residence under the British Raj. This was the climax of all three conferences, and was a grand occasion. The Indian Government's leading personalities, with the two Grand Lamas, the principal members of the conferences, the motionless sentries in splendid uniform stationed at intervals around the room, and the orchestra's bold music made a mosaic of colour and sound gorgeous by any standard. But it was on leaving that I experienced the crowning moment of my trip to India. Outside the brightly lit ballroom was a pillared hall almost in darkness, through which one passed on the way out to the waiting cars. There, in a softly lighted alcove stood the famous standing image of the Buddha of the fifth century, which is perhaps the best known image in all India. I knelt with others on the marble steps of the alcove and looked up into that face. Suddenly I saw much more than the features graven there. It was beauty beyond the form of beauty. Then I came back, as it were, and hoped my friends were not waiting for me. Then I was lost again, and again saw what was utterly there. . . .

Soon our party had to break up, Colin to do more work on the film

he was making for the Society, Carlo to take the train journey to the
sacred places arranged for the W.F.B. delegates, and I to go home.
But on arriving in Bombay once more I was asked by Bhante
Sangharakshita, on behalf of a Dr Dunshaw Mehta living on Mala-
bar Hill, to speak that night to his small Society of the Servants of
God. Of course I agreed, and found the largest room in the house
stripped of furniture and covered with linen sheets. Visitors came, as
I sat between the windows on a cushion with our doctor host and
Bhante; Hindus, Mohammadans, Parsis, Sikhs and English Christians came until they filled the room. I was introduced. What could
I say? I had deliberately emptied my mind and waited. 'Let me
begin', I said, 'with Parabrahman' (the Absolute). Gently I came
down, along lines in common with all present, and at the end climbed
up so far as my own experience could take me. That hour was a
fragrant, unforgettable farewell to India.

19
Silk and Unorthodox Medicine

On returning to England from my somewhat breathless 'year of destiny' I had much to consolidate, without and within. I had to pick up the reins of government of the Saddlers' Company; take up again my practice as No. 1 at the Old Bailey, and my sittings at Guildford and in Kent; and supervise the rapid expansion of the Buddhist Society and its circle of new Buddhist groups. I had also become President of the Shakespearean Society, more than ever concerned to disprove, if necessary, the claims of the man of Stratford, and to find the real author of the greatest poems and plays in the English language.

In the summer our friend, the Reverend Sohaku Ogata, who had been of such great help to me in Japan, paid us a long visit. He reorganised the Zen class into something approaching the Zendo of a Japanese monastery and played an active part in the summer school, by now held every year at High Leigh, Hoddesdon. There he played the Japanese flute for us, and ended every piece with the fascinating 'dying fall' which I had noticed in the speeches of the Dalai Lama and the Panchen Lama of Tibet. While in England he wrote, and we had published, *Zen for the West*, and he created a deep impression on us. Someone behind his back christened him 'Sunny Boy', which was a compliment, for the man of Zen is or should be full of smiles, and true laughter is proof of the end of fear, fear of life or death or anything between.

He was followed in the spring of 1958 by the charming and erudite Dr Shinichi Hisamatsu. His importance to us was that he was a lay roshi, or spiritual teacher, who had obtained his *inka* or seal as a roshi on the strength of his inner attainment, without ever having been a monk. A roshi, therefore, need not be someone from the inside of a Rinzai Zen temple, and like Dr Suzuki and Mr Jamshed Nasserwanji, the businessman of Karachi already described, he could use in the world his experience of the plane beyond duality.

In the same year Alan Watts arrived, after twenty years absence in the U.S.A. where he had become well known for his excellent work, *The Way of Zen*. In London he attended Carlo Robins' Meditation class and the Zen class, and gave a series of lectures at the Caxton Hall. He also found time to help Dr Graham Howe, who often lectured to the Society, in his interesting venture, The Open Way. While he was still here, and on the very day of our annual Wesak Festival, Dr Suzuki arrived. In 1953 he had visited England, in the course of a long tour of Europe, with his pretty and most efficient young secretary-companion, Miss Mihoko Okamura. He lectured to the Society and elsewhere, and was of enormous value to the Zen class. He had come again in 1954, and having flown the Atlantic, sitting up all night, at the age of eighty-four, came straight to the class. We could not ask him for a full lecture but he wrote up later what he had to say in a deeply interesting article on the *Mondo*, the unique Zen question–answer form of training. This was published by the Society in 1969, with a dozen of his other talks and articles, in *The Field of Zen*.

But now in 1958 we had him for a substantial period. He stayed at the Rembrandt Hotel, and having his ink and brushes with him, he made for us four brush-writings of famous Zen phrases. He practised on a folded copy of *The Times*; would that we had preserved these pages for posterity! Alan Watts, Dr Irmgard Schloegl and I spent much time with him at the hotel, and the frontispiece to my *Zen Comes West* is the only photograph of 'Sensei', teacher, as we called him, with Alan and myself, perhaps the three names most closely associated with Zen Buddhism in the West. This was a wonderful period in our lives, to live within the aura of this deeply spiritual and lovable old gentleman. He was full of fun, but at all times willing to answer questions about the whole object of his life, Zen, and his efforts to help the West to lift their minds towards the ultimate totality.

When we bade farewell to him at London Airport we knew that this was the last that we should see of him in this life, although I was corresponding with him about his books until 1966, the year in which, at ninety five, he died.

Towards the end of 1958 I was sent for by the Attorney-General, Sir Reginald Manningham-Buller, who reminded me that I had been a Treasury counsel for twenty five years, with the overtone that this was enough. I was offered a choice of positions then vacant, but being perfectly happy where I was I refused them. Weeks went by and I then had another summons, with what amounted to a request to resign. It seemed that the Attorney-General had certain promotions of his own in view, but the effect was that I was offered silk, that is, to be made a Q.C., and as the alternative was near-unemployment I accepted. Most barristers have in mind that they will in due course apply for this honour. I was certainly in a minority in having it virtually thrust upon me and in regarding it as a step down rather than up in my legal career. Be that as it may, in the following April I was among those summoned before the Lord Chancellor; I took the prescribed oath of loyalty and went in procession with a dozen others round the High Court in the Strand. In each Court I was 'called within the bar', to the front row, which is reserved for Silks. I was much troubled by the fact that the beautiful silk stockings, worn with my silk knee-breeches, kept falling down, and I envied a fellow Silk who had borrowed a suspender-belt from his wife and so dealt with the problem efficiently.

As a Silk I could no longer prosecute at the Old Bailey, for the work of the Director was, as already explained, in the hands of the team of Treasury counsel. I could defend, which seldom appealed to me, and prosecute for the Crown when occasionally offered a brief on Assize. But having early formed a conceited opinion of my ability at the Bar I had never cultivated work on my 'home' Circuit around London, and preferred to wait for work at the Old Bailey, where it came. A Silk cannot take pupils, but I had taken many in my years at the Junior Bar. One, Miss Jean Southworth, was of outstanding worth and is now the only woman Q.C. at the Old Bailey. She was and is that somewhat rare being, a charming woman with a first-class legal brain. They may be found in science and in medicine; they are rare at the Bar, for the brain must be visible in the subtle art of advocacy as well as in arguing law. Certainly, I had expressed the view that in a difficult fraud case I would rather have Jean South-worth as my junior than the available men.

I had only two cases in the High Court as a Silk. The first, which lasted ten weeks, was that of Auten v. Rayner, in which a totally irresponsible young man brought a series of accusations of fraud against a Colonel Rayner, for whom I appeared. Each accusation was dismissed by the judge as having no foundation. The pleadings ran to two hundred pages. I never got down to reading them all, which proves that I was a most unconventional lawyer.

The second case was in 1960. A Mr Frank Bentley called at my chambers on behalf of Mr and Mrs George de la Warr to ask if I would defend them in an action of fraud. This concerned their sale of a diagnostic instrument pertaining to the field of radionics. The instrument was an elaboration of the 'black box' made famous by the remarkable discoveries of Dr Abrams in the U.S.A. and his follower, Dr Drown. I had never visited the de la Warr Laboratories at Oxford, nor had I met the de la Warrs; I was tired and the defence would clearly need much preparation. In the end, however, I agreed to take the case. They were desperately in need of help, and I had special knowledge which perhaps no other leading member of the Bar possessed.

Radionics is one of the many forms of 'fringe' or unorthodox medicine about which I knew a good deal. Puck and I, in the forty five years we lived together, had never had a doctor in the house, meaning by the word doctor a registered medical practitioner. We had managed efficiently with osteopathy, herbalism, homoeopathy by advice on the telephone and, after we learnt of it through this case, radionics.

My first and convincing knowledge of osteopathy was already described, when Puck all but dragged me to her osteopath, Dr Ralph West, after I had injured my fifth lumbar vertebra at Cam-bridge. But for him I should have been a bent cripple by the age of thirty. In 1938 I broke my neck diving. Ralph West died soon after-wards and I went through the war and out to Japan and back before the pain drove me to mention it to Dr Jean Johnston, D.O., a tiny American woman osteopath with fingers of steel. She sent me for an X-ray, and told me later of what happened. A colleague of the radio-logist saw my negatives hung up to dry and remarked, 'I didn't know you photo'd stiffs.' 'Stiffs, nonsense,' replied the radiologist; 'that man drove here from the Old Bailey and back to court.' 'Nonsense to you,' said the friend; 'that man's dead!' The atlas, top vertebra of the spine, was deeply split from the top almost to the bottom. In two months of intensive treatment Dr Johnston got it together again, but it took five years before it was entirely healed. But for her I should at best be wearing a collar for life; more probably, I should be dead. Again, in 1956, just before going to Guildford for the plum cake episode already described, I fell from a ladder and broke my right shoulder-blade in three places. Dr Johnston raced to the rescue, strapped it up, and took me to a surgeon two days later to approve her strapping. He said, 'I could not have done it better myself.' In due course that injury too was healed. Is it surprising, therefore, that I am deeply impressed with osteopathy? Since then I have periodic treatment to keep the skeletal frame in good condition, with the result that I have few old man's troubles, and at seventy-five can without strain turn a compost heap, or refix tiles on the roof. I therefore find that the theory of osteopathy makes sense. If the joints are in order the great majority of our aches and pains will not arise; or if they do, in such accidental cases as tennis elbow or a slipped disc, generally they can be quickly removed.

For internal ailments Puck and I were content with the help of the herbalist Mrs C. F. Leyel. Herbs are the oldest form of medicine and still sufficient for millions of human beings today. With her background of medical knowledge, she prescribed for a wide range of patients, and ordered them their 'ten drops three times a day' of herbs made up in the Society's dispensary. She knew that the herbs would be more than palliatives; they would eventually remove the cause of the trouble, although the process would be slower than the 'bullying' methods of drugs. Herbs help the body to heal itself; drugs at best replace nature's methods and thereby weaken its own inherent power of recovery.

Later, when Mrs Leyel was ill, we had help from Dr George Lawrence, who after thirty years as a G.P. had turned to homoeopathy. This was the system founded by Hahnemann in the late eighteenth century on the principle of giving the patient a very minute dose of the diagnosed cause of his ailment. Hahnemann also insisted on treating the whole man, not merely the obvious symptom, and was therefore in the line of true healers. Dr Lawrence worked by diagnosing with a pendulum over a large chart of the human body and a spot of the patient's blood. Puck or I would telephone him in Wargrave in the morning and describe symptoms. In an hour he would ring back. 'It's your old enemy,' he might say to me; '*staph. aureus*. I have telephoned Nelson's,' Nelson's being the homoeopathic chemists in London. That afternoon Puck would call for the tablets and I would be taking them that evening. In this way we coped with all manner of troubles over the years. We were not using orthodox medicine but a power released on a plane as much higher than the physical as thought is above one's muscle power. If an expert ana-lysed, say, *carbo veg. 200* he would find nothing but sugar. But it worked!

Dr Lawrence, at the age of ninety, founded The Psionic Medical Society, of which Puck and I were founding associate members. This drew together homoeopathy and radiaesthesia, a name taken from the French for their form of dowsing. The relationship is obvious, for both admittedly use the same supra-physical factor, as found in all elements of E.S.P., which I call psychic power. With the aid of his training in electronics, George de la Warr drew these together as the motive power in his various radionic instruments. Just where this non-physical plane lies in the total 'force-field' of man's complex constitution is little known in the West, but having studied for some fifty years, in both Theosophy and Indian philo-sophy, the various planes or levels of man's consciousness, I was better able to understand the nature, purpose and functioning of the de la Warr instrument which I was called upon to defend.

By 1936 George de la Warr had reached the position of Assistant County Engineer for Oxfordshire. During the war, while on sick leave, he gave long thought to the subject of 'energy fields', the rela-tion of electronic and psychic energy. He began organised research, and sank much of his capital in the Laboratories. At this time he knew nothing of the work of Dr Abrams and Dr Brown, and his own research was of his own devising. His wife, Marjorie, became a skilled helper in his work, and in 1948 the two were joined by Leonard Corte, known for his own experiments with the radionic camera. The whole field of work was expanded to cover not only human health but that of animals and agricultural products.

The de la Warrs called the level of the mind on which their

instruments work 'pre-physical', known previously in English as the astral or etheric, and in other parts of the world by other names. They believed, as others have long believed, that it is on this plane that disease is born, and that the disease will only be cured, or be helped to cure itself, by treating it on this plane, whence the benefit will in due course appear in the physical body.

I am not competent to describe in detail the diagnostic instrument sold to the plaintiff in the action. It is as difficult as a computer for a newcomer to understand. In brief, it is a convenient means of establishing rapport or 'resonance' with the patient, the link being a specimen of blood or sputum placed in the instrument. The operator 'tunes in' to the wave-form or radiation of the patient by means of setting a series of 'rates', empirically compiled over the years, for the different parts of the anatomy, disease or psychological state of the patient. Experienced fingers find by a 'stick' on a rubber pad on the instrument just where treatment is needed, at pre-physical level, and a smaller instrument is then used, if the patient asks for treatment, where the patient's specimen is 'tuned' in to the appropriate magnetic field, allowing transference of energy to take place.

Needless to say, fifty years' research by Dr Abrams, Dr Drown and George de la Warr, and since the trial by scores of doctors, physicists and other scientists, cannot thus be described in a paragraph, but as defending counsel I did not have to describe it. The plaintiff had to prove fraud, meaning in this context that the de la Warrs did not reasonably believe that it worked.

The instrument, like many others, could be bought by anyone whom the de la Warrs thought would be able to use it intelligently and who had developed the necessary psychic faculty in the field in which it operates. The basis of the action was that a woman, a somewhat stupid woman it seemed to me, had bought an instrument after satisfying Mrs de la Warr on these two conditions. Of the hundreds sold, no other person had ever complained that the instrument would not work. Only two, who found they could not use it properly, had asked for and were promptly given their money back. This woman, however, did not ask for her money back; she sued or, as I thought more likely, was persuaded to sue for damages for fraud, and the fraud alleged had to be proved.

The details of the trial have no place here. There was much sneering at the claims of 'pre-physical' diagnosis and treatment, and the defendants and some of their witnesses showed under cross-examination that they were pioneer researchers in a field where at times they were all but lost, a not uncommon experience for pioneers, whether in darkest Africa or the deeps of the human mind. The range of George de la Warr's invention was astonishing, and groups of qualified researchers are today following up in different fields discoveries which he was the first to proclaim. Many a time when Puck and I were dining with them, George would produce a handful of pennies on the table cloth and demonstrate, in the placing of them, his latest discovery in field-forces. As I said to the Judge in the course of my final speech, he never gave himself time to 'salt down' one discovery before he was off in pursuit of another, which does not make for an accurate and scientific recording of information found.

First I called the de la Warrs, their principal assistant Leonard Corte and their daughter Diana, to give evidence. I killed the allegation of fraud, as the learned Judge agreed in his judgment, when I followed this by calling a long line of distinguished witnesses to speak to the high integrity of the defendants. I then called five doctors, men and women on the Medical Register, who told the Judge that they could use for their patients any system of diagnosis and treatment they chose and had chosen and learnt to use the instrument sold to them at the de la Warr Laboratories. How then could it be said that a woman who admitted that she was told how to use the instrument, in demonstrations and with literature, was defrauded because she found she could not use it properly? In his judgment the Judge said that he accepted that the defence witnesses were telling the truth as they believed it, that no fraud was proved, and found for the defendants. The trial cost the plaintiff not one penny, but the de la Warrs £11,000.

For me an unpleasant part of the trial was the presence in court, sitting in a group behind the plaintiff, of some five doctors, gloating it seemed at every point made for the plaintiff, and furious, as I saw for myself, when their action for fraud – for it had all the appearance of being their action – failed. This savoured of the witch hunting of an earlier age. Why should they hope to smash the de la Warrs and their work in the field of medicine? Why not examine, as literally hundreds of doctors, scientists and physicists from all corners of the world have since examined in detail, the work of the Laboratories, where the overworked principals were ever ready to explain and demonstrate their instruments and plans for research? George de la Warr died in 1969, but his widow, struggling to expand still further their joint work in spite of the rising cost of it, still treats some two hundred patients at a time, each with a separate instrument, and, with Leonard Corte and a small staff to help her, carries on.

What of the future, not merely radionics but of the tension between orthodox and unorthodox forms of treatment? In England the General Medical Council has a statutory duty to protect the public from unqualified practitioners, and to license those whom it holds to be qualified. But medicine, like all branches of human knowledge, is changing year by year, and the 'nonsense' and 'quackery' of today may be acceptable tomorrow. Already there are conferences of many kinds where the orthodox and unorthodox sit side by side to examine new discoveries. The rule that a doctor may not 'delegate' the care of his patient to an unqualified practitioner is more and more loosely applied. Where the latter is in fact controlled by the governing body of his own form of treatment, the co-operation can in fact be full. As long ago as 1935 a body of osteopaths, fully qualified in their own American university but practising in England, applied for a Charter, which would protect the use of the term. They failed, being few in number, but the Privy Council suggested the formation of a Register of those held to be well-qualified. This was promptly created, and those accepted on the register are allowed to use the initials M.R.O. The word osteopathy, however, is still unprotected, and the practice is still unrecognised by the Health Service. Instead, in the name of physiotherapy, unpleasant things are done on skeletal injuries – methods which those whose hands are trained for such treatment would not dare to use. Worse, there are doctors who, after a few weeks of watching demonstrations of osteopathy, feel themselves at liberty to give their patients a hopeful 'click' and expect this to provide relief.

Let us hope that the word osteopathy will soon be protected, and that the benefits of this, at best, immensely helpful form of treatment will soon be freely available to the general public through the Health Service. One solution to the general problem is surely obvious. Let the G.M.C. continue to protect the public from the untrained and therefore potentially dangerous quack. Let all groups of unorthodox practitioners who wish to be recognised create their own governing bodies, with standards of training and proper behaviour clearly defined for members. These new organisations would not be under the control of the G.M.C. but would remain independent in their several specialisations. In this way, those worthy to be recognised would acquire the privileges of such recognition, and the untrained man would, by the absence of the appropriate letters after his name, be recognisable as such.

Our knowledge of the complex entity called man expands every year, and no doctor can keep up with the ever-increasing branches of the parent tree of medicine. Let the doctors be more willing to consider any form of treatment which might help their patients, and let those not on the Register hasten to acquire their own appropriate proof of qualification, and so join with the doctors in their common enterprise, the health of the nation.

20

To India for the Dalai Lama

My attention was soon to be concentrated on Tibet. The history of Buddhism in Tibet is well known from the autobiography of the present and possibly last holder of the title of Dalai Lama, *My Land and My People*. For centuries this isolated country, much of it at 16,000 feet, twice the size of France but with a population of only two or three million, was closed to the outside world, and is closed today. We know that in the seventh century King Shrongtsen Gampo was converted to Buddhism by his two Buddhist wives, from China and Nepal, and in the face of bitter opposition from the indigenous Bon religion opened his country to Buddhism. At some period the kings were replaced by grand lamas as the effective rulers of the country, and in the seventeenth century the fifth of these received from the Emperor Kublai Khan of China the title of Dalai (Great Ocean) Lama. Successive holders of the title either died young or were nonentities, but the thirteenth was a powerful figure, as shown in the biography by Sir Charles Bell. When he died in 1933 a search had to be made, according to the accepted formula, for his successor, and the present Dalai Lama describes in his autobiography how he was found. He was born in north-east Tibet on 6 June 1935 by our reckoning, 'just before sunrise', as his mother told me when I met her in Dharamsala, and, being recognised as the reincarnation of his predecessor, was at the age of four brought to Lhasa to be enthroned as the fourteenth Dalai Lama. From that moment he was educated intensively to be ready for his adult responsibility as the religious Head and secular King of Tibet. At the age of seven he was clearly an exceptional child, as can be seen in a photograph of him enthroned. If one may read a child's face, there was here a blend of vision and strength which he would need to the full in the years to come.

In the early fifties there were already mutterings of impending trouble from China, and when the young man came to India in 1956 for Buddha Jayanti he had long talks with the Prime Minister, Mr Nehru, about the best course for him and his country to pursue. Soon after his return to Lhasa the tension became acute, and as President of the Buddhist Society I was destined to become in a small way involved. Puck and I were already in close touch with the young Maharajkumar, or Crown Prince, of Sikkim who owing to the poor health of his father was the *de facto* ruler of the country, assisted by his sister, Princess Pema, known throughout that part of the world by her nickname Cocoola. I would see them whenever either was in London, and had met the Crown Prince in New Delhi during Buddha Jayanti. I may have helped them with some of the problems besetting them, such as the handling of the press on the Sikkim-Indian relationship which was already a cloud on the horizon. One evening Cocoola came to see us to ask if the Buddhist Society could do anything to help the Dalai Lama to resist the pressure from China. She thought it might strengthen his hand to know that he had Western Buddhist support. I suggested that we could ask him to be Patron of the Society, which might help him as well as being a very great honour for the Society. She agreed at once, and I drafted a long letter of invitation which she said would be taken by a secret route to Lhasa. I signed it on behalf of the Society, and Cocoola, in the best tradition of pure melodrama, slipped it into the bosom of her dress and rose to go.

But she first asked more of me, that I should go to Lhasa and there press my support as from the Buddhists of Europe. If I went I should go by jeep over the Natu La from Sikkim, about half way to Lhasa, and would then have to proceed on mule-back over very high passes indeed. I agreed, and put the proposition to the Foreign Office. They killed the idea out of hand. I should be stopped, they said, within fifty miles, and on one excuse or another at least be turned back, or at the worst just 'disappear'. Thus one more adventure ebbed away, but at least it was fun to have considered it.

In 1959 came the invasion of Tibet and the Dalai Lama's flight to

India. What happened thereafter is sickening to read about. It is well to realise that the great mind which we so admire in others is our own – 'there are no others' – but equally our own is the mind of those who murdered thousands of Tibetans, rich and poor, with ghastly cruelty, destroyed their temples and their homes and all for no more reason than that they were 'the enemy'. Some seventy five thousand Tibetans escaped with the Dalai Lama, about fifty thousand into India and the rest into Nepal and Sikkim. Their plight was terrible: they were without money, food and clothing; without employment which they could understand; and in a climate which to them was incompatible with health. What could the Indians do for them save give them a ration of food and permission to use what empty buildings they could find? In London Mr Francis Beaufort-Palmer founded at once the Tibet Society of the United Kingdom, with three very different objects in view. First, to rouse public opinion at the United Nations and everywhere where men would be horrified by the rape of a harmless and beautiful country. Here the President, Sir Olaf Caroe, with long experience of North India, did what could be done. Secondly, to afford relief to the refugees in India, Sikkim and Nepal with money, clothes, food and other necessities, and in due course to help arrange their future lives for them. And thirdly, for those concerned with religion, to help preserve Tibetan Buddhism, and to learn more about it than was then known in the outside world. Here was the irony of the invasion, that a large number of learned lamas escaped with the refugees and have been working ever since to translate, write and teach so that the wisdom of Tibetan Buddhism might be passed on to the younger generation of refugees, and to a large number of men and women of other races anxious to learn and practise what it contains. But for the invasion, we might not know of the profound teachings of the many schools, now being taught in the West in gompas (monasteries) founded in increasing numbers year by year. The Tibet Society has done, and is still doing, noble work in all its three fields and is working hard today from its London headquarters.

In September 1960 I myself was brought into the field of Tibet in India. I received a letter from the Dalai Lama's elder brother, Thondup, asking for my opinion, as 'a leader of Buddhist thought in the West' on a scheme which the exiled Pontiff-King had evolved as 'a remedy for the existing spiritual ill-health of mankind'. It was in fact such as organisation as already existed, the World Fellowship of Buddhists. The writer must have known of it, but may have held it in low opinion. There was in it, as I had already complained, too much talk and not enough Buddhism. In my reply, however, as requested by his brother, I gave my views at length as to how he, in his extremely difficult situation, might act to best advantage and put to best use his available resources. For the next twelve months we discussed the list of suggestions which I had initially put forward. Some proved impracticable, and others unacceptable to the Indian Government. The principal point remaining was the creation of a Council of Tibet, to co-ordinate the Dalai Lama's work for the refugees and the preservation of Tibetan Buddhism, always taking infinite care that it should not seem to be the court of a king in exile who was scheming to return, for this would embarrass his host, the Indian Government, in a way which he was most anxious to avoid. Yet, as he wrote pathetically, how else could he do what might be done to save his people? I then advocated a lecture tour of India in order that thousands, millions it might be, would see him as a great spiritual leader. He would not need to mention his political plight, and thus embarrass Indian relations with China. I took the opportunity, when meeting Mr Nehru again in London, to ask his views about a more extended tour of Buddhist countries. He preferred separate visits to each, and I saw the force of the difference.

In our correspondence on these and a dozen other matters, the time came when personal conversation became essential, and I was invited, at the expense of the Dalai Lama's two elder brothers, to visit the camps, settlements and hospitals in India and Sikkim and 'see for myself', before reporting my discoveries and views to the Dalai Lama in his Indian home at Dharamsala.

At Easter, 1962, therefore, I flew out to New Delhi. I went as a Vice-President of the Tibet Society and President of the Buddhist Society, but thought it prudent to call at the British Embassy to make the purpose of my visit clear. Having thus cleared the lines, I called on Dr Radhakrishnan, then Vice-President of India, to ask his views on the subjects about which the Dalai Lama and I had been corresponding. On the suggestion of a lecture tour in India he was quite clear: 'The Dalai Lama is a holy man. It is his business to preach.' Having thus got the blessing of the Vice-President and the Prime Minister on at least one aspect of our discussions, I flew to Calcutta and then up to Bagdogra. This is the airfield at the foot of the Himalayas from which there is a road up the Teesta valley to the control point at the only bridge over the river. I was driven over the bridge and up to the famous Himalayan Hotel at Kalimpong. It was then run by 'Annie-La' who, I was told, was one-quarter Scots, one-quarter Tibetan, one-quarter Lepcha and one-quarter Nepalese. But whatever her lineage, I learnt from her, in the famous lounge whence many an expedition started for Tibet, a great deal of what I wanted to know. As we were sitting there Bhante Sangharakshita walked in. He was the English bhikkhu, now also a Tibetan monk, who, from his bungalow–monastery in Kalimpong, edited the journal published by the Maha Bodhi Society of Calcutta. I asked how he knew I was there. 'I phoned them at the bridge to let me know when you passed,' he replied and, imperturbable and smiling as ever, took charge of me and my affairs in Kalimpong. With him I visited the admirable school for refugees run by Dhardo Rimpoche in an old Bhutanese palace; and he took me to see the Rani Chuni Dorji, sister of the Maharajah of Sikkim and widow of the Prime Minister of Nepal, who seemed to be one of the most powerful figures in the area. From her I gathered more information, and then made a round of high-ranking lamas with Bhante as my interpreter and guide. There were leaders of all four schools of Tibetan Buddhism in the town, and I was deeply impressed with many of them. Being 'incarnations', they might be old or as young as the Dalai Lama. One, aged ten, received me with a dignity, intelligence and air of royalty which one does not expect in a child, and I made my obeisance as to one of an inner development superior to my own. Khamtrul Rimpoche (Rimpoche is a title of high rank) was already becoming the printer for the refugees, and later opened a printing press on a large scale.

Having seen what I wanted in Kalimpong, I drove with Bhante down to the bridge and up to Darjeeling. We passed through miles of the famous tea plantations and were refreshed with occasional views on the horizon of Kanchenjunga, whose summit is but a few feet short of Everest's.

In Darjeeling I was taken in charge by the Chinese wife of another of the Dalai Lama's brothers, Mrs Gyalo Thondup. I described her in my diary as 'the most dynamic and utterly efficient woman I have met in the Orient'. She had planned and opened a beautifully run school for 350 of the refugee children, added an Arts and Crafts Centre where they made and sold a variety of Tibetan articles, and stimulated the opening of a Tibetan theatre. I called on other schools and centres, and attended the theatre, before being summoned by Princess Cocoola to Gangtok. For some reason, my telephone conversation with her from my hotel in Darjeeling to the Palace of Sikkim, across hundreds of moonlit miles of inhospitable, snow-clad mountains, impressed my poetic mind enormously. Bhante and I left for Gangtok next morning and on the way we called at the famous monastery at Ghoom. It belongs to the Gelug-pa or Yellow Hat sect of Tibetan Buddhism, founded by the famous Tsong-ka-pa in the fifteenth century, to which both the Dalai Lama and the Panchen Lama belong. I was met by a blast from one of the great trumpets or *radongs* whose booming voice can be heard for miles across the mountains, and was charmingly shown round by the Abbot. Bhante left me at the bridge and I then drove through wild and glorious scenery to the frontier of Sikkim where, as I had no written pass, some casual telephoning seemed to be sufficient. And so to the lovely Guest House of the Palace in Gangtok, where the silver thread of a river flowing 1000 feet below the window, and immense views in all directions, made the visit in itself a joy.

The following day I began a tour under the guidance of Princess Cocoola, who had placed herself in charge of the many thousands of Tibetan refugees in Sikkim. Their presence there was a serious problem. This tiny Kingdom, wedged between Tibet, Bhutan and Nepal, was self-supporting, but could ill afford to add to its population. Tibetans were alien to them, for, although the reigning family were Tibetan by blood, the inhabitants were a blend of Lepcha, Bhutia and other races besides the native Sikkimese. I learnt a good deal of the state of affairs from Thondup, the Crown Prince. Not unnaturally, he was more troubled by the military situation. The Chinese were already encamped on the Natu La, the 14,000-foot pass into Tibet which, at eleven miles distance, could be seen in detail, and Indian troops were already being drafted into the capital to be ready for what might come.

I moved about the bazaar in the one main street of Gangtok with Cocoola and saw how from a tiny office she tried to cope with the refugee situation. I noticed with interest, for these customs are dying out, the respectful gesture with the tongue with which Tibetan men greeted the Princess. It is not 'putting the tongue out' but, as it were, filling the front of the mouth with the tongue, a relic, I understood, of pronouncing a term of respect which itself had died out. I called at the Palace and exchanged ceremonial *kata* or silk scarves with H.H. the Maharajah. He showed me his studio where, with views out of every window to delight the heart of any landscape artist, he was painting in his own style, and holding exhibitions of his work in Calcutta. But his health was failing, and he died the following year.

With Cocoola I visited the Tibetan Temple in the palace grounds, where the young Prince was later married to Hope Cooke, the American girl, who was at once called Hope-la (everyone is '-la'. I was Toby-la, and Cocoola's smallest child, for want of any other name, was Baby-la!). In the temple a service was in progress, and I was fascinated to hear the long trumpets, conches and stringed instruments. They were not, as I first thought, each making impromptu interpolations, but were playing according to a written score, as one finds on the music-stands of any Western orchestra. This was my first visit to a Tibetan temple and I was later shown the library of manuscripts in their pigeon-holes, and the lovely altar with a great variety of *tanka*, the Tibetan painted scrolls or banners now increasingly well known in the West.

Time was getting short, and after giving a lecture at the Institute of Tibetology, I bade farewell to my host and his able son and daughter and drove down to Kalimpong. As I left I received the present I most wanted. This was the national Sikkimese garment, the *chuba*, a long gown which is buttoned across the body and up to the right shoulder. It is worn with a sash so that some of the front is pulled up from beneath to make a pouch for articles of all descriptions. The sleeves are long, and I loved the gesture of raising the arms to shake them down, so as to leave the hands free for action. Cocoola's husband, Pheunkang-se, at the last moment gave me a *chuba* of his own, and I wear it frequently at home in the winter, complete with a scarlet sash of Sikkimese hand-woven silk. I know nothing warmer or more comfortable or more dignity-producing, even when alone.

.   .   .   .   .

In Kalimpong I made a further round of calls on leading lamas, and the next day was up at five for the long drive down to the airfield. In Delhi I had a long talk with Tsepon Shakabpa and his advisers, during which I summarised my impressions and planned my visit to Dharamsala. The details fifteen years later are of no importance, but I finally killed the cruel stories that the Dalai Lama had escaped with enormous sums in bullion and had secretly invested them in the U.S.A. I learnt from his financial adviser that the whole of such gold and silver as he had brought with him had been invested in Indian securities in Calcutta, and the income soon made known to the appropriate authorities.

Soon I took the night mail to Pathankot, the rail-head for that part of the Himalayas, and was driven by car to the Rest House at Dharamsala, about 7000 feet up, and some hundred miles north of Simla. It was clearly at one time a British hill-station where bungalows had been built for the hot weather. Backed by the forested hills, it looked out over glorious views on to the plains below. It was here that the exiled Dalai Lama of Tibet lived, very simply, in a bungalow beautifully furnished with Tibetan art. He was surrounded by his family, his staff, and members of his one-time Cabinet from Lhasa. Here also was a school for refugee children run by his elder sister, the nucleus of a monastic settlement for some of his chosen monks, and a herbal clinic. The climate, which ranged from some four feet of snow in winter to the gentle heat of summer, was ideal for the Tibetans, and when a move was suggested either to Mysore or to Dalhousie it was quickly turned down.

The Dalai Lama was learning English slowly, and with the aid of Sonam Topgay as interpreter we got on fast and well. He had developed a great deal in the previous six years in his knowledge both of Indian ways and Western culture. As I wrote in my diary, after several interviews, 'he had a quick mind, enormous charm, a keen sense of humour which bubbled out at intervals in his deep laughter' and he was imbued with Buddhist principles in a way which roused my humble and profound admiration. His task was still extremely difficult. He had to tread a middle way between the preservation of tradition and the necessity of progress; between the life of a grateful guest and that of an exiled autocrat; between the delegation of some powers into democratic control and the maintenance of sufficient authority to prevent the trouble caused by squabbling factions. Above all, he had to preserve and indeed make better known Tibetan Buddhism, while listening to the criticism of modern minds.

For many hours we thrashed out my long list of findings and suggestions, but at lunch our conversation could become less formal. As I am no scholar, it was embarrassing to be asked by such an authority for my views on Nirvana and Paranirvana, and I doubt whether he was satisfied with my suggestion that 'we shall know when we get there'! But on his being traditionally an incarnation of Chenresi or, by the Sanskrit name, Avalokiteshvara, our minds could move together; and when we were face to face the transmission of awareness was more profound.

In due course I was taken round the Tibetan area. I called upon the Dalai Lama's tutors, who had escaped with him. The senior, Trijang Rimpoche, and the junior, Lingtsang Rimpoche, each received me on the conventional throne-bed in his own house, and impressed me again with the wisdom which shines out of acquired experience. I lunched with the members of the Dalai Lama's Cabinet, most of whom had escaped with him. All were keen with questions, and avid of ideas for the improvement of the Tibetan conditions in India and for hastening a return. And so to the school, then run by the Dalai Lama's elder sister, who died soon after – one would think from overwork. The conditions then were terrible, but now I gather they are enormously improved. On the last day I was allowed to sit on the lawn and watch His Holiness conduct a service on the veranda of his bungalow for some twenty of his senior pupil-monks. The power–humility of the teacher, the veneration–adoration of the monks, the locked tension of the sacred ritual left me shaken, and I felt some actual transmission of the power released. Then came the moment of farewell, a rapid summary of views and plans, and promises by me to help as best we could from the Buddhist Society in London. I gave His Holiness a Buddha image of the Wei dynasty of China. He, in addition to the silk kata, which now as I write hangs about the shoulders of a Tang figure of Kwan-Yin, gave me in return an antique bronze Tibetan figure of the Buddha which has, I know not how or why, blue eyes!

And so, after a run down in the car to Pathankot which must be one of the most beautiful drives in the world, I returned to New Delhi, and after dining for a final talk with Mr Shakabpa and his family, took my plane for home. I reflected that I had done what I could. In the last fifteen years, much of what we discussed has been adopted, and I am glad that as the years have gone by my karma has allowed me to see more of this tragic, lovable and noble-minded man.

21

Reconstruction, Sarnath and Sikkim

After that immensely interesting but exhausting tour of India for the Dalai Lama, I returned to find changes in my circumstances and in myself. I wrote my report on the Indian journey, sending the first copy to His Holiness. It was published in the *Middle Way*. I attended the school for Tibetan refugee children at the Pestalozzi Centre in Sussex, where they were in the care of Spencer Chapman. As he knew Tibet well, he was an admirable teacher to introduce his pupils into the Western way of life. As it happened he had little difficulty, for the Tibetan children took to our ways at once and became very popular with neighbours and visitors alike.

At the Bar I realised that my uncomfortable life as a Q.C. might be ending. I was made a Commissioner at the Old Bailey, which meant that I would sit there as a judge whenever an extra judge was needed. The pressure of work was growing fast, and available courts were inadequate. Some in the High Court in the Strand were converted to our use, but whenever a case ended a long delay would ensue while counsel, witnesses, jury and defendants went by bus or taxi (or prison van) from the Old Bailey to the High Court, where conditions for all alike were most inconvenient.

The need for new courts speeded up the plans for a large addition to the Old Bailey buildings, originally erected in 1907. However, it was not until 1973 that the new building, with its marriage to the old, was ready for use. The word 'marriage' is appropriate. The Old Bailey must be one of the most complex buildings in the world.

Judges and the Lord Mayor and Sheriffs walk in and out with no contact with any other section of the hundreds of people who use the building on any day. They have their own rooms and luncheon arrangements, and ushers guide them through a labyrinth of back corridors to one of the eighteen courts available. Prisoners are brought into the building by a different entrance and taken to the cells; they, too, have their own rooms and food facilities, as have the officers who look after them. Barristers have their own entrance, their own rooms, luncheon Mess, with separate facilities for men and women. The administrative staff, the Probation Service, the Press and the shorthand writers also have their own facilities. People queueing for the public galleries use yet another entrance and have their own cloakrooms and refreshment facilities away from contact with anyone save the jury bailiffs. All these perform their duties in the building largely without communication with each other, save in the common arena under the public eye, the Court. Imagine the problems arising when this remarkable building, no larger than many a modern store, is extended in each of its non-communicating corridors into another complex of the same size. Add air-conditioning, a loudspeaker system, and the increasing need for security, and one may honour indeed the architects and engineers who made the marriage possible, with the minimum delay.

The Buddhist Society was entering another phase. We started a Correspondence Course in basic Buddhism, in response to requests from prisoners; it was widened to include those living too far from a group which they could visit in person. Of course the scheme produced its own problems, for Buddhism is a vast field of human activity, with no dogmas and no orthodoxy of belief or behaviour. Each student, beginner or advanced, inevitably has his own speciality, which might be Theravada, Tibetan Buddhism or Zen. The answers of a tutor from one school might differ widely from those of another, and those responsible for the Society's policy of making known the basic principles of Buddhism cannot know what any tutor is in fact teaching any correspondent. The same applies to the Buddhism being studied and taught in many of the widely spread Groups affiliated to the Society.

These Groups were on the increase. They were forming and re-forming in various corners of the country, for the first time independently of the efforts made from London. The most important of these was the Western Buddhist Order. Its organising brain, director and spiritual leader was Bhante Sangharakshita, with whom I had spent so much time in India, and its purpose was an idea new to the West. Its need arose from the failure of many attempts to found a Western branch of the Sangha, or Buddhist Order, that of the Theravada school. Englishmen from time to time 'took the Robe', and with shaven heads and the yellow robes of the Order tried to observe the 227 Rules which bind these bhikkhus in their several countries. For the most part they failed. Some left and married, as indeed did many of the monks and lamas coming to England from the East. Some just lost the impetus which made them join the Order; others having entered the Order in the East, stayed and lived there and are living there today.

Bhante (which means 'teacher', like the Japanese Sensei) has tried to build up a new form of Sangha, more appropriate to the West, where the shaven-headed beggar makes no appeal. When he first explained the idea to me, it reminded me of a phrase used by W. Q. Judge, who was one of the three founders of the Theosophical Society, about 'wearing the yellow robe internally', which might be interpreted as applying the highest ideals of the Buddhist life to that of the householder. The Buddhists have a term *upasaka* which means a lay disciple of the Buddha, self-appointed, who strives to keep the precepts of right living all the time. Whether man or woman, old or young, Bhante thought that an effort might be made to form a nucleus of such people in England. This was his Western Buddhist Order, and I gave it my full support, for I never felt the least enthusiasm for an English branch of the Sangha. Its members could not beg in the London streets; they would therefore have to be supported. They could not obey the rule of not handling money, or how would they take a bus ride? They could not keep to the five garments of the rules, for in England they need woollen clothes and warm socks. Nor could they eat before noon if accepting hospitality. Bhante's idea removes these disadvantages, and the Order is spreading rapidly. He himself is a first-class lecturer, writer and meditation teacher and the prospects are good. May it encourage more and more who accept the basic principles of Buddhism to apply them constantly, at all times and in all places, and – more important still – in all the situations which face the average citizen hour by hour, from trouble in the office to a bus which does not come, from a sick child or a lost job to trouble with the authorities.

The Western Buddhist Order was the first substantial Buddhist organisation to be born beyond the ambit of the Buddhist Society, but it was not the last, and I rejoice at the number of new groups and schools and meditation centres which are appearing year by year, and the increasing demand from existing schools and colleges, conferences and government-sponsored units for lecturers on Buddhism.

This period of reconstruction and development included myself. It is not easy, looking back, to apply dates to periods of new aware-ness, often consisting of suddenly 'seeing' – a favourite word in Zen Buddhism – a condition of mind long felt. I had lectured and written so much on the principles of the inner life, using words for want of a better means of expression, that it was all too easy to let new growth of spiritual knowledge remain at the level of words, that is, of con-cepts; but one moment of intuitive awareness can be the reward of a year of intensive thinking. The stimulus of the Indian tour produced in me new elements of knowledge; I would like to call it wisdom, for I mean knowledge beyond logical proof or the need of it.

First, I found, the mind is involved in an unceasing war between self and Self. Precise definitions of these terms are irrelevant, for the fact becomes the important element in every day and hour. The Self was becoming the dominant force in me, whether I called it the Light within, the Buddha-Mind within or the Christ-principle. It is that which on its best behaviour *knows*. The lower self, on the other hand, I came to regard as a yapping, only half-trained dog beside me, diminishing in size, I noted, as the years went by. I amused myself by making it objective to the extent of saying loudly at times, when its demands were too outrageously expressed, 'Shut up!'

'I want' is voiced internally a thousand times a day. 'I should' is often the unheeded because incompatible reply. I want my lunch, to look at television, to keep for myself things others ask for, of my time or energy or money. I want to be first in the queue for a bus or a job or an honour. My 'Self' – not yet total Self but a pale reflection of the totality within – tells me, as if I needed telling, that I should do something different, in the interests of someone or something other than my self. The conflict rages, and is always with us, recognised or not. But the sharp awareness hour by hour of the clear distinction between the two becomes more and more unmistakable, unarguably clear.

The second principle was a deepening understanding that the Buddha was right in teaching that 'all things are inseparable from suffering', and the cause of suffering is very largely the desires of self, my yapping dog. This light of perception came, I think, from a new view of compassion, which means 'to suffer with', as an infinitely higher force, or the one Force on a higher plane, than love, our human, sadly personal love. I now saw Compassion as impersonal, even cold as distinct from the heat of emotion. *The Voice of the Silence*, I saw, is right: 'Compassion is no attribute. It is the law of Laws – eternal Harmony, a shoreless, universal essence, the light of everlasting right, and fitness of all things, the law of Love eternal.'

If this is so we suffer, as we grow, not less but more. We learn that we are one with the world's suffering as with its joy. We lie in the gutter with the drunken thief, even as we sing with the angels in heaven. How then be swayed by pleasure/pain, or seek 'my' happiness? But though 'weeping may endure for a night, joy cometh in the morning', and I was beginning to feel a little of that joy.

Another Conference of the World Fellowship of Buddhists was appearing on the horizon, but first I indulged in what I believe to be a peep back into my distant past. This took place at Easter 1964, when Puck and I joined Phyllis Naylor, our astrologer friend, and her sister for a week in Rome. I went straight to the Forum and the Senate House, and took photographs of the rostrum where Mark Antony made his speech on Caesar's death, and where a thousand other orators have no doubt held forth at this Speakers' Corner of its day. We visited St Peter's, where the entrance down to the tomb was for me the only live and 'charismatic' corner of the building. The art of the Middle Ages did not appeal to me, and the emanations of the Colosseum, the worst blot on the Roman character as I view it, were horrible. But near it was a fascinating church, St Clement's, on the surface a basilica of the twelfth century. From it one descended to a church of the fourth century, but this was not all, for recent excavation had revealed below this again a Mithraic temple, in excellent condition, of the first century. Here was vertical history indeed. I came back again and again to the Forum for it was alive with memory, albeit memory unspecified.

Pompeii has always excited the imagination, but for myself I was more impressed with Herculaneum, perhaps because it is less visited, and its own vibrations therefore less worn down; or it may be because it lies now in a vast pit from which the modern houses may be seen about the rim. The Roman houses of Herculaneum are larger than those of Pompeii; sometimes they include the first floor, and one has the feeling of really standing in a Roman room. I enjoyed taking a photograph of Puck standing behind the bar of a 'pub' at the corner where even the jars remain intact.

And so to England, and forward by some fifteen hundred years. It is a remarkable fact that the coroner's report on the inquest of Christopher Marlow, who was killed in 1594 in a Deptford inn, has survived, and that the actual method of the killing is described in detail. It was suggested that the method was impossible and that it should be tested. At a joint meeting at the Caxton Hall, the Marlowe Society and members of the Shakespearean Authorship Society staged a reconstruction of the murder. I took the chair as the coroner, and after hearing my reading from the report, a group of young men from the audience put themselves into the appropriate positions on benches and chairs. Could someone have stabbed Marlowe as described, which involved the killer reaching round from a recumbent position to stab the poet in the chest? It could be done, and to strengthen our belief, it was done again! So that, for what it is worth in the history of England, was that.

The Marlowe Society celebrated the birth of its hero far more splendidly that did the Shakespearean Authorship Society the birth of the man of Stratford-upon-Avon born in the same year. It was understandable because the one belief held in common by all our members was that Shakespeare never wrote a line. The Marlowe Society staged a splendid Elizabethan banquet in the City. The menu included grilled mullet, venison, sucking pig and roast swan, followed by 'marchpayne Saltytte' and cheese seasoned with herbs. We drank, of course, mead and malmsey, and threw scraps of our food to 'beggars' most realistically whining at our elbows. The salt was coarse-ground in a common dish and the bread stone-ground whole grain. But what to wear? The women came in splendour, for which portraits provided ample precedent. The men did what they could, but I was determined to be a lawyer. I made large 'bands' out of a cotton handkerchief and, as I see from a photograph, I wore my Silk's gown and on my head a French beret. The result at least allowed me into the banquet.

At last came the Seventh Conference of the World Fellowship of Buddhists. It was held at Sarnath, near Benares where the Buddha, as recorded in the Pali Canon, preached the first sermon. The site had been excavated under British expert supervision, and is now beautifully preserved. The Conference headquarters at the famous Clark's Hotel in Benares can seldom have seen such a mixed gathering, with Buddhist monks of high and low degree from Mongolia and Japan, Vietnam and Tibet, Thailand and Ceylon, and leading Buddhists from all corners of the world.

A Tibetan abbot appealed to my love of immediate action in the building of a gompa at Sarnath. While others talked about how to raise funds, he acquired a trolley full of bricks. These he spread on the ground, and in a shallow trench began to build a wall with them. The response was immediate, and within six months innumerable experts and amateurs had produced a most impressive temple.

While the delegates were assembling I was asked with others to speak at a symposium at the famous Hindu University of Benares. As all speakers know, it is not easy to adjust oneself to an audience of unknown culture and calibre, but the Buddha was a Hindu and deeply venerated by all India, so this occasion was not too difficult. A far more exacting test occurred when Mr Rohit Mehta, then General Secretary of the Theosophical Society in India, with whom I was staying, asked me to address a meeting of his Theosophical Lodge. At the last minute, as I was taken to my seat on the platform, where I sat alone cross-legged on a cushion, I was told that my audience would be about 'one-third heavy-weight Hindu scholars, one-third the sixth form of the local Theosophical Girls' College, and the rest members and friends and all sorts'. Where was the Middle Way for a talk to all of them? I decided to keep close to the basic of principles of Theosophy, and survived even the questions. But I had an experience of what now must be ancient history when, lecturing to a small society in South India. I felt fresh air behind me, and found it was a genuine punkah-wallah slowly moving his enormous fan above my otherwise perspiring head.

All at the Conference were delighted when the Vice-President of India, Dr Radhakrishnan, arrived with the Dalai Lama. Here at least was a step towards the tour of India which I had advocated for him in 1962, and the welcome to these visitors was warm indeed. We listened to the reports of delegates, and splendid speeches, and I played my part in the work of the committees. There was much talk of what should be done but little of who would do it, or how and when. Puck and I made new friends and strengthened our links with old ones, and so the Conference ended, and we entered on a holiday which turned out to be the most perfect five days of our lives, with Princess Cocoola in Sikkim.

We flew to Calcutta and thence to Bagdogra, where a royal car was awaiting us. At the frontier into Sikkim the car broke down, and we were told that another was coming down from the capital. While we waited as darkness fell, we examined and talked to our first yaks. Then a military jeep arrived. The driver was determined to show what a jeep could do and, while Puck and I clung to each other in desperation, he rushed us up the mountainside, taking bumps and hollows as they came. We arrived at the Guest House, half frozen and exhausted, and were welcomed by Cocoola herself. An enormous log fire burned in the hearth. Then came a typical Tibetan dinner and, to our surprise, an excellent bottle of burgundy. Afterwards there was a tableau I shall not easily forget. On the hearthrug lay Cocoola's Baby-la, on her tummy. Beside me, her nanny was threading beads bought in the bazaar to make up a rosary for Puck. Beside her, Puck and Cocoola, and her family tailor, who had been brought in to make a chuba for Puck. Solemnly, his pigtail curled about his head, he measured Puck and remembered the measurements. He promised the completed garment for the following night and withdrew. It came, and fitted to perfection.

Then began five days of pure delight. The Crown Prince, now the Maharajah, and his American wife Hope-la invited us to lunch in the Palace. We then watched an archery competition on the Temple lawns, for it was a feast-day when the people at large are welcome there. We went to the bazaar with Cocoola and haggled over pieces of local craftsmanship we wished to buy. We called at the school, now better organised but still too crowded, with two classes in each room with the teachers at either end. Cocoola spoilt us with something new for breakfast every day, yak-milk yoghourt, or *tsamba*, the local food which is based on parched barley and will sustain a man for long journeys. At a temple I was offered Tibetan tea, which is made of Chinese block tea, rancid butter and salt. Eyes watched me to see, I think, if I would spit it out. I liked it, to my hosts' relief and my own surprise, so long as one thinks of it as soup and not as tea. But had I not said the same of Japanese ceremonial tea which Dr Suzuki had offered me in his house in Kamakaura after the war? I went with the Chögyal (the Buddhist title of the Maharajah) to the Officers' Mess of the Indian regiment stationed in the town as the front-line defence of the capital, and with him visited the monument to his older brother who was killed flying in the war. The Chögyal was himself a monk at the time, and was brought to the office of Crown Prince with what to him was sudden violence, a fact I think of some significance in the development of his character. Cocoola, indifferent to the threat from China, was planning to build a house up the road which led to the Natu-la, the high pass where the Chinese guns were trained on the palace night and day. I photographed the famous pass in the sunlight and in snow, and fear that it may yet have its place in history. Puck found a silversmith, and sat on the floor to compare the tools each used in the handling of silver, while I tried to get a worthwhile photograph of Kanchenjunga, veiled in the heat-haze seventy miles away.

A highlight of this visit was a trip to Rumtek, the monastery eleven miles away at which the Karma pa, next senior in rank to the Dalai Lama in the schools of Tibetan Buddhism, had made his home and, later, international headquarters. He was dignity incarnate, blessed us as distinguished visitors, and gave us each the traditional knot of red silk to carry his blessing on our way. We were to see him later in London.

22
Thailand and the Journey Home

I remembered the final scene in Gangtok when giving my attention to 18 June 1965. This was the 150th anniversary of the battle of Waterloo and near enough the 750th anniversary of the signing of Magna Carta. Lady Parker, wife of the Lord Chief Justice, proposed a charity ball at the Law Courts in the Strand, at which guests could appear in fancy dress of either period. The result was a huge success. Puck and Carlo 'managed', as women can, with something vaguely appropriate, and I found a picture of a gentleman of about 1215 and saw that I could imitate his attire. The chuba which Cocoola's husband had given me was remarkably similar, a Nepalese cap might have come from the gentleman in the picture, and a silk scarf worn across the shoulder completed a remarkable likeness. The fourth member of our party, Edward St George, came as 'a Bhutanese gentleman visiting England at the time', complete with a short sword in a silver scabbard.

He was a remarkable young man, a member of my chambers who, somehow being in Katmandu at a time when the country was in fact closed to foreigners, wished to explore eastern Nepal, of which very little was then known. How could he get permission, he was asked. 'Can't I ask the King?' he inquired. No one had thought of that. He asked and was promptly given permission, and made a pleasant journey. There is much to be said for the simple mind!

When, in 1962, I was having tea with the Rani Chuni Dorji in Kalimpong she was obviously anxious and waiting for news. The situation in Bhutan, but a few hundred miles across the mountains, was serious, and her son, then Prime Minister as her husband had been before him, was already involved in a crisis which culminated two years later in his murder. Then a message came by telephone – from Edward St George! Somehow he happened to be at the scene, although this country too was closed to foreigners, and he had promised to send what news he could obtain.

Soon after the ball came the Society's Summer School at full development, one hundred and fifty eager minds at High Leigh, Hoddesdon, from most parts of the U.K., with visitors old and new from the Continent. I was never on the committee of management, and was therefore free to help, observe and comment as I chose. My part was usually to begin with a talk on the field of Buddhism, for my specialisation, as I would explain, was not to specialise. I see the vast field of Buddhism, its metaphysics, philosophy, mysticism, psychology, morality, action and art, as one vast whole, stemming, all of it, from the teaching which the Buddha chose of his wisdom to give mankind. Such was the tree, and the schools of Buddhism are the branches of it. In the same way, since I first read *The Secret Doctrine*, I have seen the religions of mankind as branches of that tree. For the rest of the week the various schools and their special teaching were considered day by day, with ample time for meditation and recreation.

There are many Summer Schools held each year in England, but none I venture to claim with the beauty which is added to our own by Miss Stella Coe, President of Ikebana International, the largest society in the West for Japanese flower-arrangement. She was told by her teachers in Japan that they could teach her no more, for she is a master of that *Do*, or Way. Day after day, at first by herself and later with a group of pupils, she would place in the meeting-rooms fresh, original and meaningful arrangements of flowers. Here is art applied with a sense of beauty to a noble idea.

Then we heard that the King and Queen of Thailand were to open a large Thai vihara (temple) at East Sheen, near Richmond. We invited their Majesties to visit the Society. It was a great moment in our history. As their car drew to the kerb, Puck presented the Queen with a bouquet perfectly matching her Thai silk gown, and we then

preceded them into the building. In the library I presented the
officers and members of the Council, and then led our visitors to the
shrine room to see the red-lacquered shrine and bronze image which
had been the gift of the Thai Buddhists in 1949. They were left
alone awhile, and I then preceded them into the lecture hall, which
was filled to capacity with invited members. In my address of welcome I outlined the history of the close association between the
Buddhists of Thailand and Great Britain, from the day when King
Chulalongkorn became the Patron of the first Society in 1907 to this
crowning occasion. The King's reply was charming and sincere.
He stayed with the Queen for tea and consented to a group photograph. Their Buddhism, we noticed, was far wider in scope than that
of many of their subjects. As the Queen put it in conversation, 'Buddhism must be taught in its simplest essence as widely as possible. It
must be a Buddhism of the heart which can ignore the differences of
ritual and of emphasis.'

And so for the last time to the East, for the Eighth Conference of the
World Fellowship of Buddhists, this time in Chiengmai in Thailand.
Muriel Daw, then editor of *The Middle Way*, came with Puck and me
to represent the Society. Thirty-five regional centres were represented, and more were accepted during the conference. A special
train took the delegates to Chiengmai, and for me it was one of the
most delightful periods in the whole trip. In the heat the carriage
windows could be left wide open, bringing to us the scented air from
the jungle. There were lively scenes at each village where we stopped.
Here were the paddy-fields, and the water-buffaloes in action; here
were men in canoes fishing for their evening meal; and here their
wooden houses on stilts above the water, in which the dying sunset
was reflected. Here, too, were the homing birds of species strange to
us, and to our delight, occasional stops to pick up vast supplies of
logs as fuel for the engine.

In the morning Princess 'Noo' Svasti was there to meet us. She
was the widow of Prince 'Chin' Svasti, and the mother of the four
daughters, all now married with children, who had danced for me
in my drawing-room in 1951. Princess Poon, daughter of Prince
Damrong, whom we had known at the Thai Embassy in London,
was now President of the Fellowship. After a splendid opening by the
Thai Prime Minister we settled down to the usual committees, but it

is all too easy to pass resolutions and very hard to find those to carry them out.

When we arrived at Chiengmai I made my own attempt to import some practical Buddhism into the conference. In the committee of which I was asked to be chairman, I introduced the Twelve Principles of Buddhism which had been so well received twenty years before. Several members supported me. But it was pointed out that such a serious step as their approval should have been on the conference agenda, allowing much time for consideration, and I had to agree. Although, therefore, one-half of the committee were prepared to vote with me I surrendered my casting vote and the matter was left there, so far as I know, ever since.

A real attempt to bring Buddhism itself into the conference was made in the evening lectures. John Blofeld gave an excellent talk on Tibetan Buddhism, and another on Zen practice in Japan was given by Dr Irmgard Schloegl, who had flown from Kyoto at the suggestion of Puck and myself to take part. Born in Austria, she gained her degree at Graz University in metallurgy and had joined the Society in London about 1950. Her interest was in Zen Buddhism, and when she was invited to Kyoto in 1960 she went for long training in Zen meditation in Daitokuji. After returning with us to London for a holiday, she went back to Japan for a further six years, finally returning to England in 1972 with her master's qualification to teach in the West the Rinzai School's method of Zen training.

But Buddhism was at least present in the sightseeing expeditions to many monasteries. There was one, a special ceremony at Wat Umong, to which the Thai population travelled for days in order to follow the final procession to the Temple led by a gorgeously apparelled elephant. We saw more of elephants when delegates were taken into the jungle to watch a group of them shifting enormous logs of teak. I left the grandstand, and creeping close got splendid pictures of the delicate footwork and trunk-work of these remarkably intelligent animals. As a climax, one of them raised and held an enormous log on her tusks and trunk and seemed to appreciate the crowd's applause.

Some months before, when I had been pressed by Princess Svasti to come to Chiengmai, I had lightly replied that I would come if I could have a ride on an elephant. Svasti 'Noo' promised, and here was my opportunity. The rest of the delegates had departed to visit a temple. Puck was sitting by a small stream talking to flowers new to her. Princess Noo called to the mahout of one of the elephants, then resting after the performance but still wearing their log-hauling harness. We climbed on to the elephant's back from a standing platform. In the absence of any other way of staying on we clung to each other and to the harness, and I was delighted to find that his neck was covered with thick hair into which one could entangle one's bare toes. We had, for the schoolboy in me, an exciting and delightful ride round and I asked if the elephant would kneel for us to get down instead of using the very dull platform. The mahout at once obliged, and down went our steed like a minor earthquake on to his knees. Noo jumped off lightly and I followed, forgetting that the back of an elephant is about as far from the ground as the roof of a London taxi. I landed on all fours but, recovering my dignity, did not forget a tip for the 'driver'. I was sorry I lacked a coconut for the elephant. Once I had fed one to a temple elephant in India. She crunched the whole nut and then delicately felt about with her tongue and spat out the tickly tuft of hair from the end of it. I almost apologised for not removing it myself.

When the conference ended, we returned to Bangkok by train where on the following day the King gave a tea-party to the delegates, and the Queen Mother, a scholar in her own right, came to our table to have an earnest discussion on the doctrine of Anatta, no-self. On the last evening we attended a reception at the Prime Minister's house, and bade farewell to our many friends, and in the morning flew back to Calcutta. Thence we flew to Madras, and I called again at the Theosophical Society at Adyar to discuss with the President ideas on publishing. I there met Miss Elizabeth Preston, who had already done much work on a shortened edition of *The Secret Doctrine*, and we made plans for me to complete it in London.

And so to Ceylon. We had intended a brief private tour of the island, but found on arrival that we had been formally invited by the Prime Minister to be guests of the Government. This was a charming thought, but for me it turned a carefree holiday into a strenuous period of much formality. I asked leave to cut a great deal of what had been arranged for me, but even so we left at 6.30 a.m. next morning for the long run to Anuradhapura. This was the ancient capital of Ceylon, and it is world famous for its Bo tree, undoubtedly the oldest tree in the world. It is a sapling of that under which the Buddha attained Enlightenment at Buddha Gaya, and as such was planted in Ceylon by the Emperor Asoka's son about 200 BC. We paid our respects to it before being hurried on to Pollonaruwa, another ancient capital, which even after a thousand years of decay still had the feel of holy ground. We stayed at the rest house built out over the lake, and at dawn walked silently about the ruined city, admiring its temples, standing statues, and above all the complex of carvings in the solid rock known as the Gal Vihara. The reclining Buddha is a remarkable work of art, as is a seated Buddha at the other end. But for me the greatest figure, one of the six finest I have seen anywhere in the world, is that most often called the weeping Ananda, standing at his master's side. It is difficult to get a good photograph and the finest I know, as the best description of its spiritual power, is in the *Asian Journal* of Father Merton. Whether considered as Ananda or as a third figure of the Buddha it breathes for me a majesty, a beauty and a spiritual strength which would take me, if anything could, across the world again to kneel once more before it.

We left this beautiful place with regret for we had to hurry to lunch with the Governor-General at Kandy. There, his official residence was a lovely abode of peace, with its garden, the tame monkeys and the brilliant birds. After more sightseeing and paying the necessary calls on the leading Buddhist theras, we drove back the next day to Colombo to prepare for a great reception in our honour at the headquarters of the regional centre of the World Fellowship of Buddhists for Ceylon. It was delightful, save that the drumming of the famous Kandyan Dancers made it difficult to hear what anyone said. Later, in the large hall, with Dr Walpola Rahula, then Vice-Chancellor of Vidyodhya University, in the chair, I made a speech not, I gather, entirely as required. I *would* talk about world Buddhism and in their minds was the firm belief: 'Here, in the Theravada of Ceylon we have it. Why look elsewhere?'

In the evening the Prime Minister invited some twenty guests to meet us for dinner in his own house. This, we were told later by Dr Malalasekera, was designed to show appreciation of the work of our Society for the Dhamma, and it was so genuine and sincere that I for one was deeply moved by it. As we left on the following morning I said to the Governor-General's aide, 'If this is how you treat us for a visit, what do you do for royalty?' He replied, 'For us you *are* royalty. . . .' Could there be a more charming and memorable farewell?

I returned to find that a booklet, *The Field of Theosophy*, containing three lectures which I had given to the Theosophical Society, had just been published, and I modestly claim it as a much-needed gift to the Theosophical movement. I had never lost touch with the parent Society, and was even then working on the third and definitive edition of *The Mahatma Letters to A. P. Sinnett*, which appeared in 1972. I was also working on *An Abridgement of the Secret Doctrine* of H. P. Blavatsky which, after my final talk with my co-editor Miss Preston at Adyar, also came out in 1966. The new booklet was an attempt to make clear the basic principles implied in the term 'Theosophy'. All teachers suffer from students interested in the teaching who prefer to write books about what they think it means rather than to study, and encourage others to study, the early writings for themselves. Does a Christian need more than the New Testament, or a Buddhist more than a vast range of the scriptures of its schools? With Theosophy the decline was rapid, perhaps because the teaching of this ancient wisdom was presented to the Western mind at too high a level. True, H.P.B. added in her last years *The Key to Theosophy* which is clear enough for all, and these, with W. Q. Judge's *Ocean of Theosophy* and *The Voice of the Silence* make just five volumes. The leaders of the movement who assumed control in the next twenty years could not resist the temptation to 'explain' to all and sundry what these volumes meant, and by 1926, when I left the Theosophical Society in disgust, not one of those books was on the bookstall at the Society's headquarters. It was therefore not surprising that other Theosophical Societies, such as the United Lodge of Theosophists, were founded to preserve and make known the teaching as given. For twenty years Boris de Zirkoff has worked in Los Angeles to produce the *Collected Writings of H. P. Blavatsky*, with texts restored to their original state before later 'editing', and in a smaller way Mrs Elsie Benjamin conducts a Corresponding Fellows' Lodge from Worthing, sending through the post in her monthly bulletin the help that scattered students need.

But something more was required, and I supported that tower of strength and knowledge, Mr Geoffrey Farthing, one time General

Secretary of the T.S. in England, in the foundation of The Blavatsky Trust, in an attempt to wean Lodges of the parent body from pseudo-Theosophy, and to give them at least a list of books which contain the original teaching. Whether an individual finds the vast cycle of wisdom offered to the world under that title to be true is for that student to decide, but at least let it be clear what is and what is not 'Theosophy'.

23
An Old Bailey Judge

By 1967 I was spending most of my time at the Old Bailey as a Commissioner, one of the permanent judges in all but name. When I heard that more such judges were to be appointed I naturally wished to be one of their number, and by indirect channels let my respectful wish become known to the Lord Chancellor, Lord Gardiner. Early in 1968 he sent for me and, while wondering with a smile how my appointment at the age of sixty-seven would appeal to others, invited me to be one of two new judges. I was deeply grateful, though sad to know that it meant immediate resignation from the Recordership of Guildford. When the appointment was announced, the Saddlers' Company kindly presented me with a new wig and gown, a judge's wig differing from that of a barrister in the arrangement of its curls and what seems to be the remains of the tonsure on its crown.

At the Old Bailey I had the choice of a court. I chose Court Four West, which was on the top floor of a block of converted offices opposite the entrance of the main building. From my earliest days as a recorder or as chairman of magistrates I had preferred a small court, more intimate and friendly than the enormous rooms of No. 1 and No. 2 of the Old Bailey and many of those in the new courts opened in 1973. I liked the jury beside me so that I could, when summing up, talk quietly and intimately and see their reactions; on the other side of me would be the witness, whose facial expression under stress would tell me after long experience a good deal of his character. And my No. 4 Court had a door at the back which opened on to real fresh air and sunlight, which I preferred to any form of air-conditioning.

I was greeted by the Bar with charming speeches, and my chambers gave me a dinner at the Garrick Club. I had some hundred letters of congratulation, many from persons I had not heard of for a great many years. The oldest, perhaps, was my father's chauffeur, Vincent, who went off to the wars in 1914 and now wrote to congratulate me in 1968.

This is no place to write at length on the duties and functions of a judge, though the public views on them seem peculiar. It may be enough to say that he does not in the true sense 'try' a case; that is the function of the jury. He is, rather, an umpire, there to see fair play according to the rules. His powers are considerable. He sits under the Royal Arms and represents the Crown, in whose name every charge of crime is presented. When the Prince of Wales had lunch with the sheriffs and other judges he expressed a wish to sit in a court for a while in the afternoon. Someone at lunch asked the judge who was trying the case which the Prince would be attending what would happen when he came into court. Would the Court stand up? 'Certainly not,' replied the judge, 'I'm his Mum!' And that is true, in the sense that the Court rises on the entrance of the judge, not out of respect for him personally but because he is in that sense and for that period the Sovereign. He exercises power over the prisoner, and can send him to the cells for impertinence; over the jury, to release any one of them for good cause from further attendance, and to be severe with those arriving late, or lacking in courtesy to the Court. He also has power over the Bar, and once, I regret to say, I had to tell a Queen's Counsel that if he did not stop interrupting prosecuting counsel, who was quite properly cross-examining his client, I would ask him to leave the court. He has power over witnesses, as to their demeanour, language used, and even manner of dress; and over the police, as a curious example illustrates. The dock, like the cells below, is notionally part of Brixton Prison, and the prison officers, once called warders, are in charge of it. The police in the well of the court have no jurisdiction over it. Once, when the prisoner before me produced a razor blade and slashed his wrists, the two dock officers had to fight to prevent him succeeding in his suicide. The police in court did nothing until I shouted to them from the bench to get into the dock and help. By thus breaking a rule I released them into action!

In brief, with one exception the judge controls the whole proceedings, from his entry into court to his leaving it. The one exception concerns the Press. Trials in this country are public trials, and what is said and done in public may be reported in the newspapers. There are now certain statutory exceptions, and the judge can always for good reason 'close the court', but in such matters as keeping out the name of the witness-victim, or someone's address, I have often *asked* the Press to omit it from their reports and my request has never been refused.

There are those who visualise a trial as being a long wrangle over law, each counsel with a pile of law books beside him. This rarely occurs in a criminal trial; in my court very rarely indeed. But should there be a point of law to be taken, it is the business of the Bar to raise it and to provide the requisite authorities for the judge to consider. But the judge must be master of the evidence as given, whether he himself believes a word of it or not. He is making notes nearly all the time, and the shorthand writer is taking down every word which, if required, will be transcribed for use in the Court of Appeal. There will be jokes at times, even from the Bench, and they do release tension. It may be unconscious humour. Once during a train strike I discussed with the jury their plans for arriving the following morning. Those living in the radius of the tubes and buses, I remarked, would manage all right, but those coming into London by steam train would be in some difficulty. I was puzzled at the jury's guffaw of merriment. As I myself arrived by car I had forgotten the advent of electrification. But jokes should never be made at the expense of the defendant. I regard that as rude, and I do not remember a defendant being rude to me.

Does a judge defend the police against attacks on them? My answer is yes and no. Yes, as against irresponsible attacks at large made in the hopes that some member of the jury will be prejudiced thereby into disbelieving their evidence. No, where there is credible evidence that some officer has fallen, in that particular case, from the usual high standard of the Force as a whole. I am prepared to believe, for example, that an officer, quite certain of the defendant's guilt, may at times exaggerate the evidence against him, or rough-handle the man who, as often as not, is successfully kicking him between the legs. But 90 per cent of the attacks on the police, a force which is still the envy of the civilised world, are completely unjustified.

Unless I was 'part-heard' I would have no idea, when I walked into court in the morning, what case I should be trying. I would listen to the indictment being read and the prisoner's plea to it, and if the plea were not guilty a jury would be sworn. It is well that there are twelve jurors, for they are a strange collection, probably a fair cross-section of the community. Male and female, old and young, well-educated or apparently of low degree in intelligence and worldly standing, it is their joint and unanimous verdict which is required. I approve, however, of the modern law of majority verdicts, for it eliminates the crank, who never believes the police, or who hates the Establishment, or even holds that 'what does a little burglary or violence matter if it does not affect me?' And it eliminates the man who has been got at, though I believe this to be very, very rare. The newly sworn members listen with great attention to the opening by counsel, who makes it clear that they are sworn not to find out the truth but to decide whether or not they are collectively sure that *that* prisoner is guilty of *that* offence.

Most trials, unless of great length, run easily for the judge. He notes the evidence, makes notes for his summing up, listens to the speeches of counsel (or does he? I make no personal confession) and then sums up.

Whether or not in the course of time I sometimes mixed my metaphors I do not know, but I must include the finest of all, attributed to a Mr Justice Kenyon. A butler had been stealing his master's wine, and the sentence contained the following magnificent lines: 'Dead to every claim of natural affection, and blind to your own real interest, you burst through all the restraints of religion and morality, and have for many years been feathering your nest with your master's bottles'!

Then comes the verdict. If 'not guilty', that is the end of the charge against the prisoner and he is discharged. If 'guilty', or if the prisoner had pleaded guilty at the outset, the trial passes into the judge's hands and the jury too can be released. No judge likes sentencing, and the reason is obvious. Here is a fellow human being whose fate, subject to a right of appeal, is now in your hands. You have two duties to perform and they are incompatible. First, you must heed the clear rights of the community whose voice you are. This mugger, raper, burglar, drunken stabber, deliberate swindler on a hideous scale should, say the people at large, be punished, and all the more so if he has previous convictions of gravity.

The defending counsel speaks in mitigation of punishment, and may support his remarks with cogent evidence. Here is the man's point of view, with the reasons for his crime and his plans for the future. Where is the middle way between these conflicting needs? Emotion should have no part in the choice. One may hate this man for his crimes, or, as I would feel, hate the crimes which he allowed himself to commit; or one may feel great sympathy for a man so tempted, or under such emotional duress. And one is remembering that a sentence of imprisonment seldom hurts the convicted man alone. His wife and family, relations, friends, employer or employees alike may suffer considerably, and in some proportion to your sentence.

To find the middle way between the demands of the community and the requests of the man the judge wants all help available. He is given, and this the public do not seem to understand, a good deal of information which is not revealed at the trial, and may never be known to anyone else in court. He will have already received a Social Enquiry Report from the Probation Service, a dedicated set of men and women who deserve from the public profound admiration and regard. He may be *shown* by defending counsel reports from the man's employers or from the governor of the prison where he is then confined, or a Borstal Report, or letters from local clergy, from his wife, or from one of the many societies hard at work in helping men and women towards decent citizenship. There may be a psychiatrist's report, or the doctor in person. Their worth is a matter of debate.

When I served for a while on the Council of the Institute for the Study and Treatment of Delinquency, I sat as chairman of a committee to draft a booklet on *Psychology and Criminal Procedure*. The committee was composed of doctors and lawyers, the latter including Gerald Gardiner, later Lord Chancellor, and the former Dr Edward Glover, who provided most of the material while I wrote most of what the committee agreed. Psychiatry has greatly advanced since the booklet's publication in 1951, and I have personally had great help from psychiatric evidence. But how far should one allow the fact that the prisoner is 'abnormal' to influence the sentence? Is not any man who has become a confirmed and violent criminal 'abnormal'? One can but add the information given to that already in hand and out of it all strive, sometimes in agony of mind, for the right sentence.

The sentence can of course be adjourned for further evidence about the accused, and in such a case I would ask counsel to help me with some clear plan for the defendant's future. If told, for example, that he had moved from his old environment of drinking and criminal companions, had a new job, was now engaged to be married, and was genuinely contrite and unlikely to offend again, I would be influenced to be merciful.

But sooner or later one is left to decide a sentence which is 'just', and I would remember my family motto: 'Be always Just'. I would put the evidence into a mental computer and rehearse aloud the factors for and against the prisoner when I sentenced him. Sometimes the sentence had to be long, but I had already seen the effect of a long sentence on a fellow human being. A friend of mine shot his girl friend and then himself. Both bullets lodged in their respective backs but both survived. He was sentenced for attempted murder to life imprisonment, which was described by the judge as merciful for it meant that he could be released at the Home Secretary's will. I visited him for five years and then reported to the Prison Commissioners that in my view he had reached a point of no return, and that further time in prison would break his character for good. He was released, and is now a normal and well-known citizen. I have reason to dislike long sentences.

It may be that my total acceptance of the law of Karma has affected my feeling for the right sentence. This law of cause–effect, well known to science, operates throughout nature, and controls human behaviour on the principle of 'As ye sow, so shall ye also reap'. But it includes the converse of the Christian doctrine, that 'as ye are reaping so did ye sow'. In brief, we are the sum total of our own causation, and will be, in the next life, this total as modified by our reactions in this life and our new causation.

The man in the dock, therefore, was, in committing the crime, the net result of a series of causes which produced the effect of the crime. In the wider, cosmic sense, he has brought himself to the dock, and will receive the sentence which he has karmically incurred. True, his birth and environment in this life were not caused in this life, but were the effect of multiple causation in his lives gone by, and thus become one ingredient in the total cause–effect before me. And his karma of the moment includes me as the judge! I, as part of my karma, have the duty to pass sentence on him, and if it is not 'right' we shall both suffer, rightly, for our several causation. The inter-action of all these causes makes one dizzy, but the law still operates, and is not 'destiny', but sense. 'As ye sow, so shall ye also reap.' Is that not reasonable, and merciful and 'right'?

Nor does the law of Karma conflict with that of compassion. They are one, and operate within the joint ambit of their effect on me. Compassion is a quality of the heart which assists in the right application of the law of Karma. There is therefore no conflict between the immutable law and the human sentence.

All in all I thoroughly enjoyed my period on the Bench, and it left me ample time for other interests. I would arrive about 10 in the morning, and cope with whatever was waiting for me in my room, and would often be free by 10.15. The Court sat at 10.30. This left me, say, fifteen minutes in which to work on a lecture, revise a chap-ter, correct proofs or finish a poem. One can do a lot in fifteen minutes, and there are many of these periods in the day. I prefer to make time my servant rather than an inconvenient master, and the precise routine of a working day was helpful. The Court rose at one o'clock and the West Court judges crossed the road to have lunch with and talk shop with brother judges as guests of the City Sheriff on duty for the day. Here we met eminent and interesting other guests, foreign judges, diplomats, and on one occasion the Queen. Then back to Court at 2, and I personally would rise at 4, finding that the shorthand writer and the jury, if no one else, had by that time had enough for the day. I would then, as I put it to someone, 'start work', on one or more of my dozen other interests and activities.

There were interruptions in this smooth routine. In June 1975 I passed a lenient sentence on a coloured youth who pleaded guilty to rape – lenient because I thought that sentence to be right, and still do. The Press blew up, apparently to orders. As a pressman whom

I had known for many years at the Old Bailey told me on the telephone, thinking I might be disturbed by the sudden outcry, 'We were told to blow it up for a bit as there was nothing else in the news; then, a few days later we were told to cut it.' In this case, as in most others, I had information about the youth of which the Press and the public knew nothing, and it was from what I read in court in the papers before me, as well as what I was told by counsel for the defence, that I formed my own view of the gravity of the rape. But the winds of fury howled about me. A Question, so I was told, was asked in the House. Articles and leaders appeared in the newspapers. Lord Elwyn-Jones, the Lord Chancellor, asked me for a report. When I went to see him he seemed as amused as I at the information that no less than six other youths had received the same sentence for rape in the previous twelve months, without a whisper of indignation, and that five others had only been fined! Of the ceaseless telephone calls and letters to my private house, mostly obscene, I only remember being surprised at the paucity of their vocabulary. One letter was all but incredible. The Borough Council of Bootle informed me that a resolution had been passed that in view of my sentence I should resign as a judge. I was with difficulty dissuaded from writing back on an open postcard, 'Where's Bootle?' Another letter did speak of blowing in my windows, but in terms of entertainment this did not match the impertinence of Bootle, wherever that is.

I sat on until the following December and into the New Year, when my career as a judge, which had begun with almost a request to be appointed, ended in pure melodrama when I was, 'as near as dammit', as an old gardener used to say, thrown out. There was some muddle between the Lord Chancellor's office and the City officials over the proper date of my retirement. One Friday afternoon the Chief Clerk, Leslie Boyd, appeared in my court and indicated that he wished me to rise so that he could speak to me in my room. I did so, and he calmly informed me that I was no longer a judge. I replied, in my usual simple vocabulary, 'Bosh. I am part-heard, I have a jury out in another case, and a sentence adjourned until Monday. Phone somebody and sort it out!' In the end I was graciously granted an extension of time until the following Tuesday, when an official farewell in the main building had already been arranged. Then I did appear in robes for the last time, and in No. 1 Court. The newly appointed Recorder, J. W. Miskin, asked the

Common Serjeant, my old friend Mervyn Griffith-Jones, to speak on behalf of the judges, and he was followed by members of the Bar and the Chief Clerk, on behalf of the building's legal staff. As I looked round the packed court my eye caught those of friends of all degree who had worked with me in the long years gone by; solicitors and their clerks, barristers' clerks, the pressmen and shorthand writers, ushers, police, Sheriff's servants and even firemen. I was deeply moved, rather more than I expected. But with the opening words of my reply I brought myself back from emotion to history. 'It is', I said, 'just fifty-five years since I walked into this court, and heard the Attorney-General, F. E. Smith, arguing a point of law with the Judge.' I hope I was not too long, and I wondered if I really had been such a judge as the speakers depicted me. I was never 'a very great criminal judge', as my father had been described when he retired twenty years before, but I had striven in my own way to emulate some of the qualities then ascribed to him.

The immediate sequence to my retirement was a burst of television and radio interviews, and though at times I was not sure whether I was talking law or Buddhism at least it was all great fun. One question of course was asked again and again; 'How do you apply your Buddhist principles to a criminal trial?' I still do not know. I am, I presume, to some small extent these principles; they had become part of the judge that was me. I answered my interviewers as best I could and soon, as I expected, sank into oblivion. There remains a typewriter and an ageing but not yet finished brain.

Youth in Age

The twilight falls. Inevitable hands
Draw the soft curtains of the fading day.
All changes, grows, grows old. Nature demands
A cycle absolute of growth-decay.
Birth follows, of the flesh, and every hour
The wakening mind, when limbs of courage leap
To fresh awareness, widens, bursts in flower
Awhile in splendour, till the body's sleep.

So life, resistless, strides upon the hills
Of our becoming and with laughing tread
Creates and uses, and in using kills,
Till every form with force of life lies dead.

The dissolution of recurring night
Awaits the body. For the spirit, light.

24
The End of a Cycle

In the summer of 1968 Puck and I returned for a tour of Ireland, and found that little of what is now Eire had changed in thirty years. The scenery was still glorious, the people as friendly as ever, and the light as soft and brilliant as I have not seen it even in the Himalayas. As I wrote at the end of a poem on Connemara:

> . . . And which is the lovelier none can say,
> The bloom on the hills at the close of day
> Or the light on the hills at dawn.

We flew to Majorca at Christmas, then little tourist-ridden, and we even bathed from the beach at the foot of the hotel. We swam a few strokes and then struggled to return before freezing up, but it was an admirable appetiser for the vast meals which followed. The next year we found Arès, a village not far from Bordeaux, where we had the most perfect bathing we ever enjoyed. A large pool, a hundred yards across, had been built in the corner of the Arcachon basin, which itself dried out at low tide. The water in the pool remained deep and warm and was refreshed at each tide with waves coming over the far wall. The sandy beach was private property and there was a tiny hotel in the corner. Our friends, Pierre and Tania Dupin, had a house in the village, and we talked Buddhism, for it was Pierre Dupin who made the French translation of my *Buddhism*. Tanya, his Russian wife, is the leading expert in France on Lithuanian, and in term-time received the language pandits of the universities for professional help. More important for us, she was a perfect cook.

There is another form of holiday, that of absorbing the peace and beauty of an old and lovely house in quiet surroundings. There are still many such in England, mostly in private hands. One such was Uppark, where Puck and I would stay with Lady Meade-Fetherstonhaugh and watch her renovating the fabric of old curtains with home-grown saponaria. Many more are available to those who can afford the amenities provided. Shrubland Hall, where Puck and I went many times, is a large eighteenth-century house in a thousand acres of ground on the highest point in Suffolk. Ten years ago we discussed with the owners, Lord and Lady de Saumarez, the best use for it, for its forty rooms had become a burden for a family of five. The decision was to turn it into a clinic, opened in 1968. Some patients/visitors like Puck and me, were content with a rest in a house of perfectly-proportioned rooms containing their original furniture; others seek what another patient vulgarly described as a fat-reducing machine. True, the diet varies according to need; for us it was light and perfectly adequate. From our room we looked thirty miles into the sunset; and without mail, telephone or visitors we found what I believe is a modern necessity, total abstraction at times from the noisy, revolving wheel of modern life.

In 1970 Puck made her last appearance at the Buddhist Society, to read an unpublished work by Dr D. T. Suzuki on the 100th anniversary of his birth; but she was failing in health. We celebrated her eightieth birthday in September 1971, with a party of old friends, but at Christmas-time her mind was failing and she began to lose contact with the world. She was taken to a nursing home in Finchley, where she was very well looked after, and for the next four years I would visit her twice a week, and she would appreciate that I was there. In December 1975 I was sent for from the Old Bailey and found her in a coma. She died on the 16th at the age of eighty-four. With help from Irmgard Schloegl, who had been staying with me for the last three years, I made arrangements for the cremation at Golders Green. There I read a Funeral Service based on that which I had written forty years before, and in January a Memorial Service was held at the Society in the presence of some seventy of her friends, many of whom had come from afar. I included in the Service a poem, 'I will go free', which Puck had written I know not when, but which I found among her papers, and it was read most beautifully by an old friend, Diana Moore. I was perhaps unwise to take the Service myself, for the strain was considerable, but who else had loved her so for fifty years? I ended, before the striking of our thousand-year-old gong, with the closing words of the original Funeral Service: 'When the day's work is ended night brings the benison of sleep. So death is the ending of a larger day, and in the night that follows every man finds rest, until he returns to fresh endeavour and to labours new. So has it been with this our sister, so will it be for all of us until the illusion of a separated self is finally transcended, and in the death of self we reach Enlightenment.'

I added, on returning home, lines which I did not write for publication, but, being true they may be included here.

FOR PUCK

One half of what for long was we
Has lived and loved and died again,
Leaving until we meet again
Only the tedium of me.

Many of the letters which I received when the news of her death was published were concerned with myself and the sense of loss which I should bear in the days to come; others spoke in terms which were often strangely the same in describing the writer's memory of Puck.

They spoke of her 'sense of hospitality, her stimulating companion-ship and her intuitive perception of others' troubles', and of her skill in dealing with them. Beyond 'her kindness and laughter and gal-lantry' some had found deeper levels in her heart and mind. They noted her 'intuitive directness of vision', 'her unique insights as well as charm'. If a few mentioned her forthright way of expressing her opinions it was by way of praise, for they admitted that her views were given to their ultimate benefit. She could teach. Martha Vaughan, one of our oldest friends and a deep student of Zen, remembered an informal group at one of our summer schools, when Puck, 'serene and gentle', spoke of the transmission of the Spirit. 'It was not *about* but straight from the source, and we all recognised it as such. She spoke as one who *knew* from her own experience that this was TRUTH.'

How sad I feel for those with no awareness of rebirth, who believe, and have to live with the belief, that their loved one is lost to them for ever. How fortunate I am to have recognised Puck at once as the companion of old enterprise, who in this life had by a few brief years preceded me into that rest and digestion of experience which for a period divides two lives. Here for me was no real parting; only a needful separation before reunion and some new job which hand in hand we shall, in our usual blend of love and laughter, just settle down and do.

I do not believe in coincidence, in the sense of two things happening without relationship, but it was strange indeed that one of those who came for the Service was my childhood friend, Rene, then Lady Burton. We planned my coming to stay with her in Kent when I was free of the Old Bailey and would now no longer be visiting Puck in Finchley. She wrote on returning home to congratulate me on the Service, but even as I read her letter the telephone rang, and I was told by a mutual friend of her instantaneous death that morning in a car crash. A fortnight later I was speaking at her own Memorial Service in Chelsea Old Church, and bade farewell to two of my oldest woman friends.

At the Society we had a remarkable series of distinguished visitors. In October 1973, the Dalai Lama came to London for a ten-day visit, and of course came to the Society. He had matured still further since we met in Sarnath in 1964, and in a talk with him at his hotel I learnt of plans for the future of his Indian home. We also had a visit from Dudjum Rimpoche, head of one of the major sects of the Nyingmapa school of Tibetan Buddhism; from the Sakya Pandita, head of the Sakya school, and in 1975 from the Karmapa, head of the Kargyudpa school, whom I had met at his monastery at Rumtek with Puck in 1964. Thus the heads of all four schools of Tibetan Buddhism had honoured us within two years.

In 1974 we celebrated our fiftieth anniversary, and produced a special issue of *The Middle Way*. The last survivor of the founders, I was awarded the annual prize of the Society for the Promotion of Buddhism, which was founded in Tokyo in 1965 by Mr Yehan Numata. I was told that I was the first non-Japanese to receive it, and regretted that I could not fly to Tokyo for the prize-giving ceremony. The silver casting of the Wheel of Life, a certificate about me and a handsome cheque were nevertheless given me by Mr Numata himself. He chose 8 April, which in Japan is honoured as the Buddha's birthday, to fly to London for the presentation. Irmgard Schloegl invited him to make it during a session of her Zen training class at the Society. The atmosphere of her class impressed me as much as Mr Numata's charming speech.

During these years I produced further works on Buddhism, including a volume called *Buddhist Poems*, although it also contained others of a different calibre and type. I was also writing from time to time for Christmas parties at home comic poems about a character called Bert, a typical low-class, humorous villain who successfully evaded the consequences of a life spent in various forms of non-violent dishonesty. These verses reached an old friend on the B.B.C., Hallam Tennyson, who offered to put them on the radio. After an introduction by me they were read by a professional actor and were very well received. But their production added an element of confusion to my correspondence and press articles about me in the first two months of 1976. By the same post I would sometimes receive letters about Puck's death, about my retirement from the Old Bailey, to which the Press added comments varying from 'the last of the eccentrics' to 'the gentle judge', or 'the Buddhist judge', and finally, letters and articles in praise of 'Bert'. This curious blend, requiring very different answers, exercised my patience and my sense of humour to the full. At the same time I was appearing on television and radio, discussing the curious blend of my Buddhist-legal career, and accepting invitations to speak at organisations of which at the time I had not even heard. Then it all came to an end, and I was left to face the future in quietude and alone. Inevitably I sat back to sum up the Society and myself.

The Society was flourishing, but what of the quality of our membership? We have produced from our midst no first-class scholar. Dr Edward Conze joined us as a Vice-President when he was already the leading authority in Europe on the Prajnaparamita, 'the Wisdom which has gone beyond'. The same applies to Dr Horner, President of the Pali Text Society, another world-wide scholar whom we did not, so to speak, ourselves produce. Perhaps the one expert of our own production is Dr Irmgard Schloegl, at one time a member of my Zen class. In 1960 she went to Daitokuji in

Kyoto to undergo Zen training at its monastery as a lay student, and finally returned in 1972 with permission from her teacher to make available in England the method of Zen training of the Rinzai School of Buddhism. This she does in her very full class at the Society, and is planning, with our full support, an independent Zen Centre which will work in conjunction with it.

Today the Centre which Puck and I visualised exists. It provides information for inquirers and a bookstall which, with its booklist, has reached a remarkable turnover. Its Journal, *The Middle Way*, goes all over the world. Lectures are provided and the Shrine Room is open to all, both at the Society and at public halls, as is the annual Summer School. Members can use the lending and reference libraries, and attend a wide range of classes at headquarters. Those living away can have the Correspondence Course on Buddhism, and write to the tutor allocated. There is a Dana Fund for those in need. This, with its total lack of dogma as to what is Buddhism, and its welcome to all who come without the least attempt to convert them to our views, provides indeed the Centre which we planned and opened over fifty years ago. At least we did not work so long and steadily in vain.

Then what of myself? My seventy-fifth birthday seemed a good moment to 'inquire within'. While I was still at Cambridge, *The Secret Doctrine* had answered my overall inquiry as to the nature and genesis of the universe, its ceaseless 'coming to be, ceasing to be'. As a way along which to reach direct awareness of this 'accumulated wisdom of the ages' I had chosen Buddhism, though my adoption of it was so immediate and strong that I would think that this was not my first life as a Buddhist. I studied the strong moral philosophy of the Theravada and, just when I was ready for something more, found the main teaching of the Mahayana. With its supreme heights of mystical-metaphysics I was for a long while unable to cope; with its doctrine of unlimited compassion, love strong-based on reason and reaching to the stars, I came to terms at once, having found and almost knelt before the superb description of it in *The Voice of the Silence*. I felt, without reasoning about it, the twofold strength of Buddhism, its Wisdom and its Compassion, the mind to seek the Truth and the heart to become one with it. If, later, I should at times peep through the dark walls of self into the light of Zen, each vision would be an impulse for greater effort to know, to love and to live accordingly.

I seem to propel myself with the aid of principles, cosmic principles which I call thought-forces, and this may one day prove to be the right way for the Western mind to approach the high truths of Religion. I am more and more using the analogy of rising, striving for a lift of my habitual level of consciousness towards the Everest of innate Totality. This Ultimate, I believe, comes forth in cycles for which, like the new concept of 'light-years', are mostly too large for the human intellect to grasp as actuality. I see the origin of these cycles as Life, the Life-force of the universe, manifesting unceasingly in innumerable forms. Each of these has its place in the scheme of things. As a Zen master put it, 'The snow-flakes fall, each snow-flake in its proper place'. Here is purpose and meaning in the Whole and therefore in each part of it. I find purpose and meaning in every form of life, and I cannot conceive of any thing as dead. There is also cosmic meaning in every event, and in each 'a finger pointing to the moon'.

I had to find my own dharma, my job to do. Karma is a blend of cause–effect so close that both are one, and I, as all other forms, am an incalculable quantity of causes precipitated in the complex globule I call me, as a compound visible effect. In the course of my present self-made cycle of rebirth what is right for me to do now? That is for me to discover, but I shall not act alone. I shall depend on others as others upon me because in the most profound phrase I know: 'There are no others.' Life is one, and all the forms of it are brother forms of it. Hence the thundering, unavoidable conclusion that compassion, ultimate love, is indeed the law of the universe, a law which rules each part of it; now, for there is no other time but now; here, for there is no other place but here, and doing this. I know this to be true. Would that I could act accordingly.

How shall I find my present dharma? Who or What will tell me what to do? I must beware of claimed Authority. If I am to 'waken the mind to abide nowhere' I must beware of bondage, whether by master, book or spoken word. I am not yet free, for I still look to the ancient Wisdom of Theosophy, and the words of Zen masters, and the works of Dr Suzuki, and find them true, and have not found one word untrue. Here is for me 'provisional authority', but I must learn to stand on my own feet, no longer leaning any way at all. But what of the inner 'monitor' which sometimes seems to give one orders what to do? Here is a dangerous concept, obedience to an inner voice, for this voice can easily be self, the yapping of the dog of self now modified to the wooing notes of a reasonable suggestion. Or it can be a form of psychic phenomenon such as the 'guides', which certainly exist, or so I believe, on the astral or psychic plane and are fully described in the records of Theosophy. How shall I know when it is Self speaking, the Buddha-Mind within? That it is the voice of the intuition giving me orders, this faculty which, when it speaks is unmistakable, making clear beyond all argument the next-thing-to-be-done? The only answer is that one *knows*, for that is the hall-mark of intuitive awareness.

On these occasions one is content to be a conduit pipe, an experience which at any level is good discipline for the ego. I felt it once when I took the chair at the Albert Hall for a judo festival. Whether the power came from behind, from the organ thundering out the National Anthem, or from the front with the 'feedback' of eight thousand people responding to my opening remarks, there was a feeling as of being a valve receiving and distributing the force released. Something of the same feeling, but from a higher level, comes when receiving orders from my Self. There is willing obedience without questioning the meaning and purpose of Totality, or the infinite unimportance of that which now contentedly gets on with the next-thing-to-be-done.

I have learnt by teaching, for thus I test what I think I know. By discussion I see how to apply it. By helping others to understand I am helped along the Way. But in all that we think and teach and do, right motive is essential. Am I teaching in order to be known as a teacher, or discussing in order to boast of my own views, or helping others for the karmic merit of such help? I must beware, for the least thought of self, as someone said, 'back-fires into the ego and blows it up like a balloon'.

For the rest, I must accept what comes. It is all equally Right, and may be dimly seen to be so by those who study karmic cycles in the process of cosmic manifestation. Above all, I must accept suffering, for thus alone we learn. Let us laugh, but let us also cry when tears have healing value. Perhaps we English do not cry enough, and thus, to our detriment, suppress the force aroused, whatever be its emotional parentage. I like the story about Soyen Shaku, the Zen master of Dr D. T. Suzuki. One day he walked past a house in which he heard weeping, for the man of the house had died. He walked in, being known to the household, and sat down and cried with them. He was asked, 'Master, how can you weep? Surely *you* are beyond such things?' He replied, still crying, 'It is this which puts me beyond such things.'

But enough of myself. What of religion in the West, and the Buddhist Society's contribution towards the need for it? For the need is clear, not only for some specific religion, to be used as a crutch or a friendly arm upon the upward way, but beyond this, a revived sense of Religion. The distinction is important. All religions are so many ways or means of rising into the heart-mind of Religion, a growing awareness of the God within, however named. Man is a religious animal and fails for want of it, and no technology, no vast array of scientific formulae can fill the empty heart. At present we bracket religion with science, philosophy, psychology and other pursuits of the mind. We even confuse religion and ideologies, and teach in the schools a series of 'religions' which include Socialism, Communism and Humanism. These are not ways to God but lie flat upon the floor of our perpetual material striving, resulting in conflict of man against man, for money, power and the ego's flatulence. Religion, I submit, is the state of heart and mind in which all else is done, and the reason for doing it. Each religion, old or new, can serve this end, and the value of the World Congress of Faiths, and other organisations bringing men and women of religious heart together, is half way to this end. But still we need, and man needs, Religion itself as the flame which lights him along the path of some religion to the common goal.

For want of Religion man is not only mentally at sea, but sick. As Carl Jung said, 'Among my patients in the second half of life there has not been one whose problem in the last resort was not that of finding a religious outlook on life. It is safe to say that every one of them fell ill because he had lost that which the living religions of every age have given to their followers, and none of them has been really healed who did not regain his religious outlook.' Until the eyes of Western man are lifted towards his own divinity he will be sick indeed, and die beneath the grinding wheels of his own technology. Meanwhile, what use is there in teaching children facts about the bodies of a few religions, ignoring the Light which gave them birth? Is this better than a kind of mind's geography? Do I want to know about five ways to Timbuctoo when I know nothing of Timbuctoo, and have no desire to go there? Let all religions be willing not merely to be friends, but side by side to achieve what Bodhidharma, founder of Zen Buddhism, called a 'direct seeing into the heart of man'. Let us seek it, for those who seek will climb the mountain side by side, each on his own path, and know that at the summit they and their paths will have alike transcended difference.

What has the Buddhist Society, my life's work, done to realise this ideal? We have made no attempt to impose on the West a ready-made set of forms called Buddhism, expecting the Western mind to adopt them. As Dr Malalasekera wrote in an article for *The Middle Way*, 'Old religions in meeting these needs [the religious needs of mankind] may have to give free formulation to their doctrines and disciplines, integrating the new with the old, tradition with science and verifying assumptions with facts. No religion worthy of the name can be merely a static conveyor of ancient thought.' My wife and I were inspired when we formulated the Object of the Society: 'To publish and make known the principles of Buddhism, and to encourage the study and practice of these principles.' We have offered principles to the West, agreeing with Carl Jung that 'What the East has to give us should be merely a help in the work which we still have to do'. We believed and I believe that these principles, studied and applied, may be acceptable as tested truths of universal value which lift the heart-mind towards the Religion of which they are but dimly illumined parts. If these, or any of them, under any name, are found of value in the war which must be won against gross selfishness and crass materialism, we shall not have worked in vain.

One school of Buddhism, however, is beyond the category of intellectual principles, however noble and profound. Zen Buddhism, that of the Rinzai school, is different from any other religious school I know. It is not concerned with knowledge, nor, in the first place, with what is often regarded as the religious life. It produces an expansion of consciousness which comes from lives of training designed to break the bonds of self, 'without reliance on the scriptures or any words to see directly into the heart of man and to attain Buddhahood'. The light of such awareness has gleamed in the eyes of holy men throughout the ages, however named. Now we in the West have been made aware of it, and a few bold spirits, largely on the information given them in the writings of Dr D. T. Suzuki, want to find it, and directly, without services or ritual, and beyond the concepts which we find wrapped up in words. As I made clear in my *A Western Approach to Zen* it is absurd to expect a body of Rinzai Zen masters to settle in Europe, and equally foolish to expect all those who wish to train under a master to find the money and time for years in a Zen monastery in Japan. Zen must be made achievable in the West according to some system of our own devising. Or at least there must be a system of valid approach to bring the student into the field of what I have called 'illumined thought', when flashes of the true awareness are more likely to appear. Who knows, before long we may produce Zen masters of our own? Has it not been said, 'When the pupil is ready the master appears'?

If it is difficult to pass through years of traditional Zen training under the guidance of a master in Japan, how much more difficult will it be for the Western mind, fast-set in an alien tradition, to succeed with some new method without a qualified teacher, and alone? But with a powerful will, right motive unconcerned with self, and a system which involves the whole man in all the day's activities, some means may be devised to provide the few with the crown of life itself, some measure of Enlightenment.

25
Towards the Centre

In the Introduction I described the arrangement of these memoirs as two parallel spines with a dozen or more collateral ribs. The result may have been unusual anatomy but it is a fair description of my life. As to the first spine, my career in Law ended with my retirement from the Old Bailey. My interest in law as such was never profound, but thanks to a blend of common law principles and common sense, applied I believe with a natural sense of justice, I was never, in some twenty-five years on the Bench in one capacity or another, reversed on appeal on a point of law. As to the other spine, my work in the field of Theosophy and Buddhism will cease for a while with my present life.

In most of the ribs my activity is ended but my interest remains. My travelling days are over, even with a car in France, yet I am still a good driver, and in the course of fifty years' driving have never been in trouble with the police. I hold that the essence of good driving is good manners, and as a proposition it has served me well. For French cathedrals and the ballet and the pursuit of Chinese art, I am content with television and my memory. For poetry, I still have a bookcase filled with the works of many favourite poets and with anthologies, and a pencil and paper are ever at hand for my own delight. Orthodox and unorthodox treatment have between them kept in use not only my ageing body but an ageing car and a much older house. All, with reasonable care, still serve me well. For the rest, when not engaged in the garden, or in the company of my friends, I have about me books and music, a wealth of beauty, and a thousand memories.

The old are apt to be lonely, and old men usually need someone to 'look after them'. I am fortunate in my Italian housekeeper and friend, Maria Genovese, who for twenty years has managed, for my wife and me, and now for me, our over-large yet elegant and peaceful home. She may be a little uncertain in her sense of time, but those fortunate enough to prove the fact agree that she is a quite magnificent cook!

And so I face retirement with content. Only the empty mind can fear retirement. I shall live, the last of my family, in London, where my forebears lived and died; it is the capital of that shrinking corner of the cultured world we knew and loved as England. Its body may look different; the heart is sound. With all respect to our immediate neighbours, it was Englishmen who won two wars when it seemed there was no alternative to surrender, and any one who feels the pulse of the last night of the Proms may reasonably hold that 'there'll always be an England', or at least for many years to come.

I now have time to work at things which are to me of more importance than those I have laid aside. I welcome time to look within, at the distance which still lies between what I am and what I would be, and the effort needed to reduce the gap. Now I can study more deeply the Wisdom which in many a published work I have attempted to describe. This Wisdom is, at our stage of development, at once the womb of laughter and of tears: laughter, for here on earth nothing is to be taken seriously; tears, for the All-Enlightened One was right. 'All is suffering' until we remove its cause, the egocentric, personal desire which rages and will ever rage until the illusion of a separate self is dead. Is this pessimism? I reject the term as firmly as that of optimism. I prefer to observe, to accept and to act accordingly, knowing joyously beyond all doubt that, as the Zen masters teach, 'It's all Right', all caused and one with its effect in what is for me the unimaginable harmony of Karmic Law.

The title of this work is not facetious, but contains more truth than I can explain, even to myself. There are of course two sides to every thing, even a circle, for the universe is built upon duality. Yet every pair of opposites is more than the two sides of a coin. It is, and never ceases to be the One from which both came. This Oneness is the Centre which, 'abiding nowhere', is each point of its circumference. Here is mystery, in a world of intuitive awareness to which, one day, knowingly, we shall arrive. At least, as we grasp both sides of the circle we shall be moving towards its centre, the Self within, which will be found to be at the same time light and life and love.

The body rests. The mind, releasing old attachment, is larger for the release. Beliefs are recognised as such, and knowledge fades before the Wisdom which appears in moments of awareness of the Self we are. If pleasure-pain fast loses its immediate value, and happiness for me in this life died some years ago, a sense of joy remains, and lights and warms a heart which dares at times to be content with something worthwhile done.

Puck was right in her last remark to me: 'There must be suffering. The heart must break.' Only when self, the cause of all our suffering is dead, will Self, the laughing, all-compassionate Self take over, and in those moments of enlightenment, love itself be crowned with light.

In a few years I shall die again, and after a period of rest, digestion of experience, and newly developed faculty, return to some point on 'the circle centreless', to seek and find the Next-Thing-to-be-Done and, with old friends and new, just set to work to do it.

Re-dedication to Puck

The lover in his love replete
Gives all, of faculty and boundless will,
To noble deeds the heart yearns to fulfil,
And nurtures them in golden light until
He lays them at her feet.

But I, un-whole, a riven part,
Have nought wherewith to build this royal array,
Have nothing left in jewelled words to say,
Have nothing humbly at your feet to lay.
You are my heart.

Appendix
Twelve Principles of Buddhism

Buddhism today is divided, broadly speaking, into the Southern School, or *Theravada*, 'the Teaching of the Elders', including Ceylon, Burma, Thailand, Cambodia and parts of India (which is not, however, any longer a Buddhist country) and the Northern School, or *Mahayana*, which covers Tibet, Mongolia and millions of the population of China, Korea, Vietnam and Japan. These schools, tolerant towards each other, are the complementary aspects of one whole.

Buddhism is called the religion of peace because there has never been a Buddhist war, nor has any man at any time been persecuted by a Buddhist organisation for his beliefs or the expression of them.

The Sangha was founded by the Buddha, and is the oldest religious order in existence today. The monks are under strict discipline, and in all schools are respected and supported by the public as setting an example of the Buddhist way of life. They spend their time in study, meditation and teaching. The colour and form of the robes differ in various countries, and some of the rules as laid down in India are varied to suit different climates.

THE PRINCIPLES

1 Each human being is responsible for the consequence of his own thoughts, words and deeds. There is no Saviour, human or divine, who can give him enlightenment or prevent him attaining it. The purpose of life is to attain complete enlightenment, a

state of consciousness in which all sense of separate selfhood is purged away. This purpose is fulfilled by treading the Eightfold Path, which leads from the 'house of self', aflame with hatred, lust and illusion, to the end of suffering for oneself and all beings.

2 The Buddha pointed out three Signs of Being. The first fact of existence is the law of change or impermanence. All that exists, from a man to a mountain, from a thought to a nation, passes through the same cycle of existence – birth, growth, decay and death. Life alone is continuous, ever seeking self-expression in new forms. This life-force is a process of flow, and he who clings to any form, however splendid, will suffer by resisting the flow.

3 The law of change applies equally to the 'self'. There is no principle in an individual which is immortal and unchanging. Only the ultimate Reality, which the Buddha called 'the Unborn, Unoriginated, Unformed', is beyond change, and all forms of life, including man, are manifestations of this Reality. No one owns the life-force which flows in him any more than the electric lamp owns the current which gives it light. It is the foolish belief in a separate self, with its own selfish desires, which causes most of human suffering.

4 The universe is the expression of law. All effects have causes, and man's character is the sum total of his own previous thoughts, words and acts. Karma, meaning action-reaction, governs all existence, and man is the sole creator of his circumstances and his reactions to them, his future condition, and his final destiny. By right thought and action he can gradually purify his nature, and so attain in time liberation from rebirth. The process covers great periods of time, involving life after life on earth, but ultimately every sentient being will reach Enlightenment.

5 The life-force in which Karma operates is one and indivisible though its ever changing forms are innumerable and perishable. There is no death, save of temporary forms, but every form must pass through the same cycle of birth, growth, decay and death. From an understanding of life's unity arises compassion, a sense of identity with the life in other forms. Compassion is wisdom in action, a deep awareness of universal harmony. He who breaks this harmony by selfish action must restore it at the cost of suffering.

6 The interests of the part should be those of the whole. In his

ignorance man thinks he can successfully strive for his own interests, and this wrongly directed energy of selfish desire produces suffering. He learns from his suffering to reduce and finally eliminate its cause. The Buddha taught four Noble Truths: (a) The omnipresence of suffering; (b) its cause, wrongly directed desire; (c) its cure, the removal of the cause; and (d) the Noble Eightfold Path of self-development which leads to the end of suffering.

7 The Eightfold Path consists in Right (or perfect) Views or preliminary understanding, Right Attitude of Mind, Right Speech, Right Action, Right Livelihood, Right Effort, Right Concentration or mind development, and finally, Right *Samadhi*, leading to full Enlightenment. As Buddhism is a way of living, not merely a theory of life, the treading of this Path is essential to self-deliverance.

'Cease to de evil, learn to do good, cleanse your own heart; this is the teaching of the Buddha'.

8 The Buddha described the supreme Reality as 'the Unborn, Unoriginated, Unformed'. Nirvana, awareness of this Reality, is a state of Awakening (to the Truth within) or Enlightenment, and is the goal of the Eightfold Path. This supreme state of consciousness, the extinction of the limitations of self-hood, is attainable on earth. All men and all other forms of life contain the potentiality of Enlightenment, and the process therefore consists in consciously becoming what we already potentially are. 'Look within; thou *art* Buddha.'

9 From potential to actual Enlightenment there lies the Middle Way, the Eightfold Path 'from desire to peace', a process of self-development between the 'opposites', avoiding all extremes. The Buddha trod this Way to the end, and faith in Buddhism includes the reasonable belief that where a Guide has trodden it is worth our while to tread. The Way must be trodden by the whole man, not merely the intellect, and Compassion and Wisdom must be developed equally. The Buddha was the All-Compassionate One as well as the All-Enlightened One.

10 Buddhism lays stress on the need of inward concentration and meditation, which leads in time to the development of the inner spiritual faculties. The subjective life is as important as the daily round, and periods of quietude for inner activity are essential for a

balanced life. The Buddhist should at all times be 'mindful and self-possessed', refraining from mental and emotional attachment to the things and occasions of daily life. This increasingly watchful attitude to circumstance, which he knows to be his own creation, helps him to keep his reaction to it always under control.

11 The Buddha said, 'Work out your own salvation with diligence.' Buddhism knows no authority for truth save the intuition of the individual, and that is authority for himself alone. Each man suffers the consequence of his own acts, and learns thereby, while helping his fellow men to the same deliverance; nor will prayer to the Buddha or to any God prevent an effect from following its cause. The utmost tolerance is practised towards all other religions and philosophies, for no man has the right to interfere in his neighbour's journey to the Goal.

12 Buddhism is neither pessimistic nor 'escapist'. It is a system of thought, a religion, a spiritual science and a way of life which is reasonable, practical and all-embracing. For 2,500 years it has satisfied the spiritual needs of nearly one third of mankind. It appeals to those in search of truth because it has no dogmas, satisfies the reason and the heart alike, insists on self-reliance coupled with tolerance for other points of view, embraces science, religion, philosophy, psychology, mysticism, ethics and art, and points to man alone as the creator of his present life and sole designer of his destiny.

Peace to all beings

Index

740327

B
Humphreys

    Humphreys, Christmas, 1901-
      Both sides of the circle : the
autobiography of Christmas Humphreys.
London ; Boston : G. Allen & Unwin,
1978.
      269 p., [8] leaves of plates : ill. ;
24 cm.
    Includes index.

    1. Humphreys, Christmas, 1901-
  2. Buddhists--England--Biography.
  3. Judges--England--Biography.
  I. Title

GA   02 MAR 79   4062065   GAPApc   78-312354